Responsibility Matters

Responsibility Matters

Peter A. French

University Press of Kansas

Published by the University Press of Kansas (Lawrence, Kansas
66049), which was organized by the Kansas Board of Regents and is
operated and funded by Emporia State University, Fort Hays State
University, Kansas State University, Pittsburg State University, the
University of Kansas, and Wichita State University

Library of Congress Cataloging-in-Publication Data

French, Peter A.
    Responsibility matters / Peter A. French.
      p.   cm.
    Includes index.
    ISBN 0-7006-0556-8
    1. Responsibility.   I. Title.
  BJ1451.F65   1992
  170—dc20   92-14728

British Library Cataloguing-in-Publication Data is available.

Printed in the United States of America

10 9 8 7 6 5 4 3 2 1

For Sandra

Contents

Preface

Mark Twain wrote in the "notice" to *The Adventures of Huckleberry Finn*, "Persons attempting to find a plot in it will be shot." I was tempted to say the same thing with respect to this book. Those looking for a sustained argument from the beginning of the book to the end may well be disappointed. It is not that sort of book. As the title suggests, my concern is to investigate various matters relating to the concept of responsibility. Several chapters focus on theoretical aspects of our responsibility practices. Others explore elements of the concept of responsibility, and some are directed at specific areas of application. Still others target more general issues in moral theory that affect the way we think of responsibility ascription. Theoretical issues are the focus of the early chapters, but also reappear throughout the book. Later chapters look at implications of and questions about responsibility in political, environmental, legal, medical, corporate, and military justice matters. Although the chapters are related in various ways, each can be read independently. Together they constitute a montage of my thinking on responsibility, a subject on which I have concentrated for much of the last twenty years.

All of that is true, but Robert Solomon has persuaded me that I would not be quite candid if I appropriated Twain's warning. (Twain himself was far from candid, in any event.) I should confess that there is indeed a sustained, if not conspicuous, argument throughout the book. As Solomon noted, many philosophers who write about responsibility see it either as a truth of some sort about the world, or like Kant, they see it in terms of a necessary presupposition of practical life. I have defended, and continue to defend in this book, the position that responsibility is but a set of practices that we use to describe and understand individual and social behavior. Responsibility matters are matters that enter into our daily lives in myriad ways that cannot be reduced to simple formulas and

principles. To explore responsibility matters is to traverse ground often left un-
trod by philosophers.

All but six of the chapters appear in print for the first time in this volume, and
those six have undergone radical revision. I do not hope to provide anything like
the last word on the issues I discuss; usually I am more interested in provoking
investigation than closing it. Still, some readers will look for more than I provide
by way of analysis of the arguments and positions of other philosophers. Some
will be concerned that I spend a considerable amount of time talking about
literature, films, legal cases, and current events. Not only do I refuse to make
excuses for using nonstandard philosophical materials, I regard them as crucial to
a responsible account of the matters I am considering. As editor of two major
philosophical journals I have had the opportunity to evaluate hundreds of papers
focused exclusively on the analysis of arguments from within the philosophical
literature. I have also contributed my fair share to that enterprise, but I want to
take the discussion of the topics of this book to a broader plane and in doing so,
open up some interesting new ways to look philosophically into the concept of
responsibility.

I am grateful to a number of people for their contributions to the making of this
book. I learned a great deal from Donald Davidson, John Mackie, H. D. Lewis,
and other teachers. Their influences are obvious. Herbert Morris's work has had
a significant impact on my thinking and methodology, as has that of Robert
Solomon. W. H. Auden's essays have made an undeniable impression on my
thinking. I have had invaluable discussions on the topics of the different chapters
with David Pears, John Ladd, Larry May, David Copp, Kurt Baier, Herbert Fingarette, Michael Zimmerman, Christopher Morris, Curtis Brown, Alex Neil, John
Martin Fischer, Kenneth Koford, and Norman Bowie. I especially benefited from
discussions with and reading recent work by Roger Scruton. Robert Curtis provided particularly helpful comments. I had the opportunity to present various
drafts of the chapters at Oklahoma State University, the University of Tulsa,
California State University, Long Beach, Millersville State University, Texas
A & M University, the University of North Carolina, and the University of
Utah. I also presented portions of the book at North American Society for Social
Philosophy conferences at Colorado Springs, Colorado, and Burlington, Ver-
mont, the American Philosophical Association's Central Division meetings in
New Orleans; Bentley College's Business Ethics conference; and the Greater
Philadelphia Philosophy Consortium. The participants in my National Endow-

ment for the Humanities Summer Seminars for College Teachers in 1983, 1987, and 1990 provided stimulating responses to early versions of many of the chapters. I am grateful to the National Endowment for the Humanities for its support. Finally, I want to express my thanks for her patience to Cynthia Miller of the University Press of Kansas.

Acknowledgments

An earlier version of part of Chapter 1 appeared in "Fishing the Red Herrings out of the Sea of Responsibility" in *Actions and Events, Perspectives on the Philosophy of Donald Davidson*, ed. E. LePore and B. McLaughlin (Blackwell's, 1985).

An earlier version of Chapter 9 appeared as "Terre Gaste" in *The Corporation, Ethics, and the Environment*, ed. M. Hoffman, R. Frederick, and E. Petry (Quorum Books, 1990).

An earlier version of Chapter 10 appeared as "Exorcising the Demon of Cultural Relativism" in *Problems of International Justice*, ed. S. Luper-Foy (Boulder, Colo.: Westview, 1988).

An earlier version of Chapter 12 appeared as "Burking a Mill" in *Ethical Issues in Government*, ed. N. Bowie (Philadelphia: Temple University Press, 1981).

An earlier version of Chapter 16 appeared as "Corporate Crimes and Innovative Punishments" in *Social Norms and Economic Institutions*, ed. K. Koford and J. Miller (Ann Arbor: University of Michigan Press, 1991).

An earlier version of Chapter 17 appeared as "Constitutionalism and Military Justice" in *Constitutionalism*, ed. A. Rosenbaum (Westport, Conn.: Greenwood Press, 1988).

1 · Principles of Responsibility Ascription and the Responsibility Barter Game

Responsibility is an important individual and communal matter because in practical terms it involves punishment, compensation costs, threats to reputation, and less often, or so it seems, praise, credit, and reward. People's lives are affected when responsibility is ascribed, assessed, or accepted.

Matters of responsibility are matters of negotiation. That is true regardless of whether the event that occasions responsibility assignment or ascription is a good or a bad one. If good, everyone wants a share of the responsibility. If bad, everyone wants as little as possible. As far back in history as we can go, philosophers have tried to identify features that delineate us as a species, a race, and a culture—rational animal, social animal, animal that lies or laughs (and, in either case, has need to), and so on. I will not add yet another trite phrase to the collection, but one thing seems certainly true of us. We spend a considerable (perhaps inordinate) amount of time trying to avoid responsibility wherever and whenever possible. Surprisingly, this is as true of the responsibility for good things as it is, not surprisingly, true when things go badly. Perhaps at some cultural learning level we had ingrained in us (a task of grandmothers? or just painful experience?) that the goodness of anything may be tarnished by revelations of unexpected consequences, and so it is safer to avoid full responsibility for it, even when it appears on first blush to be wonderful. Morality also preaches modesty and humility and that no one stands utterly alone. So it may be good form to give some credit to others for our successes. (This no doubt explains the yawning length of Academy Award shows. The winners usually take some of the credit that is offered, but prudently note that their contributions were not all that significant, unless there's big money to be made. In that case, the share they claim increases dramatically.) Most of us have been taught to inoculate ourselves against the prospect of a turn of the worm, a change in fortune, the future day when what seemed so good turns out so bad and everyone is looking for someone to blame. And who is responsible for this? As bad things seldom turn out to be good ones in disguise, an escape from the tentacles of responsibility always seems the order of the day.

The problem for most of us, excepting moral masochists, is that responsibility does get doled out. The strategy is either not to be in the line at all or to find a way to get as little dumped on one's plate as possible, trading off to others as much responsibility as one can. Consequently, the Responsibility Barter game (RB) is probably the most common experience ordinary people have with morality. Grand philosophical theories about THE GOOD, maximizing utility, gaining virtue, and doing one's duty enter into the barter game only in oblique ways. They play a role in marking out what is good or right from what is bad or wrong at a theoretical level, and they are legitimate sources for appeals, though their authority is not always accepted. But when people get down to the business of moral assignment of responsibility, the questions of goodness or badness, rightness or wrongness, have been at least tentatively answered, more often than not by appeal to intuition, custom, or common agreement. Then the game begins.

As with most social games we can ask a number of questions, the answers to which expose the structure and play of the activity. What, for example, is the goal of playing? What are the rules? How is the game played?

In most of our popular games the goal of each player (or team) is to score more points than other players (or teams). There are games, however, in which winning is not tallying the highest score. In golf, for example, the winner is the player with the lowest score. Golf and RB share the goal of finishing with less rather than more, but there are too many disanalogies to make much of the comparison. In golf the course is the given and the player tries to tour around it in the fewest possible strokes. The best possible score on an eighteen-hole course would be eighteen, a hole-in-one off every tee. There is an unavoidable minimum number of strokes against a player. RB begins in earnest after the identification of an event as good or bad, so there is also a given or a base situation with which RB players must deal. In RB, however, there are no established units by which scores are kept—no strokes, points, or runs. The minimum achievable score is zero, though it is seldom attained if the player is really in the game. RB also involves carryover from previous instances of the game, but then golf includes handicapping of players based on previous performances. It is also rather difficult to know exactly when an RB game has begun and when it is over, and numerous RB games even involving the same players can continue simultaneously. The analogy with golf is tempting but no better than one that could be made with Hot

Potato or other games in which the winner's goal is to end the game with nothing or as little as possible.

We play RB to reduce liability, compensation costs, social discomfort, and so on. There are powerful economic, psychological, social, and legal reasons to do so. Hence, the basic reason to engage in RB is rational self-interest. "X is responsible for y" can have the illocutionary force (to use J. L. Austin's term) of an accusation, a verdict, an 'exercitive,' an expression of an attitude, and a simple causal identification—all at the same time. It is no wonder that avoidance of responsibility has become almost an art form, one that is learned and practiced relatively early in life and honed to the end.

J. L. Austin credits Aristotle with the discovery "that questions of whether a person was responsible for this or that are prior to questions of freedom."[1] "Prior" here might be taken in two ways, and Austin probably meant both. They are practically prior in that we seldom ask if someone was acting freely unless we are concerned with pinning responsibility for something on him or her. We assume that people in normal circumstances do what they do freely, that is, their actions are not performed under constraint, inadvertently, or under duress. It is only when events go wrong or when they go exceedingly well that we investigate whether the persons who brought about those events were in control of their actions. Questions of responsibility are also theoretically prior because they provide the conceptual superstructure in which questions of metaphysical freedom or moral freedom are conceived. Theoretical substance aside, at least for the moment, Aristotle's "discovery" reveals the tactics of responsibility ascription. It tells us that to find out whether someone is to be held responsible for some event, we should determine whether some excuse for the person's behavior is acceptable. Aristotle focused on whether or not the action in question was performed under compulsion or due to ignorance.[2] But as Austin noted, "in considering responsibility few things are considered more important than to establish whether a man *intended* to do A, or whether he did A intentionally."[3] It is widely assumed that an adequate understanding of intentional agency should include or at least entail the concept of a morally responsible entity and yield an underlying principle of responsibility ascription. That assumption seems to recommend itself as a starting point in our attempt to understand how responsibility ascription works.

J. L. Mackie called the prototypical version of that principle the "straight rule of responsibility."[4] It says that "an agent is responsible for all and only [its] intentional actions." Although he did not endorse this principle without modifications, I will refer to it in this pristine form as Mackie's Rule. According to Mackie's Rule, ascriptions of responsibility are proper only when made about things capable of intentional action: intentional systems. An intentional system may be defined, following Dennett,[5] as a system some of whose behavior can be explained and predicted by relying on ascriptions to the system of beliefs and desires (or hopes, fears, intentions, perceptions, expectations, and so on). It is irrelevant to something's being an intentional system that its behavior can also be adequately explained in a purely mechanistic way. To be an intentional system, as Dennett stresses,[6] an entity need not have any particular intrinsic features that are referred to when it is called intentional. It need not have, for example, any "real" beliefs or desires. It merely has to "succumb to an intentional stance" adopted toward it. In other words, it must make sense to ascribe intentional predicates to some of its behavior, and that is only to say of it that it has reasons for doing some things, or expects certain outcomes, or wants certain ends, or seeks, or hopes, or whatever. The conditions of something's being an intentional system can be more fully explicated in terms of Donald Davidson's account of agency.

For an entity to be treated as a Davidsonian agent, some of the things that happen (some events) must be describable in a way that makes certain sentences true, sentences that say that some of the things the entity does were intended by the entity itself.[7] Such an account is remarkably similar to the basic requirements for what Dennett calls a "first-order intentional system."

An identifying feature of an attribution of intentionality is that it is referentially opaque: that it is intentional in one description of a particular behavior does not mean it is intentional in all true descriptions of the event. Hence a perfectly good account of an entity's behavior may be purely mechanistic, while at least one true description of that behavior says that the entity acted to bring about some state of affairs, or because of certain expectations, or desires.

As long as there is one true description of the event that says it was intended by an entity, the event is an action of that entity. In this way intentionality is used to sort actions out of the larger category of events. For example, if I dump out a cup of coffee believing it is tea and wanting to dump out the tea, then dumping out the coffee, though not what I intended, is an action of mine.

Mackie's Rule allows only *intended* actions as appropriate subjects of responsibility ascriptions. But we are commonly held accountable for actions unintended under the relevant description (though intended under other descriptions). An extension of Mackie's Rule or, rather, a restatement of it in terms of actions seems advisable. It could be rephrased to read: "An agent is responsible for its actions." Whether or not those actions were intended under the relevant descriptions plays more of a role in mitigation than in structuring the basic rule of moral responsibility ascription. For example, if I really intended to dump out tea but mistook the coffee for tea, I might be forgiven or lightly reprimanded and required to make a fresh pot. In more serious matters forgiveness may be harder to garner by appeal to "intention under a different description"—for example, "I didn't know the gun was loaded."

Though this alteration may appear to shake the foundations of Mackie's Rule, an important link to intentionality is preserved, for it is intentionality ascriptions that drag the doings of entities into the class of *their* actions, and it is for actions (at least those that are or produce untoward events), in the first instance, that moral responsibility is ascribed. However, I do suspect, as I suggested earlier, that when praise is the issue, only intentional actions qualify. In any event, praise is somewhat restrained if it turns out that the good outcome was not intended but occurred because of what was intended.

Whether or not an entity is an intentional agent depends on the possibility of describing its movements as results of the reasons for their occurring. When we describe them by reference to desires, we describe them as intentional actions. Intentional agents then, or (as I prefer) moral persons, come into existence at various levels of description or, more to the point, via descriptions. Whether or not an entity is a proper target of moral responsibility ascriptions, that is, a moral person, depends on rules of redescription that allow us to say that a movement of a body was intentional: for example, pitching a baseball or stabbing the person hiding behind the arras. Those rules, which I have elsewhere called licenses of redescription,[8] are cultural, linguistic, historical inventions.

If an entity were never to do anything that could be properly redescribed as the result of its having certain reasons, desires, or expectations, no matter what it did, it would not be a member of the moral community. By the same token, if a machine's behavior could be so described (like, for example, a game-playing computer's moves, which might be attributed to its strategies), then the machine is a Dennett intentional system or a Davidsonian agent and might qualify as a moral person. I have argued elsewhere (and will say more on the subject in chapters thirteen and sixteen) that corporate entities with certain kinds of decision structures (those having not only standard recognizable procedures but also delineatable policies) can satisfy the requirements of Davidsonian agency.[9]

Although Davidson is concerned with explicating human agency, there is nothing in his account that requires that the primitive actions (movements of our bodies, which is all we ever do when we act) be performed by the entity to whom the relevant intentionality is being attributed. He simply argues that for every action, in some true description it is intentional and in another it is a basic bodily movement. In a corporate case the primitive action (for example, writing a signature on the bottom of a piece of paper) might be located in the body of a senior officer. (That action is not, of course, really primitive. We should talk instead of a hand moving in a certain way.) There may be a number of intentional descriptions that are true of that event. One may attribute to the senior officer the intention of signing the document knowing full well that doing so has the procedural effect of corporately doing something. At yet another descriptive level it may be true that the corporation intentionally or deliberately did something (raised the price on its products for example), and that it had certain corporate reasons for doing so (consistent with its basic policies, including profit maximization) that are quite distinct from any purposes the executive might have had in signing a paper.

When primitive acts (bodily or physical movements) are redescribed, there seems to be no built-in restriction on either the number (or layers) of descriptions before the focal, intentional one is reached or the number of intentional acts performed when a single primitive movement occurs. Each description must be true and accord with appropriate description rules. We could imagine a situation in which the muscles of a hand contract, pulling a lever, releasing a storage tank of untreated chemical waste, and polluting a canal in a residential area, even though the lever puller's only intention (if he had one at all) was to pull the lever as ordered by his superior. Furthermore, we stipulate that the lever puller had absolutely no intention of polluting the canal, though that is certainly one of his actions, assuming he intentionally pulled the lever. If he were incapable of doing anything intentionally (suppose he was under a hypnotic trance or that he was really a robot programmed to pull the lever at a specific time every day), then pulling the lever and polluting the canal would not be actions of his. What this robotic lever puller did, however, could be redescribed. If the company in question had adopted certain policies about waste disposal and/or had reasons for getting rid of its waste in such a fashion, then the lever puller's actions were not his actions but corporate actions. The fact that an action was performed by a robot, whether one of metal and wire or one of flesh and blood, does not imply that it was not an action of whatever programs or controls the robot.

This sort of expansion of what I take to be a Davidsonian account of intentionality raises hurricane signals for many moral philosophers, because it entails that the moral community is not metaphysically basic or substantial. Its members are not identified in the way those of natural communities are. Instead, the moral community itself is a product of a certain kind of description or, rather, redescription.

Intentionality, the standard criterion of agency, is intensional, though the expression of agency is extensional. Davidson notes, "The relation that holds between a person and an event, when the event is an action performed by the person, holds regardless of how the terms are described. Therefore, we can without confusion speak of the class of events that are actions, which we cannot do with intentional actions."[10] Hamlet, for example, intentionally killed the person hiding behind the arras in Queen Gertrude's room, but he did not intentionally kill Polonius, though Polonius was the person hiding behind the arras. Hamlet had no intention of killing Polonius or of orphaning Ophelia. His intentions with respect to the event seem to have been to kill the king, to kill the person hiding behind the arras (whom he believed to be the king), and to frighten Gertrude. There was only one event, so Hamlet's intentionally killing the person behind the arras is extensionally identical to Hamlet's killing Polonius. If there were a class of intentional acts, we would be committed to saying that what Hamlet did, one and the same action, was both intentional and not intentional. This tends to support a revision of Mackie's Rule in terms of actions rather than intentional actions.

Clearly Hamlet was the agent of Polonius's death. Killing Polonius was one of his actions. Should he be held morally responsible for Polonius's death? I suspect that most of us would say yes, even though it was not his intention. It would badly bend the concept of intentional action to rescue Mackie's Rule by treating every act done intentionally under some description as intentional. As long as we intuit that Hamlet is morally responsible for the death of Polonius, we will have to abandon the idea that persons are morally responsible for only their intended actions.

Consider another example: I know how much you prize a cup of coffee before entering an important meeting. Your cup has been filled with coffee, but you have not yet arrived. I find your cup but think it is filled with tea, which I know you dislike. I dump the contents of the cup down the drain, intending to pour a fresh cup of coffee for you. You enter as I discover that the coffee pot is dry and you identify the residue in the sink as coffee. Clearly, I dumped the cup intentionally, believing it was filled with tea. What I did was intentional, though what I did was dump the cup of coffee and I did not do that intentionally. Am I not responsible for the loss of the coffee? I hope, however, you will forgive me since I thought it was tea. But Laertes will not forgive Hamlet for killing his father just because Hamlet thought the person behind the arras was the king, and there seems to be no reason he should.

As noted earlier, praising a person for a good outcome and holding him or her morally responsible for a bad one are not symmetrical, even in what seem like similar cases. Suppose someone had laced the coffee with arsenic. I think it is tea, dump it, and it is later learned that I saved your life. It is unlikely I will be praised for saving your life, though saving your life was what I did.

More closely parallel to the Hamlet case, suppose that I am passing a lake and see someone drowning. I am convinced that it is Rob, a dear friend. I toss caution to the winds, dive in, and save the drowning person who, it turns out, is Jim, my most bitter and despicable enemy. I tell Jim, who offers me a healthy reward, "If I'd known it was you, I'd have let you sink. The only reason I jumped in was to save Rob. My intention was to save the person drowning who I thought was Rob. It was most assuredly not to save you, you swine." Do I deserve moral praise for saving Jim? You probably would be reluctant to extend it when you learn of my reasons for going to the rescue. To be worthy of moral praise, a person is expected to have specifically intended to perform the praiseworthy deed. However, we hold persons like Hamlet morally responsible for untoward events over a much greater range of their actions. We appear to be much more concerned with controlling and preventing untoward or harmful occurrences then we are with patting people on the back for the good things they do or examining their mental states when things have gone awry. Again we have reason to endorse the modified version of Mackie's Rule: an agent is morally accountable for its actions.

Although intentionality allows us to sort actions out of the class of events, it is not as central to the attribution of responsibility as is usually supposed. It seems that we look at intentions more closely when we are evaluating excuses put forth to mitigate penalties than in the primary ascription stage. In a way, that is also what happens with praise. Praise is withdrawn if the intentions were inappropriate. Punishment or blame may be lessened if the intentions were good, but the result was still an untoward event. In fact, it seems that praise and blame (affected by consideration of specific intentions) are matters apart from or following after attributions of moral responsibility. Ophelia and Laertes may not blame Hamlet for their father's death quite so much when they learn he had no intention of killing the old man, though he is still morally responsible for Polonius's death.

These principles of responsibility ascription are the basic rules of the Responsibility Barter game in that they serve as the justification for ascriptions and the grounds for appeals. To be a player, however, one must be a member of the moral community. Davidson makes a persuasive case against a traditional way of distinguishing the members of the moral community from those who are not legitimate RB players.[11] If I lace your coffee with arsenic with the intention of killing you and I succeed, did I not cause your death by poisoning your coffee? The temptation, of course, is to agree, but agree to what? It sounds as if the claim is that I, the agent, caused something, your death. Most basically, what I caused was my hand muscles to contract in a specific way. That muscle contraction caused the poison to be put in your coffee. The implication is that there are two distinct kinds of causality: regular event causality (when, for example, contracting hand muscles causes poison to drop in your cup) and agent causality (a special power that intentional agents, that is, persons, have to cause parts of themselves, like hand muscles, to do things). Surely if there is such a thing as agent causality, being an RB player should require the capacity or power to agent-cause.

Davidson has conclusively demonstrated, however, that agency requires nothing like agent causation. Primitive actions are basic bodily movements, such as moving a finger. It may well be true that I cause my finger to move in a certain way by contracting certain hand muscles, and I do that by making a certain event occur in my brain. It looks as if the movement of my finger, rather than being primitive, is the result of more basic actions. But that is not the case, for doing something that causes my finger to move does not cause me to move my finger; it is moving my finger. Davidson's argument takes this form: suppose that causing a primitive action is to introduce an event separable from and prior to the action. This prior, distinct event must either be an action or not an action. If it were an action, then the action with which we began (the one we pronounced to be primitive) was not primitive. If it were not an action, then we slip into trying to explain intentional agency by appeal to the obscure, if not utterly senseless, notion of a *causing* that is not a *doing*. The whole idea of a special kind of causation that is a mark of agency and a requirement for full-player status in RB, a Cartesian mental ability that computers, corporations, and other nonhuman intentional systems are supposed to lack, is contentless, useless, and unnecessary. The relationship between my moving finger, the arsenic being put in your coffee, and your being poisoned is simple event causality. No appeal to a special brand of causation (that is, the causing of cerebral events that is not itself an action of the agent) is required to explain why I am the cause of your poisoning. As Davidson notes,[12] even if I must make certain brain events occur and I am utterly unaware that they must occur to move my finger, moving the finger is all that I do, and I do it under at least one description intentionally: the description of the event as intentionally putting arsenic in your coffee, that is, poisoning your coffee in order to kill you.

It is certainly true that most of us do not know that we are making things happen in our brains when we move our fingers. We could even be ignorant of the fact that we have brains, like the Scarecrow in *The Wizard of Oz*. What is needed for action is that we know what we do under some description. All I need to know is that I am moving my finger or that I am poisoning the coffee for the event to be an action of mine under all of its descriptions, including the neurophysiological ones.

Searching for the identifying characteristics of moral persons (RB players) is not looking for occult mental powers. A Davidsonian agency account conjoined with the modified Mackie Rule does not, then, exclude nonhuman intentional systems from membership in the moral community. Mackie's Rule as modified, however, is inadequate to satisfy our intuitions about responsibility. Nor does it correspond fully with what happens in RB.

Mackie's Rule holds that the necessary and sufficient condition of being morally accountable for an action is having intended it. Already we have modified the rule to include actions of the agent that were not intended under the relevant description. Having intended *something* is then a necessary condition for moral responsibility, but it is not necessary that the action being targeted was intentional.

The earlier discussion may have left the impression that all intentional systems should be admitted to moral citizenship, that all are legitimate RB players. That, however, is clearly not consistent with our basic intuitions about responsibility. Dennett maintains that most animals and even some plants can qualify as first order intentional systems.[13] I have been accused of providing an argument that not only qualifies corporations for moral citizenship, but admits cats and dogs as well.[14] The fault lies not directly with the Davidsonian agency condition, but in reliance on an inadequate account of the principles of responsibility, the rules of RB. A drastic remodeling to satisfy ordinary practice in RB is required before we reexamine the Davidsonian agency condition.

One way to describe what Hamlet did in Gertrude's room is to say that he orphaned Ophelia. He most certainly had no intention of doing that, but it seems reasonable to say that he was willing to do that, as he was also willing to stab Polonius if, as it happened, Polonius rather than the king was the person hiding behind the arras. The idea that being willing to do something does not entail intending to do it is embedded in the concept of negligence.

Imagine that my practicing the piano disturbs the neighbors and from past experience, I know that it does. I do not intend to disturb them—I am not that kind of person—though surely I am willing to do so in order to improve my piano-playing skills. I hope that this time I will not disturb them. It would be odd to say that I intend to disturb the neighbors when I hope that I will not. No one tries *not* to carry out his or her intentions. Hence, there should be a distinction between what one intends to do and what one is only willing to do when one intends to do something else. That distinction, however, is not acknowledged as fundamental in ordinary moral responsibility ascriptions in RB. Generally we are held accountable for doing the things we were willing to do though we did not intend them.

Davidson's theory of agency can, of course, assimilate things done willingly but not intentionally because they amount to redescriptions of the person's intentional behavior. Negligence (understood in terms of being willing without intending), then, is usually an action of an agent. Such cases could be covered by Mackie's Rule if it were modified to focus on actions rather than intended actions. At any rate, persons are held morally responsible not only for things done intentionally, but for things they were willing to do as well.

There are a number of other cases in which things not done intentionally are nonetheless likely to cause trouble in RB. J. L. Austin argued that we can distinguish, in some cases, persons doing things deliberately from their doing them intentionally.[15] I suspect that there may be some overlap with cases of willingness, but Austin-type cases are worth at least brief mention. Consider my rushing to get to the airport to catch a plane to Bermuda. I am off on a well-earned holiday, and it's the last flight of the week. I am running a bit late, so I hurriedly back my car out of the driveway. Then I stop short, seeing my youngest child's favorite doll lying directly in my path. I realize I could get out and move it, but that would cost precious time. It is just too bad. I have a plane to catch. I drive over the doll, crushing it, and speed off to the airport. Now, following Austin, it seems right to say that I deliberately drove right over my child's doll. But I did not do it intentionally, that is, it was not any part of my intention to destroy the doll. Of course I did not do it unintentionally either. It was incidental to my intentions. But I am not only causally responsible for destroying the doll, I should be held to account for it in RB, as well. When someone does so, I will no doubt try to lessen my responsibility load by maintaining that my daughter should not have left the doll in the drive and that I just had to get to the airport. That strategy might work—at least I might not be thought such a monster—but it should not get me off the moral responsibility hook. Had my intentions involved doing something laudatory or morally commendable, such as rushing to the aid of an injured friend, deliberately driving over the doll would probably have been forgiven or excused and the slate wiped clean, or mostly so. This example only confirms that we can be held morally accountable for what we do deliberately but not intentionally; otherwise, excusing or forgiving would not be a sensible RB move with respect to the incident.

I suspect that further investigation will show that doing something deliberately but not intentionally is commonly distinguished from being willing to do it. After all, to do it deliberately I must have deliberated about it. I may be described as willing to do things that I have hardly thought about, such as disturbing the neighbors when I practice the piano, which I did neither deliberately nor intentionally. At any rate, Mackie's Rule needs to be broadened to allow deliberate actions even if they are not intended actions in order to remain consistent with common usage and intuitions. Again, Davidson's agency theory anchors the required modification. Deliberately running over my child's doll is one of my actions because "drove over the doll" is a true description of what I did intentionally under the description "drove out of the driveway." Responsibility then remains firmly attached to intentionality by merely modifying Mackie's Rule to encompass more than just intentional actions. Collateral or second effects involving the intentional acts of others may demand other adjustments to Mackie's Rule, but the link to intentionality can still be preserved.

Mackie's Rule with all of these alterations I call the Extended Principle of Accountability or EPA.[16] It is basic to RB, but it is also likely to be viewed as extraordinarily rigid insofar as it admits all of the actions of an agent into the scope of moral responsibility. In other words, as long as an action was intended under some description, it is an action of the agent and thus something for which the agent can be held responsible. Only a limited range of behavior would be exempt. Such a latent tyranny of moral responsibility, however, is checked and balanced at the appellate level of excuse evaluation in RB. What EPA clearly indicates is that certain popular excuses such as "I didn't mean that," "It was unintentional," "That wasn't what I wanted to do," are not necessarily exculpatory or even mitigatory in RB. That is especially true when RB is played over serious matters involving injury.

EPA, however, is not adequate for another class of cases in which moral responsibility is commonly assessed. Those are cases in which something untoward occurs that was unintended, unforeseen, or not willingly done under any true description—cases in which ascriptions of moral responsibility would be inappropriate according to the EPA. These cases have the further feature that after a period of time the perpetrator fails to change the behavior that resulted in the untoward event. Under such conditions moral responsibility for the earlier event is often reassessed and ascribed to the perpetrator. This is done in full recognition of the fact that at the time the untoward event occurred, it was not intended by the person nor was it something the person was willing to do. It was not an action of the person. In effect, moral responsibility may be assigned specifically because the perpetrator, subsequent to the event, failed to respond to its occurrence with an appropriate modification of the behavior that had as an outcome the unwanted or harmful event. I have called this the Principle of Responsive Adjustment.[17]

PRA captures the idea that after an untoward event has happened, the persons who contributed to its occurrence are expected to adopt certain courses of future actions that will prevent repetitions. We have strong moral expectations regarding behavioral adjustments that correct character weaknesses or habits that have produced untoward events. PRA, however, is more than an expression of such expectations. It allows that when the expected adjustments in behavior are not made, and in the presence of strong evidential support for nonadjustment, the persons in question are to be held fully morally responsible for the untoward event. PRA does *not* assume, however, that failure to mend one's ways after being confronted with an unhappy outcome of one's actions is strong presumptive evidence that one had originally intended that outcome. The matter of one's intentions at the time the event occurred is closed. If it was not intentional when it occurred, nothing after the action can make it intentional. PRA expresses the idea that refusing to adjust practices that led to an untoward occurrence is to associate oneself, for the purposes of RB and morality in general, with the earlier behavior. In this respect PRA captures more of the richness of our ordinary notion of moral responsibility than EPA by uncovering the principle that explains our practice of reevaluating persons with regard to past events even when attributions of intentionality are defeated for some reason or other. RB is a tough game in which players must be always ready to excuse or justify themselves, even after they may have thought they had put an event behind them. More importantly, though, PRA reveals that the plea that one did not intend to do something is often very ineffective in avoiding responsibility.

PRA should not be read as suggesting that some future intention can affect a past event or that a future intention as manifested in a future course of action could have the effect of making a past event intentional when it was not originally intentional. "Backward causation" is not entailed in PRA. By intentionally doing something today, however, a person can make something that happened yesterday an event for which that person should bear moral responsibility. A person's past is captured in the scope of the person's present and future intentions. PRA insists on that.

F. H. Bradley writes, "In morality the past is real because it is present in the will."[18] PRA expresses this elusive notion. The idea is that adjustments in one's behavior to rectify flaws or habits that have actually caused past evils or to routinize behavior that has led to worthy results are required by moral considerations. In other words, the intention that motivates a lack of responsive corrective action or the continuance of offending behavior affirms or loops back to retrieve the behavior that caused the evil. By the same token, failure to routinize behavior that has produced good results divorces that behavior from one's "moral life." Intentions certainly reach forward, but they also may be seen as having a retrograde or retrieval function by which they illuminate a past action that was not, at the time of its occurrence, an action of the agent. A present intention to do something or to do it in a certain way can draw a previous event into its scope.

Davidsonian agents need not be viewed as purely prospective, ahistorical, or even abstract centers of action. They have lives, pasts that form the context out of which their present intentions emerge.

Suppose that RB player Sebastian gets drunk and in a stupor drives his car over Quincy's property. Assume that Sebastian had no intention of damaging Quincy's property, that nothing he did while inebriated was intentional. After regaining sobriety and learning of his misadventures, Sebastian quite deliberately returns to the local pub and gets roaring drunk. Sebastian knows his own past well, including the fact that he got drunk on one occasion and destroyed Quincy's property. Nonetheless, he embarks upon the same course. Though he might not have been assessed moral responsibility for the damage he did on the first spree (he was, after all, under the influence) had he subsequently modified his behavior, he did not do so. Thus, by PRA he has made the crucial early events not an out-of-character happenstance, but very much in character and hence something for which he may be held morally responsible. PRA captures, at least to some extent, the Aristotelian idea that we do not hold people morally responsible for unintentionally "slightly deviating from the course of goodness"[19] as long as they do not subsequently practice behavior that makes such deviations a matter of character.

The most radical element of PRA is surely that which provides for a retrieval of past unintentional behavior in a present intention to do something. Joel Feinberg identifies a feature of act descriptions known as the "accordion effect."[20] Like the musical instrument, the description of a simple bodily movement can be expanded in different directions by causal linkages and other associations. For example, the act of pulling the trigger of a rifle might, through a series of redescriptions, be expanded to the description "the killing of the judge." Accordions can be drawn apart in both directions. The description of Sebastian's present act of getting drunk may be associated to his past behavior by the ordinary relations "like yesterday," "as before," or "again." It is the case that Sebastian, in our story, intends to get drunk *again*. The action intended under that description clearly retrieves the previous behavior, though it certainly does not make the previous behavior an intentional action at the time it occurred.

Sebastian might counter with the plea that he had not intended to get drunk under any such accordioned description at all. He only intended to get drunk *simpliciter*. Such a plea, however, can be rejected by RB players on the grounds that unless he is of diminished mental capacity or suffering from amnesia, Sebastian's grasp of what he is doing is formed within a mental or personal history that is not present-specific, and his descriptions of his actions are formed within that history. "I intended only to get drunk, not to get drunk again," is too restricted an intention for what he is doing. There are limits on excludability by appeal to semantic opacity in the playing of RB. If Sebastian quite intentionally makes his way to the pub in order to get roaring drunk, he intentionally goes to get drunk again, or like yesterday, and his doing so affirms the previous episode insofar as it takes it into the description captured in the scope of the intention.

PRA insists that people learn from their mistakes, that the pleas of mistake and of accident cannot be repeatedly used to excuse frequent performances of offensive behavior. "It was an accident" will only work if the event was not the result of behavior that is repeated after the original offending event. "It was inadvertent" or "it was a mistake" will exculpate only if corrective measures are taken to insure nonrepetition. Such excuses can be, and often are, reevaluated after observing the individual's actions subsequent to the event. But it would be wrong to decide in such cases that the individual must have had the relevant intention in the first instance of the offending behavior. We may grant that no error was made at that time in describing the event, but the event has taken on a new description in the light of subsequent action.

The application of PRA may be read as saying that a person should be held morally responsible for a previous event to which that person had unintentionally contributed if he or she subsequently acts intentionally in ways that are likely to cause repetitions of the untoward outcome. A strict set of temporal closures need not apply to PRA. For example, moral enlightenment many decades later may demand reevaluation of an event that was not originally thought to be bad or harmful, and PRA will require moral accountability from the perpetrator if, after enlightenment, no behavioral adjustments were made.

There is another important aspect of this principle that is intuitively appealing. Suppose we consider all of those things for which a person can be held morally responsible as exhausting that person's moral life, the life which, when regarded as a complete moral biography, can be morally judged or evaluated as Aristotle suggests, "in a complete life," against a standard of moral worth or virtue. PRA forces incorporation of originally unintentional pieces of behavior into a person's moral life, because it does not allow persons to desert their pasts. It demands that present and future actions respond to past deeds. It forces us to think of our moral lives as both retrospective and contemporaneous, as cumulative. It does not let us completely escape responsibility for our accidents, inadvertencies, unintended executive failures, failures to fully appreciate situations, or bad habits, by simply proffering excuses. The PRA-countenanced response to such pleas, in certain cases, will be "Yes, it surely was unintentional, but you have done nothing to change your ways. You have seen the earlier outcome and you have not altered your behavior to guard against recurrence. Hence, you must bear the moral responsibility for the earlier untoward event." The ordinary notion of moral responsibility, then, operates over more than isolated intentional acts considered seriatim, as Mackie's Rule implies. The moral integrity of a person's life depends upon a moral consistency that is nurtured by PRA.

PRA is not divorced from a firm foundation in Davidsonian agency for at least two reasons: First, it is directed to subsequent intentional actions of the person as well as to the earlier unhappy event; and second, the capacity to respond, the response itself (in the relevant moral sense), must be expressed in intentional action. The two principles of moral responsibility (EPA and PRA) constitute the superstructure of accountability and are primary rules of the Responsibility Barter game. EPA captures F. H. Bradley's insistence that a deed cannot belong to someone unless it can be properly said to "issue" from his will[21] and Aristotle's view that virtue and excellence depend upon the voluntary nature of actions. While PRA embodies Aristotle's conviction that persons are "themselves by their slack lives responsible for becoming men of that kind and men make themselves responsible for being unjust or self-indulgent . . . ; for it is activities exercised on particular objects that make the corresponding character."[22]

EPA and PRA together imply that if an entity is to be considered a moral person, it must, minimally, be a Davidsonian agent with the capacity or ability to intentionally modify its behavior patterns, habits, or *modus operandi* after learning that untoward events were brought about by its past behavior. The modification condition involves the reflexive capacity that Dennett includes in his definition of "second-order intentional systems."[23]

The term "responsible" speaks in favor of this view of a moral person. To be responsible is to be able to make a response.[24] [There is a notable archaic use of "responsible" as an actor who undertakes to play any part required by the company. Someone in the theatre who could answer any call was a "good all-round responsible."] Understanding "responsible" in terms of "response-able within the Responsibility Barter Game" carries the concept further from Mackie's Rule than even PRA takes us. To be able to respond one must be an intentional agent, but the person who is able to or must respond may have had little or nothing to do with the entity that caused the untoward event, let alone intentionally caused it himself. Parents run into this dilemma with regularity. A child, whether intentionally or not, breaks a neighbor's window. Who must respond? Who is able to respond? The child's parents. They are not responsible for breaking the window, yet they are response-able. Used this way, moral responsibility is associated with tasks, stations, and status. Being responsible for x, in this sense, does not necessarily imply that one did x or did x intentionally or did something y intentionally that could be redescribed as doing x. It would be ridiculous, for example, to extend the redescriptions of the parents' act of conception to include the child's wanton breaking of windows. It is enough to assign responsibilities to roles or to task holders. However, many of the moral responsibilities (and the legal responsibilities) of mature moral citizens, full-fledged RB players, are of this task or role variety. Mackie's Rule, EPA, and PRA are not adequate, separately or in combination, to account for this kind of responsibility. Assignments of these responsibilities are made only to persons who are capable of the kind of responses PRA demands.

2 · Responsibility, Retaliation, and TIT FOR TAT

Edmund Pincoffs schematizes the elements of a standard ascription of responsibility.[1] He notes that to ascribe responsibility is for one person to identify a second person as the cause of an event (usually a harmful event, but sometimes a happy one) because of some action performed by that person in light of his or her position or role or station, and because that person cannot provide an acceptable justification or excuse for the action.

Rather than tinkering with his formula, I want to mount an attack on Pincoff's skeptic. My argument is that at least one of the practices that supports and is supported by the concept of responsibility incorporates a principle of retaliation. This principle provides some of the glue that bonds a moral community because it will be the preferred strategy regardless of the moral theory individual members adopt.

Pincoffs identified three social practices that utilize the responsibility ascription formula. One is determining who merits punishment or reward. The second is setting the targets of (usually financial) burden shifting, and the third is identifying appropriate subjects of blame and praise. Although these three uses of responsibility ascriptions may often converge on the same person with respect to the same event, they are distinct practices. To ascribe responsibility for the purpose of punishing is a very different moral enterprise from ascribing it for purposes of assessing the costs of harms or injuries suffered. And both of those practices are separable from using it to identify whoever is at fault when things go wrong. Notice how we regularly draw these distinctions. In the case of the *Exxon Valdez*, for example, Exxon was assessed the financial burden of compensating the state of Alaska as well as those whose livelihoods depend on the wildlife in Prince William Sound, while the captain and the corporation were blamed for the oil

18

spill. Punishment could have been meted out to the captain but not the crew, or only to Exxon.

Responsibility ascription, following Pincoffs, can be schematized as follows:

> Event C occurs. A imputes C to B because B did act D and B occupied role E and had no defense or only a mitigatory excuse for having done D and A imputes C to B in order to justify either (1) punishment of B for C or (2) placing the burden of compensation on B because of C or (3) finding B morally at fault, that is counting the doing of D and producing C against B's character.

Moral philosophers writing about responsibility tend to focus on one or the other of these reasons or purposes for ascribing responsibility. F. H. Bradley,[2] for example, emphasizes punishment. Utilitarians often settle on matters of compensation, while Aristotle[3] provides the *locus classicus* of the character evaluation usage.[4]

The practice of holding people responsible for things that happen, hence the concept of responsibility itself, depends for its sense on the purposes or ends to which we put it: the practices in which it is integral and which also depend on it. If there is no reason to punish people or if there is good reason to view punishment as unjustified, or if we cannot justify the sort of burden shifting that is characteristic of our compensatory system, or if the evaluation of character is unfair or unwarranted or inappropriate, then the skeptic will have shown that responsibility ascription is either meaningless, useless, silly, perverse, or a waste of time. Hence, the ascription of responsibility, no matter how complex internally, ultimately depends for its sense on the continuation of these practices. The sense of responsibility-ascribing, then, depends on the adoption of a certain set of practices and institutions in a community.

The skeptic introduces doubts about whether responsibility ascriptions can ever be justified. The skeptic believes that adequate and morally defensible alternative practices will serve the same purposes as the ones that support holding people responsible for things or that those purposes themselves are not appropriate or justifiable, so that the practices and institutions designed to meet them should simply be terminated. The skeptic then has at least two lines of attack: target the three practices by offering morally better alternatives that do not utilize responsibility ascription or show that the very purposes for which the practices exist are dependent upon philosophically untenable beliefs.

A skeptic taking the second tack might argue that punishment and blame are cruel and immoral because people cannot avoid doing what they do (an argument to be examined in chapter four). In *The Laws* Plato argued that crime is a symptom of a kind of social disease, a miasma or pollution. Criminals do not do evil willingly. Plato writes:

> The unjust man is presumably bad, but the bad man is involuntarily so. Now it never makes sense that the voluntary is done involuntarily. Hence the man who does injustice appears involuntarily unjust. . . . Everyone does injustice involuntarily.[5]

How then can we justify punishing anyone for his or her offenses? It would surely be neither just nor noble to inflict pain and suffering on someone who acted in a criminal fashion because of an affliction. Furthermore, if what is just is always noble, how could suffering what might be supposed to be a just punishment really be just? Plato argues:

> If we agree that something one undergoes is just, but shameful, the just and the noble will be in dissonance since the just things will be said to be most shameful.[6]

Punishment is intended to be shameful to those on whom it is inflicted. Even though suffering unwarranted punishment (such as being tortured for one's political or religious beliefs) might be ennobling, it could not normally be described as noble. But if punishment is not (or seldom) noble, it cannot be just. Plato's solution to the problem is ingenious, if a bit ingenuous. He admits that punishment is a morally unacceptable way of dealing with offenders but argues that there is an appropriate treatment for such persons: therapy. If our way of handling convicted criminals is not punishment but therapy intended to cure their diseases and rehabilitate them, then the principles of justice and nobility will be satisfied. This will especially be the case if, as Plato believes, the cause of their involuntary unjust actions is ignorance and the therapy is education. What could be more noble than educating the ignorant? It is irrelevant that the form of the therapy adopted may be very like and even harsher than the usual punishment. No matter how much suffering is inflicted, it will not be punishment because the offender is not held criminally responsible for the offending event. The crime is nothing but evidence of the need for the therapy. Nor is blame assessed. After all, the afflicted cannot control what they do, driven as they are by the disease. It is important to note, however, that Plato does believe in holding the offender responsible for compensation. He writes:

If . . . it should become evident to the judges chosen for the occasion that one of these circumstances obtains [these amount to various conditions that would explain involuntariness], and he should be judged to have broken the law while in such a condition, let him pay to the full exact compensation for the injury he has done someone.[7]

So even though he has an alternative to retributive punishment, he will need the basic responsibility ascription formula to generate appropriate compensation targets.

Can we simply substitute theraputic practices for punishment without losing one of the basic moral categories? The concept of wrongness is surely such a category, but embedded in it, as J. L. Mackie notes, is the very idea that "a wrong action calls for a hostile response."[8] I will call this the rule of retaliation or RR. Insofar as the identification of some actions as wrong is a mark of morality, RR should be fundamental to any morality. However, RR advocates, indeed mandates, harm-causing—hardly what one would expect of a moral rule! After all, morality focuses on the prevention of harm-causing, not the requiring of it. RR's apparent antithetical stance to the body of other moral rules and principles may have led philosophers like Plato to shun retributive punitive measures, seeing them as ignoble and so unjust. A close reading of Plato, however, suggests that he really does not reject RR. He looks instead at the reasons for wrongful action and tries to channel the hostile response toward rehabilitation. He does not deny that the wrongfulness of the actions requires retaliation, and many of his proposed "educational techniques" for criminals are indistinguishable from the traditional punishments attributed to Solon's legal code.

How can RR be optional in a moral system? Mackie maintained that, minimally, an act is wrong if it causes harm, is forbidden, and requires a hostile response. All three elements must be present and necessarily connected for full-blooded wrongness. In a boxing match, for example, one fighter may do considerable harm to another, but as long as the match is conducted within the sporting rules, the harm is not forbidden and so is not wrong. It is, in fact, often praised.

Mackie explained our acceptance of RR in terms of "an ingrained tendency to see wrong actions as calling for penalties."[9] He saw this rule as a product of feelings of resentment that are to be accounted for in sociobiological ways. The case for RR can be persuasively made without relying on sociobiological assumptions. There is, I think, a provocative similarity between Mackie's proposals and Locke's description of the rights people have in nature. Included among the Lockean rights is the right to retaliate or punish. Still, I am uncomfortable with grounding RR on any Lockean natural rights. I will turn instead to that other great classical British political theorist, Hobbes, in search of the defense of RR.

Imagine in a Hobbesian state of nature one person, Tom, is harmed by an invader, John. John has poked out Tom's eye while trying to steal food. Tom grabs a stick, chases John, pokes out one of his eyes, and takes back the food. John should be relatively certain that his earlier aggressive actions provoked Tom, and the harm Tom caused in response to the harm he endured will probably discourage John from repeating the raid. Apart from any question about a right to retaliate, both should realize that retaliation benefits the retaliator. Hence, if people commit themselves to acting prudently, they will have overwhelming reasons to independently adopt retaliatory strategies. (That does not exclude the possibility that there will be occasions when the prudent thing to do is run away and retaliate another day.) The retaliatory strategy, however, has a tendency to escalate, a problem noticed by the earliest legal codifiers. After all, why should Tom stop with the poking out of one of John's eyes? Why not both eyes and five teeth?

As far as we know, the talion principle (*lex talionis*) first appears in the Code of Hammurabi. (It seems not to be present in the purely compensatory code of the Sumerian UrNammu.) A striking application is found in section 229:

> If a builder constructed a house . . ., but did not make his work strong, with the result that the house which he built collapsed and so has caused the death of the owner of the house, that builder shall be put to death.[10]

In the Hebrew Book of the Covenant the familiar formula is found:

> If . . . hurt is done, then you shall give
> life for life,
> eye for eye,
> tooth for tooth,
> hand for hand,
> foot for foot,
> burn for burn,
> bruise for bruise,
> wound for wound.[11]

Some legal historians, including Maine, view the talion principle as barbaric and primitive, but I think that is a misinterpretation. It is significantly fairer than a purely compensatory model. The wergeld system of the Anglo-Saxons, for example, favors those with the wherewithal to pay. The rich might inflict injuries and pay compensation, while the poor cannot afford to do so and so are killed for the slightest offenses. The talion principle also works to limit retribution and end spiraling blood feuds. In fact, the principle, as Boecker notes, "originated in the administration of justice characteristic of nomadic tribes."[12]   Its dominant purpose is to control the extent of retaliatory response, and it can do so across different populations because it is a principle that can be (and was) acceptable to a variety of tribes. Hence, as Wagner argues,[13] the talion principle is a basic, reasonable principle of international law. Insofar as Tom and John exist in a state of nature comparable to the relationship between nomadic tribes, the talion principle should recommend itself to them. What it says is "only one life for a life, only one eye for an eye, only one tooth for a tooth, etc."[14] In effect, in the language of game theory, it counsels the adoption of a TIT FOR TAT strategy in human relationships such as those characterizable in iterated Prisoner's Dilemma games.

Strictly speaking, the talion principle is reactionary. It does not directly counsel not invading, so it is not a perfect translation of TIT FOR TAT or vice versa. Invading, in fact, is the rationally dominant move for either party to make if (1) he does not expect the other to be able to retaliate *or* (2) he does not know the other has adopted a retaliatory strategy, *or* (3) this is not an iterated game.

Robert Axelrod has shown that TIT FOR TAT is a relatively successful strategy for players of iterated Prisoner's Dilemma games.[15] Our story involves two humans in a state of nature, so let us define Tom's and John's two choices: to cooperate with his neighbor (that is, let him alone to plant, sow, build, and enjoy the fruits of his labors) or to take a hostile action against him (to invade and deprive him of those fruits as well as his life or liberty). If Tom and John cooperate, the two should create a stable, relatively secure communal environment. It will always be true, however, that if one is cooperative and the other is an invader, then the invader will reap the greatest immediate benefits and the cooperator will suffer. It appears rational, then, to be an invader rather than a cooperator, but if each attacks the other, neither will benefit, both will suffer. The dilemma is that rationality, defined as acting to maximize one's interests, will lead both players to the worst rather than the Pareto optimal outcome.

When the dilemma is iterated, does the rational strategy change? Be an invader, make a big profit; be a cooperator, try to achieve social stability. What sort of long-term strategy should Tom and John adopt with respect to their interactions?

John, let us say, reasons that the number of plays in the game is unimportant. He has no idea how long Tom will stay in the neighborhood, so each play is as likely as another to be their last engagement. He knows he will always do better if on their final interaction he invades. As that is true of the final play, it will be true of every other play. This is commonly referred to as the rollback argument. On the last play there is clearly no reason for John to try to persuade Tom that he is cooperative. But Tom knows that as well, so the last play isn't really the last play in which choosing to cooperate is a lively option. The second-last play is. But no, the same argument applies, and so the lively option of cooperating rolls back to the third-last play. And so on, until one returns to the first play, where it will also be rational to invade, and no cooperation between John and Tom will be achievable by appeal to rationality.

But John and Tom have no idea when their last interaction will occur, so the rollback cannot be started. Still, it does not seem to be rational for either to cooperate on the first move.

Assume that Tom is about to make the first move. He would prefer a long-term cooperative arrangement with John to a single invasion success. More than likely, that would be followed by a retaliatory invasion by John. Still, Tom has no way to insure that John will not regard any cooperative play by him as an invitation to invade. Invading, after all, is the rational move. Tom is no fool. He has read the *Leviathan*:

> It is a precept, or general rule of reason, that every man, ought to endeavor peace, as far as he has hope of obtaining it; and when he cannot obtain it, that he may seek, and use, all helps, and advantages of war.[16]

And Hobbes here echoes Shakespeare's Henry V:

> In peace there's nothing so becomes a man
> As modest stillness and humility:
> But when the blast of war blows in our ears,
> Then imitate the action of the tiger.[17]

What strategy should Tom adopt? Following Hobbes's recommendation and his own realization that he is likely to do better over the long haul if both he and John cooperate, Tom decides on two simultaneous actions. He will cooperate and announce a strict retaliatory policy if John does not also cooperate. Simply, he will cooperate on the first move and then on all subsequent moves do whatever John does on his previous move. Tom adopts TIT FOR TAT. Actually there is no need for him to announce his intention to retaliate unless he wishes to deter John from invading on the first move. His actions will reveal his strategy. John, let us say, decides to take a short-run rational approach and invades on his first move. He realizes that after the first move he will be locked in a retaliatory spiral with Tom. Still, invading on the first move will put him ahead of the cooperator, though he cannot expect to realize the gains of mutual cooperation in the long run.

Axelrod[18] has shown with tournament studies that TIT FOR TAT players cannot do better than those playing other strategies, and they cannot do better than dyed-in-the-wool cooperators. But a TIT FOR TAT policy will produce far better results against all other strategies when those using other strategies also interact with each other. To illustrate, let us add another player to the situation, Mary, and assign to her the strategy of occasionally invading to grasp an advantage and invading in response to an invasion. Suppose she interacts at various times with both John and Tom. She and John will be in a constant noncooperative state, and each of her invasions of Tom will be paid back in kind. So on the whole, Tom will do better than both John and Mary in approximately the same number of engagements.

The reason for that outcome is that TIT FOR TAT is what Axelrod[19] calls a "robust strategy." Unlike the other strategies, except for a saintly communal co-operative commitment, TIT FOR TAT is stable across a population of players. There-fore, if all the players in a region have adopted TIT FOR TAT as their approach to interactions with each other, then no other strategy can do better. Players using other strategies will not remain in the region.

But can a TIT FOR TAT enter a group whose members are all like the invader John? Will Tom's strategy gain the upper hand? No, because he will always be retaliating, and so he will be indistinguishable from the others. If, however, Tom can win over some allies—a small cluster of like-minded players—TIT FOR TAT can gain prominence. Even if there is only a 5 percent chance that a TIT FOR TAT player will meet another TIT FOR TAT on any given interaction, this rule will do better than the norm (of always invading).

Peter Danielson has shown that TIT FOR TAT is a strategy that will achieve cooperative stability for both Egoists and Universalists. "Indeed," he writes, "it would not be an exaggeration to say that TIT FOR TAT is a natural moral law."[20] Axelrod's proofs that TIT FOR TAT recommends itself to Egoists are based on his famous tournaments of iterated Prisoner's Dilemma. TIT FOR TAT won the first tournament by beating fourteen other strategies. It is easy to see why this should be so. If we eliminate all but the Always-invade, Always-cooperate, and TIT FOR TAT strategies (for the sake of simplicity), it is clear, as cited by Danielson,[21] that if each entrant plays the others 200 times, the Always-invader will win by a very slight margin over TIT FOR TAT. That would seem to confirm the view that Al-ways-invade is the Egoist's best strategy, but that is only because the field is too restrictive. In a tournament against a number of strategies, TIT FOR TAT dominates.

This is because TIT FOR TAT gets a far higher score against cooperative strategies than Always-invade can register. TIT FOR TAT is itself a cooperative strategy, so even in the match against Always-invade and Always-cooperate, this characteristic of TIT FOR TAT is evident. Always-invade scores poorly against the retaliator and not well against itself. Its only major successes come when it is matched with the dyed-in-the-wool cooperator. TIT FOR TAT, on the other hand, gains high scores against the field. Hence, if one adopts an Egoist position, TIT FOR TAT recommends itself. Axelrod's book, in fact, provides a strong argument for what we have always tried to tell our students: being nice to others accrues greater long-term benefits to oneself. There are strong self-interested reasons for not acting as Hobbes described people in nature. There is one problem with this idyllic picture: it ignores the possibility of only one Always-invader in a community otherwise composed of TIT FOR TATs and Always-cooperators. In short, as Danielson writes, "If an Egoist asks, 'Why won't [Invading] go well in general?' the answer is not the hypothetical, 'What if you were made to play against yourself,' but, 'Others may in fact have the same idea.' "[22]

Here the issue of collective stability comes to the aid of TIT FOR TAT. No one wants to argue that there is a best strategy, but some strategies, as mentioned above, may stabilize in a community. TIT FOR TAT is such a strategy, while Always-invade is not. A community of Always-invaders (Hobbes's state of nature, I suppose) can resist the entry of all other strategies "so long as the newcomers arrive one at a time."[23] However, we have already seen that TIT FOR TATs can successfully enter and sustain themselves in such a community in very small clusters, and that they resist the onslaught of any number of Always-invaders. So again, TIT FOR TAT should be, according to Axelrod's propositions, the strategy of choice of Egoists.[24]

What of Universalists? Axelrod's argument is rather persuasive, if somewhat tentative. He equates universalism with something like the Golden Rule which, he acknowledges, one is likely to interpret as counseling Always-cooperate and not the retaliatory stance of TIT FOR TAT. Turn the other cheek. But one soon runs out of cheeks. The Always-cooperate strategy is itself "an incentive for the other player to exploit you."[25] It encourages the Always-invader and so destabilizes the community. TIT FOR TAT, however, not only furthers one's own interests, it helps others, in Axelrod's terms, "by making it hard for exploitative strategies to survive."[26] That seems to be the point of the Universalists' moral theory. Hence, they should embrace TIT FOR TAT rather than the unstable Always-cooperate stance. Importantly, TIT FOR TAT does not offend against the idea that one should act as one wishes to be acted on, "Do unto others as you would have them do unto you." I am committed to not initiating invasions as I do not want to be invaded, but I would be willing to universalize a retaliatory strategy as I would expect retribution for my trespasses.

The TIT FOR TAT strategy is, then, the most stable for any population. In short, a strategy that seeks cooperation, never initiates invasion but responds hostilely to hostility, then immediately returns to cooperation once the other has done so, is the most collectively stable strategy that a people can adopt. It is no wonder Hammurabi and the early Hebrews incorporated it as a central element of their legal codes. It is the basic moral strategy, and what appear to be vastly different ethical points of view should endorse it.

The Universalist might be a bit "softer" than the Egoist in adopting TIT FOR TAT against strategies like TESTER (a first move defector who cooperates and then plays TIT FOR TAT on subsequent moves if the other player defects; "otherwise it cooperates on the second and third moves and defects on every other move after that"[27]). As Danielson writes, "Our Universalist will use a responsive stragegy like TIT FOR TAT only if the gain from his victim's learning to cooperate outweighs the social cost of teaching him."[28] In general the Universalist will adopt TIT FOR TAT only when convinced the relationship is long-term. It is important to re-member, however, that the Egoist and the Universalist will not converge on a single strategy in noniterated Prisoner's Dilemma situations. So, though I think we can say with confidence that the rule of retaliation is *a* basic moral rule, we cannot extend the same confidence to the claim that it is *the* basic moral rule.

Mackie maintains that retaliatory policies and behavior "will naturally be ac-companied by the development of retributive emotions directed towards the sources of injury."[29] Insofar as the invader (or noncooperator) disrupts the stabil-ity of society, resentment against the invader is to be expected. Cooperative retaliation by a community of TIT FOR TATs is very likely to develop. That commu-nity may be expected to emphasize notions of cooperation and nonharm in the principles and rules it adopts for intercommunal life. Hence, though founded on a rule of positive harm-causing (RR), their morality will be dominated by princi-ples antithetical to such positive hostile displays.

What Mackie called the "paradox of retribution"[30] (that a retributive principle of punishment, though inconsistent with and not derivable from our other moral principles, cannot be eliminated from our moral system) is dissolved. RR is foun-dational in the sense that it is a precondition for the stable community to which the other moral principles and moral aspirational ideals are addressed. That may also explain why Locke found it necessary to make the rule of retaliation a natural right. Insofar as TIT FOR TAT (and RR) must incorporate responsibility ascription to identify proper targets of retaliation in multiple-member communities, responsibility ascription is crucial to morality. Regardless of whether or not we establish a compensatory system or evaluate each other's characters, responsibility ascription cannot be eliminated as long as we would sustain a stable moral community. Even Gandhi accepted the rule of retaliation, though he required nonattachment in its application.

3 · Losing Innocence for the Sake of Responsibility

"Our squad of Mustangs was flying escort for B-l7's over Belgium. I was on the point. Three ME-109s came at us from out of the sun. It was one hell of a dog fight. Jimmy Craig was hit and bailed out. He was up there in his chute, settling down easy, when this Kraut pulls away and takes dead aim at Jimmy. I couldn't believe it. You never shoot a guy hanging in a chute. But that's what he did. He cut him in half. I swung round on that bastard's tail and picked at him until he bailed out. His chute opened. I watched him floating there just like Jimmy. I wanted to see his eyes. But he had goggles on. Then I shot that son of a bitch out of the sky."
"How'd it feel?"
"It felt good."
"Really? . . . Well, you were there."
"No . . . Okay, . . . I cried."
—Conversation with a fighter pilot at a reunion, 1989

Lost innocence seems to create problems that moral philosophers have almost utterly ignored despite its apparent significance in each of our lives. Theologians, novelists, and poets have made loss of innocence perhaps the central theme of Western culture. Where would psychiatrists be without it? And the moral philosophers? Concentrating on guilt and punishment, no doubt. Innocence is a very elusive moral notion, one better looked over than looked at, loaded with the sort of emotional complications that resist the clear and clean principles of philosophers. Theologians and novelists rush in where wise folks fear to tread!

At least one philosopher, Herbert Morris,[1] has made a notable contribution to our understanding of the phenomenon. I hope to build on his analysis and carry matters further by arguing that loss of innocence is a prerequisite for membership in the responsible moral community. I suspect that the reason for this lack of philosophical attention is that innocence is a morally ambiguous notion. Is it a good thing or a bad thing? With respect to criminal activity, being innocent is, of

course, a good thing. And under our law everyone is supposedly presumed innocent until proved guilty. In ordinary legal use innocence is simply the absence of
guilt. But that cannot be all there is to the innocence that is meant when we talk
of innocence lost.

Losing innocence and gaining maturity are generally associated with being
liable to be held fully morally responsible for what one does, individually or collectively. Innocence, in the sense I am using it, is not merely an excuse or an
alibi; it is a matter of status.

Innocence is often identified with moral purity when it ought to be associated
with moral virginity. Moral purity, if there is such a thing is determined by evaluating someone from the perspective of or against the standards set by moral
rules and principles. The morally pure always act in the morally prescribed fashion. Moral virginity is the condition or state of not being a proper subject of
those standards. One can be a moral virgin while acting in ways proscribed by
moral principles and rules.

The *Oxford English Dictionary* defines innocence as "the state of being untaint-
ed," but also as lacking knowledge. Moral virginity may sound like a desirable
state, but our cultural/moral traditions insist that it must not be allowed to persist
for too long in any member of the community. So how good can it be? From the
point of view of contract, it is a socially unsteady state, one in which persons are
legally treated as undependable or, more importantly, unaccountable. At best, it
is something to be tolerated only for a limited time.

Let us, following Morris, examine one of the culture's earliest lost innocence
myths. Eve and then Adam ate of the fruit of the forbidden tree of knowledge of
good and evil and "the eyes of them both were opened, and they knew that they
were naked"[2] and they felt shame. As Morris points out,[3] the meaning of this
biblical passage is not self-evident. It becomes all the more mysterious when we
consider that the ingestion of the fruit supposedly brought Adam and Eve knowledge of good and evil. Is that not what all of us want our children to learn? The
law requires it as a test for criminal liability.

Perhaps their *awareness* that they were unclothed constituted the loss. The
sheer fact of their nudity alone, however, could have had little to do with the
matter. They were not wearing clothing from the first. What is it to become
aware of one's nakedness and that of someone else? Surely Adam and Eve had
seen that they wore no garments before they ingested the fruit. The business
about their eyes opening is metaphorical. They were not, presumably, literally
blind before the Fall. In fact, if they were, they would have much less to remember, and so regret, about their loss of paradise.

Seeing *that* you or someone else is naked, however, is not just a matter of seeing an unclothed body. It requires a conceptual acquisition. To see that you are naked is not simply to see the obvious, but to see that which was unremarkable as remarkable. J. L. Austin wrote of the principle of "no modification without aberration,"[4] which John Searle modified and expanded into what he called "the assertion fallacy."[5] Searle's point was that in a normal situation it is inappropriate to assert that it is normal. To remark that "Mary is breathing" is usually out of order. Insofar as being unclothed was not only normal but the only state they had experienced, for Adam to say, "Eve, you're uncovered," would have been equally inappropriate before the Fall. "It is inappropriate to assert of a particular standard or normal situation that it is standard or normal unless there is some reason for supposing, or for supposing someone might have supposed, etc., that it might have been nonstandard or abnormal."[6]

Adam and Eve had seen each other unclothed from their first meeting, but they did not see that they were naked until they ate the fruit of the tree of knowledge of good and evil. After the Fall, had Eve remarked to Adam, "I'm naked, and so are you," she would not have been committing Searle's assertion fallacy. Such an observation would have been, in the circumstances, remarkable, an assertion worth the asserting, though the state of their undress had not changed since their creation.

Suppose we ask Eve (before the Fall) what she sees as we direct her attention towards Adam. She reports that she sees a naked man. But does she see *that* Adam is naked? The answer is not as simple as it should be. In mid-June 1991, in Texas, a child with normal eyesight looking at the western sky in the early evening might have reported seeing a crescent-shaped white object and three white dots of different degrees of brightness. But the child could not have seen that those dots were the convergence of the planets Mars, Venus, and Jupiter, the dawning of the Age of Aquarius, unless the child possessed a good deal of knowledge about astronomy and popular culture. *Seeing that*, as opposed to seeing, is knowledge-dependent.

N. R. Hanson wrote " 'Seeing that' threads knowledge into our seeing."[7] From every "I see that" an "I know that" can be unpacked. The biblical passage speaks of Adam and Eve knowing that, not seeing, they were naked. Coming to see *that* or to know, unlike merely seeing, depends on the acquisition of concepts and even theoretical information. Acquiring concepts is more than acquiring a vocabulary. There are layers of understanding the possession of which is not always evident from the proper use of the vocabulary in ordinary discourse. Innocents sprinkle their discourse with the language of sexual experience in ways that are perfectly in order, syntactically and semantically, but provide no measure of their acquisition of the concepts. Acquisition of a conceptual structure, such as the one that includes or focuses on nakedness, causes one to see *that* something one had long seen one way takes a description one had not previously used with respect to it. Eve's seeing *that* (or knowing) Adam is naked is quite a different thing from her seeing him naked. In the latter case, she merely "lays eyes on" him. One can, for example, see someone kidnap a child without seeing that the child is being kidnapped.

The nakedness of the principal characters in Eden is not the element that makes the situation nonstandard for them once they've eaten from the tree of knowledge. The crucial element that would make remarkable Eve's remark that they are naked must come from some other source than their nudity. It must come from a conceptual enrichment that is somehow associated with the kind of knowledge they gained by eating the fruit.

One might object that the point of the story is not so much gaining a special kind of conceptual knowledge, but discovering what is entailed in a divine prohibition. Suffering the consequences of disobeying God is, of course, a memorable way to cement the lesson in human consciousness. In such an account, Adam and Eve lose their innocence not by acquiring a new way of conceptualizing and so describing their experience, but because their defiant behavior exposes them to the range of human possibilities and freedom. Their grasp of their own power is expanded, but the new options available to them are terrifying. By ordering them not to eat the fruit, Kierkegaard notes,[8] God reveals to them that they could eat it. And if they could, they might. The prohibition provokes a radical experience of freedom which, Kierkegaard claims, involves dread. According to Donald Palmer,[9] Sartre mentions a woman who dreaded her husband's leaving for work because she feared that after he left she would sit nude in the window looking out on the street. Because she knew she was free to do it, she dreaded she would do it.

There is one obvious problem with the prohibition/disobedience conception of loss of innocence. We have all seen children playing at the beach. Their mother shouts at them, loudly enough for everyone on the beach to hear her (including the children), telling them not to throw sand at each other. But they keep doing it all the same. They understand the prohibition, they know the authority that issues it, and they are guilty of disobedience. Perhaps they even sense that the prohibition would not be uttered if they could not do it. If sand throwing were morally wrong, they would be guilty of wrongdoing, but it hardly seems that in or because of this situation they will lose their innocence. When the mother catches and spanks them, they might even feel guilty for disobeying, yet retain their innocence. The episode does not cast them into the community of morally responsible persons, though it could, I suppose, provide a nudge in that direction.

They might learn that their freedom to act can have unpleasant consequences when it confronts authority and power, but the lesson does not have the catastrophic consequences of Adam and Eve's disobedience of God's prohibition. I doubt, however, that the divine nature of the authority is the important factor. Most of us lose innocence without countermanding the direct orders of God.

[As something of an aside: I have difficulty with God's role in the story. What actually was God's point in forbidding the eating of the fruit? Was it to teach Adam and Eve something about the extent of human freedom? Was it to test their ability to follow orders? Was it to protect the realm of the gods from overpopulation? After all, the fruit of two trees was forbidden, and the expulsion was as much a way of preventing humans from eating of the fruit of the tree of life as it was a punishment for disobedience. Furthermore, what were the forbidden trees doing in the Garden in the first place? One must also assume that God (or the gods, as the plural is used in the third chapter of Genesis) is (are) not innocent. "Now that the man has become like one of us in knowing good from evil, he must not be allowed to reach out and pick from the tree of life too, and eat and live forever."[10] Matters better left for some other occasion!]

The only plausible cause of the loss of innocence in the Eden story that also would have applicability over the spectrum of human biographies is the acquisition of conceptual knowledge. By conceptual knowledge I mean knowledge of good and evil, not just knowledge of the extent of one's freedom—that would support the *Oxford English Dictionary*'s definition of innocence as a kind of ignorance. What is involved is not ignorance of the possibilities of action, but ignorance of the possibilities of description. So, even if God had not forbidden eating the fruit of that tree and Adam and Eve ate it, they would have lost their innocence but been guilty of nothing.

The problem of understanding innocence is complicated by the different ways in which we use the concept. There are innocent actions—those not in violation of the appropriate command, law, rule, or principle. And there are innocent persons—persons not yet admitted into the moral community, moral virgins. As noted above, deeds alone have little to do with innocence or its loss. Innocents can kill, lie, steal, have sexual intercourse, and retain their innocence.

Innocents may exist, from the moral point of view, in something akin to Hobbes's state of nature, the state of "war of every man against every man . . . in which nothing can be unjust. The notions of right and wrong, justice and injustice, have no place . . . [for] [t]hey are qualities that relate to man in society, not in solitude."[11] Hobbes could have said that they are qualities that relate to mature people, not those still in innocence. Certainly Hobbes would agree that innocents may contract. After all, humans in his state of nature are premoral, innocents of a sort, who contract while in nature to form the state. But innocents must be converted to moral citizens or their contracts will always be avoidable by them; that is a basic capacity principle of contract law. Any attempt to maintain a society of innocents is doomed because of the instability of their contractual relations. Hence, although rational innocents naturally in love with liberty may form themselves into social units to escape the misery of their solitary, brutish condition, they must be forced from their innocence and made moral, the keeping of contracts insured by the sword if necessary for the common benefit. (That is one of the themes of *The Lord of the Flies*.)

And what of sex? In novels and films the advent of sexual experience is typically identified with the end of innocence, but that is unconvincing. Surely Adam and Eve could have had sexual intercourse in the Garden before the Fall. Innocent sex. It is not sexual intercourse, or even its products (wanted or unwanted), that thrusts people into adulthood's responsibilities. The crucial factor must be the conceptual shift that promotes describing familiar things in a new way, a way that is laden with the language of responsibility.

Sean O'Faolain wrote a marvelous short story in which innocent nuns and monks on a summer holiday in Ireland spend many carefree hours in song as, with childish delight, they undertake learning Gaelic and the traditional Irish dances. Evening sessions in their rooms and moonlight cruises on the lake, though boisterous, never overstep the bounds of propriety. Nonetheless, they are sternly rebuked by the local curate. "Glory be to God, . . . to think that this kind of thing has been going on . . . for weeks. . . . Perhaps we think we are back in the days of the Reformation? . . . Singing? Dancing? Drinking?"[12] The monks and nuns become intensely ashamed of their behavior and live out the rest of the summer in virtual reclusiveness. Some years later the curate confides, "They were only children. Such innocents! . . . Of course, I *had* to frighten them!"[13] The story is entitled "The Man Who Invented Sin."

If losing innocence is identified with gaining a certain kind of knowledge, at least two types of questions are in order: the how question and the what question. How is such knowledge acquired? Ingestion of fruit may have salutary effects on one's need to summon a physician, but it is unlikely to be the primary route for acquisition of the relevant knowledge. And secondly, what actually does one need to learn or to be taught to lose innocence? What is the content of the requisite knowledge? Surely the knowledge in question is not gained by deductive logic.

The Bible says "their eyes were opened." A metaphor, but how is it to be understood? One gets the impression of a sudden dawning, the switching on of a faculty like the switching on of an electric light. People can lose innocence in a moment in an experience that triggers a different way of seeing the world and the humans, especially themselves, in it. Such dramatic moments do not happen for all of us, yet we lose innocence. Perhaps we should think of the eyes being opened as simply acquiring or adopting a different way of interpreting our environment. Some things may be exposed that before were hidden, others appreciated in different ways or for different reasons. Some things previously prized may now be discarded, others now held in high regard that before were not even noticed.[14]

I said that one may either acquire or adopt a different way of understanding things when one loses innocence; the two are not equivalent notions. One can acquire something in a number of ways; in some the individual is passive. Adopting, on the other hand, is an active business which suggests that the loss of innocence is the result of a deliberate act or acts. Many of us do set out quite purposefully to gain knowledge, but we usually cannot be described as setting out to adopt a conceptual point of view. I suppose that some people do go on such quests (some cultural anthropologists, for example) but it would be unfair to characterize the activities of, say, ordinary teenagers in such terms. More likely than not, people set off to experience what they have heard about only in whispers and euphemisms and wind up acquiring an unexpected understanding of things. Unfortunately, they often wind up acquiring other things as well—things they had not bargained for and with respect to which everyone is asking, "Who's responsible?"

The metaphor of the eyes being opened suggests that when people lose innocence they undergo a Gestalt shift, seeing the old hag where earlier they had seen the young woman, or the rabbit now where before the duck was evident. But such an account does not fully capture the important elements of the experience. I would rather suggest that those who lose innocence learn in a very personal way how to redescribe their situations, their experiences, and their actions. In effect, they learn first hand or in the first person how to appropriately use the language of responsibility with respect to themselves. Herbert Morris says, "loss of innocence really consists in nothing more than a different feeling about what has been before one all along. Nothing new is learned; something new is *felt* about what is already known."[15]

The feeling dimension cannot be denied. Typically the feeling is intense and probably propels the epistemological shift. But the feeling itself is, I think, produced by learning the redescription. One feels differently about things because one describes them in a radically different way. Because they are described differently, one knows something more than one previously knew. At the very least, one knows that this sort of behavior takes a moral description and that acting in that way has moral consequences. But there is much more involved than a feeling, no matter how intense. In fact, I suppose one could lose one's innocence without experiencing any intense feelings at all.

What then is lost? The idea of loss itself contributes to the conceptual problem. First of all, unlike losing a toy, lost innocence is essentially connected with a gain. It is probably also the case that one does not know one has innocence until one loses it. It is part of the concept of innocence that to be innocent is not to know you are. Hence, we are in the curious position of only prizing innocence after we can no longer claim it. As long as one has it, it is normal to seek the experiences that result in its loss.

I have said that the process of losing innocence is one of learning how to redescribe things. But once the redescription has been learned, one loses the option of seriously using the illusions of innocent description. There is a linearity about the path of this redescription which makes the process different from Gestalt shifts. This shift is irreversible. It is also important to note that the shift is a cultural artifact, not at all a natural occurrence guaranteed by biological processes such as aging. Seneca, in one of his letters to Lucilius writes:

> Nature does not give us virtue: The process of becoming a good person is an art. . . . The innocence of primitives was due to ignorance and nothing else. . . . They lacked the cardinal virtues of justice, moral insight, self-control, and courage. Corresponding qualities had a place in their primitive lives; but virtue only comes to a character which has been thoroughly schooled and trained and brought to a pitch of perfection by unremitting practice. We are born for it, but not with it. And even in the best people, until you cultivate it there is only the material for virtue, not virtue itself.[16]

To say that the loss of innocence requires the acquisition of a disposition to describe events in a particular way is to suggest that the innocent, even if they possess the requisite concepts of morality, lack an understanding of the appropriate application of those concepts or of the use of those concepts in their own cases. Most basically, innocence means not having the training to use moral conceptual descriptions with insight. But there is much more. "An essential requirement of lost innocence is experience of a certain kind."[17] That is why the innocent cannot really imagine what they will acquire when they lose their innocence; it is what makes their attempts to understand so humorous to us and serious to them. The irony of innocence is that we strive so hard to lose it not knowing what it is, and then spend entirely too much time trying to reclaim it, to hide in it, and to be shielded by it. Innocence, it seems, is only valued by those who no longer possess it. In *Brideshead Revisited* Sebastian speaks of burying treasures from his happy youth and then spending his adult years digging them up and "remembering."

Jane Austen's *Pride and Prejudice* may be understood as revealing Elizabeth Bennet's progress from illusion to reality, from innocence to maturity. Austen seems to see innocence as self-deception, as living in a fantasy world governed by comfortable illusions. At the Netherfield ball Elizabeth reveals her immaturity and ignorance by teasing Darcy and laughing at him behind his back. Wrapped in childish romanticism, her sexual attraction to Wickham blinds her to the real characters of both Wickham and Darcy. But when she receives Darcy's letter, Elizabeth is suddenly thrust into the harsh light of reality. "Everything that happens in *Pride and Prejudice* . . . pivots around that crucial moment when Elizabeth comes to realize that she has never known herself."[18] Elizabeth loses her innocence when the letter disassociates the child Elizabeth from the woman.

Elizabeth cannot appreciate Darcy while she is under the spell of Wickham, whom she sees only as her illusions would have him. Maturity is outgrowing Wickham like an old dress. Although the letter is the crucial moment of her passage, the change into adulthood is hardly self-annihilating. Elizabeth grows up. Her immaturity naturally passes without a total disruption of her identity. She does not become something or someone other than she was. She realizes instead that, despite what she believed, she had not previously known herself or most of the people in her world. "Til this moment, I never knew myself." The immature Elizabeth fancied she could easily understand complex people, but on reading Darcy's letter she discovers herself exposed for the first time. The experience for her is remarkably like that of Adam and Eve. Her eyes are opened, she sees her figurative nakedness, and she is ashamed in Darcy's presence as she realizes how her life before the loss of innocence was "blind, partial, prejudiced, absurd."

So for Jane Austen loss of innocence is a good thing, not something to look back on with regret. Why then is it often viewed as so terrible? Because most of us do not share Jane Austen's confidence in the continuity of self. Many of us sense that it is the very illusions of our innocence that sustain our identities. Being robbed of them or having them corrupted by maturity or by events that hasten maturity is a clear attack on ourselves. Like another great heroine of English literature, Catherine Earnshaw, we fear maturity because it might radically transform us.

In *Wuthering Heights* Cathy is terrified at the prospect of involvement in a world she does not control, yet she realizes that it is inevitable that she must enter such a world. To combat the loss of self she associates with maturation, Cathy projects her innocent self onto Heathcliff to keep "from losing it altogether. As Cathy sees it, Heathcliff . . . personifies childhood . . . he is indifferent to the physical and cultural constraints . . . responsible for the disturbing changes in identity that she . . . experiences once she reaches puberty . . . and he cannot avoid loving her."[19]

She tells Nelly, "He is more myself than I am . . . I *am* Heathcliff."[20] Cathy, by identifying her innocent self with Heathcliff, tries to fight against the loss of innocence, but she has already lost the battle, and her self has been lost as well. "I wish I were a girl again, half savage, and hardy, and free, and laughing at injuries, not maddening under them! Why am I so changed? Why does my blood rush into a hell of tumult at a few words? I'm sure I should be myself were I once again among the heather on those hills."[21] Only death returns Cathy to those hills, and even as a ghost she is Catherine Linton, not Cathy Earnshaw. She has been irreparably altered by maturity. She may try to cover her loss with the trappings of innocence, but the result is ironic. Innocence is not salvaged. Her plight reminds me of the final scene of the film *Full Metal Jacket*, in which young soldiers altered by the savagery of war march off, not to the tunes of glory, but to the melodies of childhood illusions: the Mickey Mouse Club song.

However, the view that losing one's innocence is simply coming to know oneself is inadequate. In the paradigm case, Adam and Eve did not gain knowledge of themselves as much as they gained knowledge of good and evil. Two great philosophers, Aristotle and Bertrand Russell, offer insights into different elements of what is involved.

Aristotle, when talking of the types of ignorance involved in assigning responsibility, distinguishes between ignorance of particulars and general ignorance of what one ought to do. For him, persons ought not be held fully responsible for their involuntary acts, and it is a certain type of ignorance that makes acts involuntary: ignorance of particular circumstances. "A man may be ignorant, then, of who he is, what he is doing, what or whom he is acting on, and sometimes also what (e.g. what instrument) he is doing it with, and to what end (e.g. he may think his act will conduce to some one's safety), and how he is doing it (e.g. whether gently or violently)."[22] Also, involuntary acts in accord with one or some of these descriptions must be conjoined with subsequent pain and repentance if they are to be among the things for which one is relieved of responsibility. Ignorance of particular circumstances as a mitigation of responsibility, however, must occur within a context of moral knowledge or what Aristotle calls knowledge of the universal. General ignorance of what one ought to do, of the principles of morality, of knowledge of good and evil, is not excusable. In fact, he says that it is grounds for censure and leads to sheer wickedness.

Knowledge of good or what one ought morally to do, however, is probably not as important as knowledge of evil or rather, of one's capacity to do and be done evil. In that sense, Kierkegaard's conception of the Eden situation in terms of the discovery of one's capabilities is far off the mark. But it is a certain type of possibility that one must come to know. Experiencing evil in the loss of innocence is grasping for the first time the possibility that things might have gone differently, and so seeing what would have been good in the situation, and so seeing yourself as capable of the evil. To do that one needs to know evil in the universal sense to which Aristotle alludes. Ignorance of that sense of evil (and therefore good) is just what characterizes innocents. They may in fact be quite knowledgeable of particulars (knowing that it is Bob and not Bill they are hitting, and that the end of the hitting will be a bruised and battered Bob), but their ignorance of the universal shields them from responsibility. Of course it will only do so for a short period of time, childhood, and adults are expected to exert considerable effort to insure that the universal is imparted to them during that period.

The recognition in oneself of the capacity to do and be done evil may promote a powerful refusal to grow up. But there is something bogus in that refusal, since the threshold has already been crossed.

I declared, resolved, and determined that I would never under any circumstances be a . . . grower, that I would stop right there, remain as I was—and so I did; for many years I not only stayed the same size but clung to the same attire . . . I did so in order to be exempted from the . . . grown-up world. . . . I remained the precocious three-year old, towered over by grown-ups but superior to all grown-ups, who refused to measure his shadow with theirs, who was complete both inside and outside, while they, to the very brink of the grave were condemned to worry their heads about . . . what they were compelled to gain by hard and often painful experience.[23]

Acquiring knowledge of good and evil (Aristotle's universal) relevant to loss of innocence must be different from the acquisition of what we might call purely objective knowledge, like knowledge of geometry, which is merely a matter of learning the rules and the angles. Suppose innocents were taught Kant's categorical imperative, all three formulations, and then Bentham's utility calculus. Would that transform them into mature members of the moral community? It might bore them to tears, but they would not be crying for the loss of innocence. Not every learning experience involving morality constitutes the crucial loss. Jane Austen is right: the loss must be very personal and not passive. The learning has to be about oneself and it has to be, in some sense, active. The illusions that are shattered must be your own and not those perpetrated on you by society. If you never believed there was a Santa Claus, it would hardly affect you to learn that Santa Claus is only a myth. You would know something, even something important, but your innocence would not have been sacrificed in the bargain. Not every kind of ignorance is innocence. To have the experience of loss, something must be at stake for the loser. The concepts of redescription one acquires must be seen as appropriately applied to oneself.

Russell drew an important distinction between knowledge by description and knowledge by acquaintance,[24] a distinction that is relevant to understanding the loss of innocence that is prerequisite to full responsibility status in the moral community. Knowledge by acquaintance, as Russell explained, is logically independent of knowledge that something is the case or what he called "knowledge of truths." Knowledge by description, however, involves "some knowledge of truths as its source and ground."[25] I can know that people ought not to do certain kinds of things, and I can know that I ought to obey authority, and I can know that there is evil in the world by description: those are "in virtue of some general principle" or principles. But to have such knowledge, I needn't become directly aware of evil. I could infer it.

Russell provides the example of a particular shade of color. Shall we take for our example the color I am now seeing while looking at this computer screen? I can say that it is blue, not a navy or a pale blue, but more of a Texas sky blue. "But such statements, though they make me know truths about the colour, do not make me know the colour itself any better than I did before: so far as concerns knowledge of the colour itself, as opposed to knowledge of truths about it, I know the colour perfectly and completely when I see it."[26] The paradigm case of Russell's knowledge by acquaintance is obviously sense-data, but he went on to extend the notion to acquaintance by memory, by introspection, and with the self. We can also have, he maintained, knowledge of universals by acquaintance. His examples are whiteness, diversity, and brotherhood. To that list I would add evil.

There is a radical difference between knowing evil by acquaintance and knowing evil by description. That is not to say that one does not learn considerably more about evil by description than one may gain by acquaintance. However, conceiving of evil through acquaintance is the foundation of that descriptive learning. Russell's principle is: "Every proposition which we can understand must be composed wholly of constitutients with which we are acquainted."[27] Carrying forward this point, we should say that a condition for a person's knowing that such and such behavior is wrong or evil is that the person must already have had a private experience of evil. Learning the principles of morality by description— and that one is subject to them—takes one far beyond one's personal experience.

That is what Russell calls "the chief importance of knowledge by description." The process of moral education, however, requires acquaintance in some manner or fashion.

Whatever Eve tasted in that first bite of the forbidden fruit, it did not have to be complete knowledge of good and evil or the destruction of all of her illusions for her to lose her innocence. All that was needed was an immediate acquaintance with her capacity to do and be done evil, that is, knowledge by acquaintance of the rudiments of Aristotle's knowledge of the universal.[28]

Making the acquaintance of evil need not be sudden or dramatic. It need not occur in a startling event in the skies over Belgium or in a sleazy motel room. Knowledge of good and evil, without the forbidden fruit, is usually incremental, and once the requisite acquaintance occurs, much of it is by description. Innocence is a scaler notion—there are degrees of it. Still, for each of us there is a threshold somewhere along the scale, and when one crosses it, when one acquires that array of concepts or that extension of a concept (like evil), one becomes morally responsible. Where that threshold is may differ from person to person. Some people will need a wider range of experience of evil than others before they are capable of the understanding necessary to respond to morality. The threshold may be crossed by different people at different points on the scale. What sets the location of the threshold for each person must be a variant not measured by the scale, perhaps intelligence or sensitivity.

The relevant experience, then, is the one in which a person grasps that he or she is a potential or actual subject of evil. The distinctive response to the experience of evil, the confrontation with what William Golding aptly called "the beast from air," is horror. It is no wonder that we weep for the loss. "With filthy body, matted hair, and unwiped nose, Ralph wept for the end of innocence, the darkness of man's heart."[29]

All of this sounds rather depressing but it is not. Loss of innocence is a necessary condition for society. Enduring civil organization, Hobbes might have said, depends on it. This might suggest that the moral thing to do is to promote the loss of innocence even in those who have barely experienced its joys. That is not my intent. Should not children have a right to innocence? If I force a child of tender years to experience evil, to learn to apply moral language in describing his or her own behavior, would I not be doing wrong? It is a curious confusion in our morality that we talk of protecting the innocent while recognizing a moral obligation to see that they are corrupted.

In common law children under seven were presumed to be incapable of criminal activity. From seven to fourteen there was a rebuttable presumption of incapacity. The only way to defeat that presumption was to demonstrate beyond a doubt that the child had actual criminal capacity. The common law rules are no longer as important in the criminal justice system because of the existence of the juvenile courts in which children are now tried as delinquent rather than criminal defendants. There is, of course, a chasm in our cultural consciousness between the concept of a delinquent and that of criminal. To lose innocence is to construct a bridge over that chasm, but it is a rickety bridge that collapses for each person after only one passage.

Statutory rape laws protect infants, even those who are physically indistinguishable from adults, from sexual encounters with adults. The age of consent has risen markedly from ten at the time of the Tudors to sixteen, seventeen, or eighteen in most American jurisdictions today. This trend is particularly notable because there has also been a decline in the age of female biological maturation since 1850 from sixteen to below thirteen. So more females than ever before are biologically mature while under the protection of laws regarding the age of consent. Insofar as the trends have gone in exactly opposite directions, we may suppose that the rise in the legal age of consent signals a strong social commitment to preserve innocence, at least sexual innocence, despite natural developments.

In moral theory in general there are two categories of entities: those that fall under the rules, principles or axioms of the morality, those who have both rights and responsibilities; and those to whom duties are owed, in whom rights are vested, but who are not required to reciprocate. Innocent children are clearly in this latter group. We protect them and give them rights that limit our treatment of them, and they generally escape moral responsibility for their actions. We protect their innocence to the point of trying to insure it. On the other side there seems to be a moral obligation for the mature members of society to cause the end of innocence, to guide children through the passage into adulthood. That obligation is recognized in the most primitive societies in carefully designed and orchestrated rituals that mark a distinct end to the validity of the appeal to innocence. In our industrialized society, ritual gave way to the dutiful parental conveyance of the "facts of life." But that too has been largely replaced by word of mouth among peers, media, and popular culture. In any event, if knowledge by acquaintance is not gained, if innocence is allowed to survive, the responsibility for such failure should be assessed against the relevant adults. If most of a generation were to fail to have the appropriate innocence-ending experiences, a collective moral guilt should be placed on the shirking shoulders of the older generation. Since there are no guarantees of that sort of experience in nature, it makes sense to talk of an adult moral responsibility to usher the innocent down the aisle of experience. The problem is that such a duty could be misconstrued as a license for child abuse. Matters here are delicate.

Surely we should not set out to destroy all of our children's (or each other's) illusions. The moral imperative to end innocence must be tempered with the restriction that only those illusions that prevent full responsible moral citizenship need be destroyed. In large measure, our illusions constitute our individual personalities. With respect to those, the child is the parent of the adult. To suffer the shattering of all or most of those illusions is to have one's identity devastated. That is not growing up. That is psychic annihilation. The nakedness in which one would be left is nothingness. No one can identify with it.

4 · Fate and Responsibility

It was a soft, sunny, Irish afternoon near Ballenskelligs on the Kerry coast. On the boat to the mystical Skellig Isles, I struck up a conversation with a middle-aged Irish woman. When I told her my name, she asked if I knew Percy French, one of Ireland's great balladeers. I assured her I did, but I was surprised that she referred to him as if he were still a living songwriter. He died in 1920. Nothing and no one seems really to die in Ireland. The long dead and the recently martyred are typically talked of as if they were just then taking a pint at the local alehouse.

She asked why I had come to Ireland. I told her it was mainly a matter of seeing my ancestral home. She asked if I was planning to visit Ulster, her home. I told her that the car rental company forbade taking its vehicles across the border. Too many of them had been used in bombings or other terrorist activities.

She reflected, with obvious resignation, on how difficult economic recovery in the six counties will be if tourists and industry continue to stay away, if Irish Americans do not invest there. I reminded her of the frequent violent attacks by the IRA, the UDA, and the RUC and incidents of mistaken identity that have cost so many lives. Only the night before a British army bus was blown up on the Antrim road out of Belfast. Four English soldiers were killed and a number injured. Two women, identified in the press as suspected members of the IRA, were hunted down at a nearby farmhouse and summarily shot to death.

She said that when she heard the news on the radio, she prayed that her niece, an IRA activist, was not one of the murdered women. I pointed out that though it sounds natural enough, it did not make sense for her to have prayed today that her niece survived on the Antrim Road last night. Either she was killed in that farmhouse or she was not. Nothing God does in answer to her prayer today can change what happened there the night before.

44

After questioning my grasp of theology, she assured me that she wasn't asking for a miracle. She understood that if her niece was killed, no one, not even God, could change that. But she was asking that, when the soldiers started shooting at those IRA women, God had made sure her niece was not there. She reasoned that God knows everything, what happened and what will happen. So God knew at the time the soldiers opened fire that she was going to pray the next morning that her niece not be killed at that farmhouse, and He may have granted her prayer at the propitious moment.

She seemed content with her explanation and turned away to contemplate the Skelligs in the distance or, more likely, to worry about whether or not her prayer had had the desired effect. For my part, I began to think about the implications of her theology. If she was right that God knows everything that will happen, then how could she not have prayed? Simply, if God knew yesterday, or forever, that she was going to pray that prayer this morning, she had to pray the prayer. She had no choice in the matter. How could anything that happens not have happened? And if her theological fatalism was correct, and no human actions are free, then why hold people responsible for what they do? Is it all a matter of fate? Is the future as unalterable as the past? In the view of her all-knowing, all-powerful God, it would seem to be. Such a God knows whether or not any statement is true, regardless of its tense, and if it is not true, that it is false. There is no maybe. That cashes out the concept of an omniscient being.

Who would deny that many, if not most, of the parameters on what each of us will ever do in our lives are set by circumstances and events utterly outside of our control? Where and when you are born, your parents, the culture in which you live, your sex, intelligence, temperament—much of what will make your life happy or miserable is decided for you or is the result of otherwise insignificant fortuities and genetic luck. That is your fate in biological terms, and it is no trivial matter, though it may be politically imprudent to make much of this point.

Fatalism appears in different guises in the culture like, for example, theories of the science of history. Hegel writes, "Spirit, the rational and necessitated will of the Idea is and has been the director of the events of the World's History."[1]

Homer places the gods in a position subordinate to a remote moral power that is primary and older than the gods: Destiny. Though the gods are not constrained by natural laws, they cannot thwart Fate. Even Zeus cannot, for example, prevent the death of one of his sons. In Aeschylus's *Prometheus Bound*, Prometheus responds to the suggestion that he might become as powerful as Zeus:

Art and skill things wondrous are,
But that which Needs must Be is stronger far.
Who guides the helm of That which Needs must Be?
The Erinys unforgetting, the Fates three
The Zeus himself, matched against these, is weak?
The doom ordained he cannot break[2]

For the early Greeks, Fate also set the boundary of right and wrong. To try to go "beyond what is ordained" was an act of wickedness for which one must expect to pay a dear price, as Homer noted in the *Odyssey*.

Despite the imagery of a hand of Fate spinning out the thread of human events and things happening regardless of our efforts, we should not forget that fatalism simply amounts to the "thesis that the laws of logic alone suffice to prove that the only actions which a [person] can perform are the actions [that person] does in fact perform."[3] Theology aside, the argument is that as long as one is committed to being logical, one must accept fatalism.

In May 1980 the signs around Mount Saint Helens were clear to volcanologists: An eruption of the long-dormant volcano was likely. Of the people living in the region, public attention focused on one old man, Harry Truman. Harry claimed he would not leave his home, even if the governor of Washington sent the National Guard to evict him.

Most of us would agree that it must be either true or false that Harry will leave his home before the volcano erupts. Either he will leave or he will not. This is an application of the familiar logical law of the excluded middle: "Any proposition whatever must be either true, or if not true, then false."[4] Before the eruption occurs, no human, not even Harry, may know whether he will leave or stay. But that is not a problem for the fatalist, for the position makes no epistemological claims.

The fatalist only argues what seems deceptively obvious: if it is true that Harry will stay, nothing he does can prevent him from staying, and if it is false that he will stay, nothing he does will result in his staying. The fatalist maintains that "a simple law of logic . . . appears to commit one logically to the view that the future is as fixed as the past . . . , so it is not now within anyone's power to alter what will happen in the future."[5]

The argument in Harry's case looks like this:

1. It must be either true or false that Harry will leave his cabin before the volcano erupts.

2. The law of the excluded middle states that any proposition whatever must be true or if not true, false.
3. Either it is true that Harry will leave his cabin before the volcano erupts or if it is not true, then it must be false that he will leave the cabin before the volcano erupts.
4. Assume that it is true that he will leave the cabin before the eruption. In that case, there is no way for anyone, including Harry, to prevent Harry from leaving the cabin before the eruption. Any attempt even he may make to stay will be thwarted.
5. Assume that it is false that Harry will leave the cabin before the eruption. Then nothing in Harry's power or anyone else's can make him leave before the volcano erupts.
6. Either it is true or false that Harry will leave his cabin before the volcano erupts, but in neither case is Harry free with respect to leaving the cabin. Harry would be free only if it were in his power to leave and it were in his power to stay. But neither action is within his power.

So Harry really has no control over his fate, as it is either true or false that he will leave his cabin before the volcano erupts.

Fatalism, as Richard Taylor notes, depends on "nothing but the commonest presupposition of all logic and inquiry; namely, that there is such a thing as truth, and that this has nothing at all to do with the passage of time. Nothing *becomes* true or *ceases* to be true; whatever is truth at all simply *is* true."[6]

To philosophers and nonphilosophers alike, the fatalist's argument sounds like a logical trick, a bit of hocus pocus. How could a mere law of logic have such an impact on the universe and our lives, let alone affect our assignment of moral responsibility? There are, as would be expected, a number of strong arguments against Fatalism. A popular argument from the past that is still invoked in the twentieth century in disguised forms by such philosophers as A. J. Ayer[7] and Adolf Grunbaum[8] is traditionally known as the "idle argument." It is meant to show that those who accept fatalism should be motivated to do nothing throughout their lives. Cicero provides a famous version of it:

If the statement "You will recover from that illness" has been true from all eternity, you will recover whether you call in a doctor or do not; and similarly if the statement "you will recover from that illness" has been false from all eternity, you will not recover whether you call in a doctor or not. . . . Therefore, there is no point in calling a doctor.[9]

The Stoic logician Chrysippus had earlier written the standard fatalist's response:

> If it is fated that "Laius will have a son Oedipus" it will not be possible for the words "whether Laius mates with a woman or does not" to be added. . . . It is fated both that Laius will mate with a woman and that he will beget Oedipus by her. . . ." You will recover whether you call in a doctor or do not" is captious, for calling in a doctor is just as much fated as recovering.[10]

Despite its popularity in various guises, the idle argument utterly fails as an attack on fatalism because it misrepresents it. But other, subtler objections have been mounted.

Fatalism is often accused of treating statements of fact as if they were statements of necessity. That something is going to happen does not imply that it must happen. It might be preventable, though it won't be prevented. On December 21, 1988, Diane Maslowski, a Syracuse University student, boarded Pan Am flight 103 at Heathrow Airport in London. The plane took off and had just achieved cruising altitude when a bomb exploded. Diane was killed as she was blown out of the fuselage. Her body was found in the town of Lockerbie, Scotland.

The statement, "Diane was going to be killed on Pan Am 103" was true, but that does not mean that her death on that plane was unavoidable. A number of events could have prevented it: she could have missed the flight; airport security might have detected the bomb; the explosion mechanism could have failed; the U.S. State Department might have shared their warning of a terrorist threat against that flight with the passengers; Diane Maslowski might have disembarked. She might be alive today if any of those things had happened.

But the fatalist will counter that all we are saying is that if she or others had taken certain precautions or if some other things had happened (if her ride to the airport had been delayed, for example), she would not have been killed in the bombing of Pan Am 103. But those things did not happen, so it is true that they were not going to happen, and that is a true statement no one will ever make false.

However, the fact that it is true means only that its denial is false, not that its denial is impossible. If it is true that Diane is going to be killed in the bombing of Pan Am 103, it is false that Diane is going to survive the bombing of the plane. But it is not impossible that she should do so; it is only impossible that she will both be killed and survive. The fatalist will point out that the logical impossibility position is unrelated to the issue which, for the fatalist, is one of human unavoidability.

Fatalism does not, and need not, affirm that the actions which are performed are the only ones which are logically possible. All that fatalism need prove is that the actions that are performed are the only ones within anyone's power to perform. . . . Fatalism does imply . . . that things would be the same no matter which of the actions within anyone's power he actually performs. Of course, this is not surprising, since according to fatalism the only actions which are within anyone's power to perform are the actions which he does, in fact, perform.[11]

But does it make sense that statements made now about the future are true now and for always? Is not the future wide open, most everything still possible? Are not statements about the future neither true nor false? The fatalist argues that the laws of logic require that we answer the first question, "Yes," the second, "No," and the third, "No." Statements about the future have truth values.

The primary source of the logic argument for fatalism is Aristotle's discussion of the implications of the law of the excluded middle.[12] Of course he was not a fatalist, but he realized that if the excluded middle law is true, there is no such thing as human freedom and for him that meant no moral responsibility.

While you climb the hundreds of steps up the rugged island of Skellig Michael, you imagine both the dedication and labor of the monks who carved them and the horrible fear that must have surged through their community at the first sightings on the horizon of the barbaric Viking marauders who would destroy their handiwork.

A monk might have shouted, "The Vikings will attack tomorrow!" And he would have been right. The fatalist would argue that if he was right, it must have been true when the monk made the prediction that the Vikings would attack the next day that there was no possibility that the attack would not occur. "All . . . that is about to be must of necessity take place."[13] Aristotle, however, was unwilling to accept such a consequence. As he could find nothing wrong with the rest of the argument, he boldly attacked his own law of the excluded middle. To do so Aristotle invoked the concept of future contingent events. He argued that if an event is yet to occur, then it is necessary and true now that either it will or will not occur, but it is not true that it will occur nor true that it will not.[14]

When the monks first sighted the Viking ships, the attack was neither necessary nor impossible; it was contingent. In that case, the prediction by the terrified monk that the attack would occur was neither true nor false when it was made. Quine, however, countered that the truth values of statements are independent of time, that the tense of the verb can be eliminated without loss of meaning.[15] "The Vikings will attack tomorrow" and "The Vikings attacked 1195 years ago" do not change in meaning when they are tenselessly rendered into an eternal statement: "The Vikings attack Skellig Michael in 795 A.D.," and that sentence is either true or false once and forever.

Aristotle viewed his allowance of future contingencies as cracking open the logical door of the principle of the excluded middle to allow in some avoidability. Lukasiewicz, however, noted that Aristotle's reasoning "does not undermine so much the principle of the excluded middle as one of the basic principles of our entire logic that he himself was the first to state, namely, that *every proposition is either true or false*."[16] That principle, Lukasiewicz maintained, is unprovable. It may or may not be believed, depending on whether or not one regards it as self-evident. If one does not, then, like Lukasiewicz, one may hold that propositions about "future facts" are indeterminate with regard to truth value.

Aristotle did not adopt a three-valued logic to avoid the fatalistic implications of his laws of logic. He maintained that the problem is not with the basic principle that every proposition is either true or false. In fact, if that is the interpretation of the law of the excluded middle, it does not commit one to fatalism. Only the interpretation that says that every proposition must be either true, *or if not true*, then false, requires the adoption of fatalism. It is the latter interpretation that is most commonly given for the law. But that version of the law is, as Steven Cahn points out, a synthetic proposition that will be false if a contingent event occurs.[17] For example, if the Viking raid is contingent, "the statement that it will occur does not correspond with reality, and the statement that it will not does not correspond with reality" either.[18] Only the statement that *it will or it will not* corresponds with reality. What is true, necessarily so, is that the future will go one way or the other. It simply "is not yet true that it will issue in one direction and it is also not yet true that it will issue in the other direction."[19]

There are several reasons not to adopt this handy way out of fatalism. In the first place, it plays fast and loose with the laws of logic, affirming the law of the excluded middle up to the point where it threatens human freedom, then restricting it because its implications are not consistent with a very popular moral principle: "a person is morally responsible for what [that person] has done only if he [or she] could have done otherwise." Harry Frankfurt calls that principle the "Principle of Alternate Possibilities"[20] (hereafter PAP). In the second place, an undermotivated temporal limitation is placed on the law. It is applied to the past or statements in the past tense, but not the future or statements in the future tense. But the future becomes the past as time passes.

Fatalism, however, implies that time is either superficial or unreal. If change is impossible and the facts are eternal, location in time is, as Quine suggested, only "a superficial aspect of reality."[21] Some philosophers have gone further; for them, time is not real at all. Kant, for example, treated time as "merely the subjective condition" in which we have intuitions."[22] For Bradley time is illusory.[23] If time has no capacity to affect the truth values of statements, as Aristotle's revision of the law of the excluded middle requires, the standard interpretation of the law should stand as read. The Aristotelian solution to the problem, recently revitalized by Cahn,[24] must maintain that time is real, that the truth value of a statement depends on the time it is stated, and hence that future possibilities "cease to be possibilities due to the mere lapse of time."[25]

In chapter five I will argue that there are genuine differences in content between sentences written in the past and the present tenses. A similar proposal might be put forth here with respect to the future tense. Such a proposal would oppose the view that eternalization preserves meaning. It could found an argument that meaning alteration defeats the notion of truth-value invariance across tenses. Though I think that such an argument can be made persuasive, I propose instead to accept the fatalist's position, as did my Irish friend, and to ask instead whether such an acceptance is compatible with holding people responsible for what they do, presumably unavoidably. The Irish woman assured me that she was both a fatalist and that she believed people are morally responsible for many of their actions. Though I first thought otherwise, I think she does not hold incompatible positions.

She told me of Mary Nellis who, during the worst of "The Troubles" in the 1970s, organized the Catholic women in the north of Ireland against the British denial of political status for the prisoners in the H-Blocks. Certainly one of the bravest, boldest people in Ireland, Mary Nellis and her band of women stood naked, wrapped in blankets, in the center of Belfast. Then they repeated the protest throughout Europe. They got their message across, and the conditions in the infamous prisons were dramatically upgraded. There were also ten young men led by Bobby Sands in the H-Blocks who died on hunger strikes. Are not they and Mary deserving of credit, praise, honor, for their deeds?

Frankfurt's attack on the PAP provides the grounds for reconciling fatalistic beliefs with the assignment of responsibility. His attack offers counterexamples that essentially depend on overdetermination. They are cases in which the circumstances make an outcome inevitable, yet they are not the cause of the outcome. For example:

A person M decides for reasons of her own to protest the treatment of the prisoners in the H-Blocks. She is then threatened by the IRA with horrible personal suffering if she does not protest. The threat is so horrible that any reasonable person would submit to it. M does protest.

Is M morally responsible for protesting when she had no alternative to doing so? It will be suggested, of course, that M had the alternative of resisting the IRA threat, so the story can be modified to make M incapable of resisting the force that would make her protest. In other words, whatever that force is, M will protest, and she will do so either because she decided to do so or because she was forced to do so, but in no case will she fail to protest. The fact that she could not have avoided protesting is a sufficient condition of her having protested. However, that may play no role in the explanation of why she did protest. Someone "may do something in circumstances that leave no alternative to doing it, without those circumstances . . . playing any role . . . in bringing it about that he (or she) does what he (or she) does."[26] Either Mary Nellis decided for reasons of her own to stand naked in her blanket in protest, or she was coerced into doing so by pressure from the IRA. We may stipulate that had she not decided to organize the protest, she would still have done so—that she was fated to do it. In any event she could not have done otherwise.

Suppose Mary had protested because of the IRA threat, but the threat had come after her decision to do it. She was not motivated by the threat, though the threat would have led to her protesting if she had not already decided to do so. Should she be held responsible? It seems right to say that she is morally responsible for protesting and therefore deserves the praise heaped on her, because she acted on the basis of her own decision. The threat did not influence her decision to protest. She acted as if the threat had not existed. Whatever coercion the IRA exercised on her was not the reason Mary protested. The coercion, despite the fact that it made her protest unavoidable by her, is not the explanation for her behavior. This example shows that coercion is not antithetical to responsibility. "Even though a person is subject to a coercive force that precludes his performing any action but one, he may nonetheless bear full moral responsibility for performing that action."[27] In Mary Nellis's case it seems clear that even if she could have avoided protesting, she would not have done so. She would have protested anyway. She did it for her own reasons. The facts of fatalism are irrelevant to the moral status of her actions because they are irrelevant to explaining or accounting for her actions.

That Mary Nellis could not avoid leading the protest does not help us understand what made her do it or anything about her. It seems clear that she did it for justice, for civil rights, and for her conception of the future of Ireland, not because she could not have done otherwise.

Frankfurt writes:

The fact that a person could not have avoided doing something is a sufficient condition of his having done it. But . . . this fact may play no role whatever in the explanation of why he did it. . .˙. If someone had no alternative to performing a certain action but did not perform it because he was unable to do otherwise, then he would have performed exactly the same action even if he could have done otherwise. . . . Thus it would have made no difference, so far as concerns his action or how he came to perform it, if the circumstances that made it impossible for him to avoid performing it had not prevailed.[28]

The point is that if our concern is the ascribing of moral responsibility, we should not place much weight on a fact that is irrelevant to explaining a person's behavior. Only the reasons a person did something in the circumstances should matter. Unavoidability does not explain Mary's behavior in the circumstances, so it is not relevant to the issues of her responsibility.

Can this example be generalized to capture fatalism? It seems to me that it can. The crucial point is that fatalism cannot necessarily be equated with causal determinism. Fatalism is the doctrine, derived from the laws of logic, that whatever happens was unavoidable. It is neither a causal theory nor a theory about how things actually occur in the sequences they do. It is neutral with respect to how an action or event comes to happen. It may admit that God knows before any event that it will happen and how it will happen and even why it will happen. But God's knowledge is not the cause or the reason why human actions happen as they do. That God knew that Mary Nellis would lead the blanket protest is not a fact about how she came to lead the protest. That God presumably knew it before it happened and for all time because all true sentences are known to be true by an omniscient God insures that her leading the protest could not have failed to happen.

One might object that God could know not only that Mary would lead the protest, but also why she would lead it. Hence the reasons she did it would also be unavoidable for her. Again the fatalist is committed to such a view, and again it is not relevant to whether or not Mary should be held morally responsible for the protest. Quite simply, God's foreknowledge is irrelevant. That God knew she was to do it or what her reasons would be to do it played no role in her doing it.

Peter Van Inwagen has argued against the Frankfurt-type analysis of PAP by providing what he claims are three principles of responsibility to which Frankfurt has not produced counterexamples.[29] Two of Van Inwagen's principles concern the power of the person to prevent the event or state of affairs from happening. The third focuses on failures and omissions. All of Van Inwagen's principles reflect on failure cases rather than successes, omissions, rather than commissions. Jack did not do x. When Jack fails to do something, it is natural to wonder if he could do it. If he could not, then holding him responsible may be, at best, gratuitous. This reasoning suggests that there is an asymmetry with respect to the way we handle responsibility ascription in cases of commissions and cases of omissions. In the case of commissions, we need to know what explains the actions of the person under scrutiny, and seldom will our quest for an explanation be achieved by merely affirming the fatalist's doctrine that the action was unavoidable. In the case of omissions, however, that the person could have prevented or insured the event does seem to be relevant to the assignment of responsibility, a matter to be discussed in more detail in chapters six and seven.

In any event, fatalism does not seem to be what John Martin Fischer calls a "responsibility-undermining factor,"[30] because its ruling out avoidability does not destroy the foundations of responsibility ascription. So responsibility may be compatible with fatalism because we have good grounds for holding people responsible for some of the things they do even if they are unavoidable.

After we returned from our trip to Skellig Michael, my Irish friend and I walked back through town, past a small shop where the headlines of the newspaper were displayed. She read furiously down the front page. Then she started to cry softly.

I scanned the story on the killings on the Antrim Road. The two women were identified, but neither was her niece. Her prayer had been answered—but how? Below the account of the events on the Antrim Road was another story, dateline Gibraltar. Three IRA operatives had been gunned down in cold blood by British agents. One of them was her niece.

5 · Time, Space, and Shame

Ethical theories are typically classed as either (predominantly) deontological or consequentialistic. Such a classification, despite the volume of ink expended on it, identifies hardly more than an intramural distinction from within a shared basic perspective, a shared network of metaphysical and meta-ethical concepts. Both of the traditional classes of theories about what one is responsible for, what one has a moral obligation to do, depend on the same basic conception of the identity and individuation of persons. That perspective, which I shall characterize as "temporal," can be contrasted with another that offers rather different grounds on which to raise the questions of responsibility. In the majority of books on ethics this second perspective, which I will call "spatial," is overlooked or relegated to a short paragraph and/or a brief footnote. In the real world, however, the spatial perspective is adopted by many of us when we evaluate each other's behavior and justify or excuse our own. Furthermore, it is (and has been) the characteristic moral outlook of a significant percentage of the world's population, those not raised in the traditions of Western liberal individualism. That tradition is characterized by the doctrines that virtue is developed through the unrestrained freedom of individuals to act as they wish; that morality is located in and focused on the individual acts of isolatable persons; that ultimately there is no way to decide between conceptions of the good, so that no person or group of persons ought to pursue the realization of a conception of the good life at the cost of the suppression of any other.

I do not claim to offer a new way to view ethics. My goal is much more modest. I hope only to propose a different way of conceptualizing differences in moral perspectives. I cannot claim to have invented the distinction between temporal and spatial perspectives, but I hope to reexpose it and perhaps reveal some of the virtues of seeing moral thinking in nontemporal terms.

55

A reading of Charles Dickens's *Bleak House* provides a helpful introduction to the two perspectives. Dickens's presentation of the two perspectives reveals the differences between them. Dickens develops the plot of the novel by alternating two narrators, each speaking in a different tense. Roughly half the book consists of the narration of an unnamed observer. It is written in the present tense from a vantage point outside the story.

> London. Michaelmas term lately over, and the Lord Chancellor sitting in Lincoln's Inn Hall. Implacable November weather. As much mud in the streets as if the waters had but newly retired from the face of the earth. . . . Foot passengers, jostling one another's umbrellas in a general infection of ill temper. . . .
>
> Fog everywhere. Fog up the river, fog down the river. . . . The raw afternoon is rawest, and the dense fog is densest, and the muddy streets are muddiest near that leaden-headed old obstruction . . . Temple Bar. And hard by Temple Bar, in Lincoln's Hall, at the very heart of the fog, sits the Lord High Chancellor in his High Court of Chancery. . . . It is but a glimpse of the world of fashion that we want on this same miry afternoon. It is not unlike the Court of Chancery but that we may pass from the one scene to the other, as the crow flies. . . . Sir Leicester Dedlock is only a baronet, but there is no mightier baronet than he. His family is as old as the hills, and infinitely more respectable. He has a general opinion that the world might get on without hills but would be done up without Dedlocks.[1]

The other half of *Bleak House* is told in the past tense by one of the major characters, Esther Summerson.

> My birthday was the most melancholy day at home in the whole year. . . . Dinner was over and my godmother and I were sitting at the table before the fire. . . . "It would have been far better, little Esther, that you had never been born!" I broke out crying and sobbing, "Why am I so different from the other children and why is it my fault?" She raised me, sat in her chair, and standing me before her, said slowly in a cold low voice—"Your mother, Esther, is your disgrace, and you were hers."[2]

After reading only a handful of chapters, one becomes aware that this dual narrative technique exposes two very different metaphysical perspectives that in turn produce two radically different moral analyses of society and the actions of people.

The present tense, as has been noted by a host of literary critics,[3] freezes the action of the scenes being described. A string of present tense descriptions is more like a slide show than a moving picture. The present is an inventorial tense, giving us structures, arrangements, associations, and objects but not flowing, connected movements. It has the power of creating a mysterious sense of unreality—a feature exploited in many novels, as well as the antinovels of Robbe-Grillet. The social world Dickens describes in the present tense narration is static and patterned, a world of people frozen in place—like the Lord Chancellor sitting at the heart of the fog and Sir Leicester in his baronial apartments. The reader is captured in a poetic "thereness" in which clusters of objects are mapped in relation to each other, suspended in time. There is no time for human intentions, extended actions, and associated motivations. Indeed, there is no time. Human identities for this narrator are station identities. Personal identity is described almost exclusively in terms of location and association, thereby forming and defining a social grid. Who one is, is a matter of where one is. This sort of narrative and its metaphysic lends itself to a moral focus on social institutions seen as ultimate bearers of responsibility, credit, and blame.

In a memorable passage Dickens writes:

> The system . . . it's the system. I mustn't look to individuals. It's the system. I musn't go into court and say, "My Lord, I beg to know this from you—is this right or wrong? My Lord knows nothing of it. He sits there to administer the system. . . . He is not responsible. It's the system.[4]

The theme of Dickens's spatialist narrator is the disgrace of a house (not Bleak House, by the way, but the House of Dedlock) brought on by the to-be-uncovered fact that people are out of their proper social places like the pieces on an incorrectly set chessboard. Although Dickens's intent was probably to show the destructive force of institutions—at least the entrenched ones—on individuals, he provides marvelous insights into the social interdependency of all levels. A few years later Bradley would powerfully affirm this social interdependency in *Ethical Studies*.[5]

The present-tense narrator of *Bleak House* shows us society as an interlocked grid of stations and associations, with the identities of people almost exclusively derived from the places they occupy in that grid. Dickens's past-tense narrator offers the alternative perspective. Because the past tense has duration, events are describable. Actions occur, have prior causes, a history, and they move on to effects. Actors endure through time and reveal plans, goals, and hopes: the elements of action that are the foci of the Kantians and the utilitarians. The moral perspective is act or agent centered. Human relations are shaped by events and, therefore, in and over time.

In *A Tale of Two Cities*, the view of personal identity that emerged in Esther's narration of *Bleak House* is expressed as "every human creature is constituted to be that profound secret and mystery to every other."[6] Thus people are what they do and how they do it, not where they are. Moral lives are causally related mental and physical events forming a chain through time. Human relations are shaped by events and, therefore, in and over time. Individuals create society, not the other way around.

Where Dickens's present-tense spatial narrator is notably clinical about the sufferings of the downtrodden (describing slum dwellers as filthy, illiterate, diseased, and dying), Esther dwells on feelings, motives, and the consequences of choices. The contrast between the two narrations is never clearer than when the corner sweep is discussed by both. For Esther he is someone to nurse, to shelter, to try to save. For the spatial narrator he is another of the innumerable denizens of the depths of the social system who must be kept in their places to control the spread of infection in the body politic.

Though at heart Dickens seems to side with Esther, it is the spatial narration that embodies the most unforgettable allegory of the novel. In writing reminiscent of Kafka, Shakespeare's *King Lear*, and Beckett's *Waiting for Godot*, Dickens shows us that human life can become dominated by expectations of a legacy that when it is awarded has been absorbed in costs. Hoping for anything better can destroy people.

British archeology reveals the impact of the conflict of the two perspectives in the lives of the most ancient of tribes. Particularly intriguing are the dramatic changes in the burial practices of the Neolithic tribes. From 3500–2500 B.C. the pre-Celtic tribes of southern Britain buried their dead in great long barrows dug out of the limestone. The building of a barrow was apparently the last stage of a complex ritual that involved laying out bodies in a timber mortuary chamber until the last member of a particular group died. All the members of the group were then buried according to their station. The barrows were dug at about the same time as the building of the famous henge monuments but before the upright stones were set in place. The structures of this period, in the words of Oxford archeologist Barry Cunliffe, "demonstrate beyond doubt the strength, social cohesion, and stability of the earliest communities"[7] in which the identity of a member was understood solely in terms of his or her place in the social unit.

Around 2000 B.C., however, burial rites in Britain abruptly changed. Single burial in round barrows became the fashion. For some unknown reason, the concept of the individual had risen to prominence. Still, communal projects such as the remodelling of the henge monuments continued.

Wonderful literary statements of both moral perspectives are to be found in eighth-century Anglo-Saxon literature, in a collection known as *The Exeter Book*. "The Wanderer" is a lyrical expression of the identity crisis of a warrior who has lost his lord, his kin, and his friends in war. All social ties severed, he has no place or identity, and he seems to have no moral responsibilities either.

A long time now, that the covering of earth enwrapped my treasure-giver, and I went thence, despondent, in the gloom of winter. . . . Only he who has experienced it can understand the loneliness of the lordless man. . . . The wine-halls crumble, the rulers lie deprived of mirth, all the veterans have fallen proud by the wall. . . . Here treasure is fleeting; here friends are fleeting; here man is fleeting; here kinsmen are fleeting. The whole fabric of the world is empty.[8]

"The Seafarer," though cursing the sea and the hardship of the mariner's life, offers the alternative theory of personal identity and worth to that founded on the mead hall-centered society of "The Wanderer." The seafarer loves to be self-reliant, adventuring solo in distant lands and oceans. In his allotted place in the system of his society, he is bored, anxious to again set sail. He is the predecessor of the liberal individualist.

No man so happy as to enjoy the land can know how I, careworn, dwelt on the wintery ice-cold waves, . . . deprived of my kinsmen. Icicles hung from me; hail lashed me in showers. . . . For me the scream of the sea-gull rather than the laughter of men. . . . No protecting lord was there to console the heart of the needy man. . . . Still, for all that, desires agitate my heart to try myself the high streams, the sport of the salt waves; always I am urged on to fare forth to seek far hence the home of alien peoples. . . . All things urge on the mind of the eager-hearted to journey, to depart far over the flood-ways. . . . No man living in comfort can know what they endure who lay their paths of exile far and wide.[9]

The wanderer has lost the stability provided by the orderliness of the social system built around its legal wergeld conception of rank and worth. For him, the world outside that system is wild, frightening, dangerous, and brutal. The seafarer, on the other hand, derives his identity not from social organizations and institutions, but from his own actions. He has not fallen from grace with the sea. Nature, rugged and demanding as it is, is elemental to the way he defines himself as an individual. With romantic fervor, he sets sail.

Temporalists tend to be defenders of some or all of the following: individual liberty, rights, self-determination, and (even) romance. Arch-temporalist John Milton in 1645 published pamphlets in favor of divorce being granted on grounds of incompatibility. Today of little note, the idea of divorce at will was then seen as nothing less than a call for the end of social order in favor of what looked to the establishment like blatant anarchy.

Temporalists see human life in terms of intentional actions and the isolatable, independent actor as the central, the ultimate moral subject. They characteristically define collectivities as aggregates that are exhaustively reducible for moral purposes to their individual members. Bentham, for example, makes a cornerstone of utilitarianism the view that "the community is a fictitious body composed of the individual persons who are considered as constituting as it were its members. The interest of the community then is . . . the sum of the interests of the several members who compose it."[10]

Spatialists focus on role, station, status, and communal unity. For spatialists, the temporalist's individual actors, when stripped of their social relations, are revealed to be not isolatable egos, but mere abstractions of no particular moral or metaphysical significance.

It is not uncommon for spatialists to shift the object of ultimate moral evaluation entirely away from individual humans to collectivities of one sort or another. Marx might be described as doing so. Bradley, though he does not completely turn his back on the individual, writes, "That objective institutions exist is of course an obvious fact; and it is a fact, which every day is becoming plainer, that these institutions are organic, and further, that they are moral. . . . Let us take the point of view which regards the community as the real moral organism. . . ."[11]

From the spatial point of view, the moral world looks something like a city. The buildings in a city mesh to form neighborhoods. A particular building could be singled out from all the rest and questions raised about its design, its materials, glass, ornamentation, and so forth. But if those questions are the only ones asked, something crucial will have been neglected: its place on the street, in the neighborhood, among the other buildings. If a building does not fill its space well or cohere with its neighbors, it can be regarded as an architectual failure. The very features that are praised when it is viewed in isolation may be reasons for an overall negative appraisal. It will be seen as "out of place," inappropriate, an eyesore, ugly. To see the building in its fullest sense, to evaluate it aesthetically as a building and not as a piece of sculpture, it must be studied in the space marked out by its relations to other buildings. Furthermore, it must serve its purpose within its neighborhood and its community. Is it functional? Is it in the right place for the purposes it is meant to serve? Is it suited to those purposes? The spatialists raise questions of moral responsibility that are remarkably akin to such architectural evaluative concerns.

Bradley argues that understanding the community as the basic moral unit has the virtue of destroying the antithesis of despotism and individualism (traditionally conjured up by the temporalist) by denying both and taking something of value from each. "The truth of individualism is saved, because, unless we have intense life and self-consciousness in the members of the state, the whole state is ossified. The truth of despotism is saved, because, unless the member realizes the whole by and in himself, he fails to reach his own individuality."[12]

Individuality for spatialists like Bradley is a far cry from the (romantic) individualism of the Humean, the Kantian, and the act-utilitarian. Individuals, as Bradley defines them, are "organs of the whole," only real because they are social entities, pulse-beats in the system. Bradley explains that an individual human being, insofar as he or she is "the object of his [or her] self-consciousness," is characterized and penetrated "by the existence of others." In short, the content of a self is a pattern of relations within a community. "I am myself by sharing with others, by including in my essence relations to them, the relations of the social state."[13]

The primary moral obligation for Bradley and most other spatialist theorists is essentially a version of the Socratic injunction to know oneself combined with the Stoic command to realize oneself in one's proper place in the natural-social order of things. Self-realization is finding one's position and acting accordingly. To find one's place requires identifying the places of others, not all others, but a significant portion of the whole grid. "To know what a man is you must not take him in isolation. . . . What he has to do depends on what his place is, what his function is, and that all comes from his station."[14]

Moral responsibility, for the spatialist, is neither a subjective matter nor an objective matter to be discovered by working a calculus or algorithm. However, it is objective in two senses: first, that whatever one is responsible for doing (one's duty) would be the responsibility of anyone else occupying the same place in society and second, it is one's responsibility or duty regardless of one's motives, thoughts, or appreciation of the circumstances.

The moral imperative for Bradley is to realize oneself in the moral world. But what is the moral world? It is the system of institutions—"from the family to the nation"—that Bradley calls "the body of the moral world," and it is the spirit that vitalizes those institutions. (In terms I have used in a related context, it is the structural/procedural and policy recognitors of institutions such as corpora-tions.[15]) In effect, Bradley champions a moral person theory that flies in the face of temporalistic methodological individualism. The first half of his famous essay, "My Station and Its Duties," is devoted to an attack on its reductionistic pro-gram. "An individual man is what he is because of and by virtue of community, and . . . communities are thus not mere names but something real, and can be regarded . . . only as the one in the many."[16]

In Bradley's account, the basic moral responsibility is to live in accordance with the requirements placed on one by the role one plays in the community. (This view is also found in Confucian ethics[17] and in the writings of the Roman Stoics.[18])

Bradley's theory provides a general outline of the spatialist's perspective, but little information on its moral epistemology. Bradley does have something inter-esting to say about how we are to learn what we should do, but it is buried in his anglicized Hegelian rhetoric and may resist excavation. Typically Bradley is classed as an intuitionist; he talks of instincts being stronger than principles and of knowing what is right in particular cases by immediate judgment or "an intu-itive subsumption."[19] But what he intends, he says, is a denial of the view that moral judgments are discursive rather than any sort of subjective intuitionist theory. In this he sounds remarkably like Hilary Putnam, who has defended the role of imagination in moral reasoning.

> Moral reasoning in the full sense of the word, . . . involves not just the logical faculties, in the narrow sense, but our full capacity to imagine and feel. . . . The sensitive appreciation in the imagination of predicaments and perplexities must be essential to sensitive moral reasoning.[20]

Bradley argues that reference to archetypical occupiers for each station is cru-cial to providing content to the duties of stations.

> The ideal self appealed to by the moral man is an ideally presented will in his position and circumstances which rightly particularizes the general laws which answer to the general functions and system of spheres of the moral organism (the society).[21]

What Bradley might mean, and what many spatialists should endorse, is that for each position or type of position in the social grid there is (or can be devel-oped) an exemplar or series of exemplars that supplies content to the moral responsibilities associated with that station. Bradley does not develop an exemplar theory of morality, but he seems to be committed to the view that in order to know what one is responsible for, what duty requires with respect to one's position or station, one needs to imbibe moral exemplars. "Precept is good, but example is better; for by a series of particulars . . . we identify ourselves on the sides both of will and judgement."[22]

Bradley notes that the custom of many ordinary people of imagining what a known person, real or fictional, of high character associated with their stations would do in their difficult circumstances is the best sort of moral reasoning. It is important to understand that Bradley is not championing role reversal, putting oneself in another's shoes or imagining him or her in yours. Appealing as that might be for Golden Rule theorists, it entails a commitment to an interchangeability of individuals that divorces them as moral subjects from their stations. Changing places for the spatialist is a profound identity shift, and it is difficult to see how, except in jest, one could use it as the foundation of moral decision making. Hence, the appeal is made internal to the station, to a model identity or exemplar that is associated with the station. When one imagines what a person one admires would do and acts in imitation, the person to whom one refers must be of a similar station. Even so, spatialists do struggle with similarity in stations because, as each position is defined by a particular set of relations, each station is, strictly speaking, unique. Nonetheless, similarities in stations, classes, or types of jobs exist in society, and more general exemplars can get a foothold. Still, Bradley often talks as if each of us could have a peculiar exemplar from which we derive our understanding of the responsibilities that are properly assigned to us.

The spatialist also has a problem with the changing of stations, moving up or down in the social world, rags to riches. Every such change must be an identity shift, and some clearly are crises. Many stations are invariably linked within institutions and must be passed through in the process of social advancement. If such stations were indexed to a time in a life, then the problem might seem to be solved, but it would not be. The temporal dimension would be introduced with all its metaphysical commitments flying in the face of spatial personal identity theory. Minimization of the temporal could be accomplished were one to deny, as Bradley does not, a continuous self through time. (Bradley needs that notion for his analysis of the ordinary conception of responsibility in the first essay of *Ethical Studies*.) A closest continuer theory of the self,[23] however, could nicely serve the spatialist's interests. Identity over time can be denied and full dependency on the spatial dimensions of station maintained. The appeal to exemplars peculiar to stations (or station types) then remains a viable moral methodology. In fact, the appeal to exemplars in setting the conditions of moral action seems to be a distinguishing feature of spatial ethics.

Spatialists will point out that ingrained in our conception of the classes of stations across the social grid are model identities or archetypes, pictures, or better, portraits of the ideal role player: the good doctor, the ideal engineer, the lawyer's lawyer, the good soldier, and so forth. Certainly these exemplars are not derived or drawn from sets of rules or codes of behavior. The good doctor, for example, is not the embodiment of the American Medical Association's code of ethics. Role model identities evince a holistic quality, a dimensionality. They are, purely but not so simply, works of fiction. They tend to be visual in their most accessible form, and they are commonly conveyed to and recalled by station-dwellers via stories, as Bradley does mention.

These model identities define the acceptable limits of the roles of which they are exemplars. They are the controlling devices of the permissible and set the outer boundaries on responsibility. They are the products of many decades of grooming, arising and thriving in the public domain. They are creations of popular as well as role-restricted culture. The good soldier, for example, is not a purely military invention. John Wayne, George C. Scott, Gary Cooper, and Alec Guinness have had as much, if not more, to do with molding the good soldier's features as have Omar Bradley and Audie Murphy. The good doctor owes a great deal to Alan Alda, the lawyer's lawyer to Perry Mason and Atticus Finch.

The spatialists see the internalizing of the exemplar by the station occupant as a matter of identity assimilation. The basic moral project is to act as much as is possible like the model identity of one's station in the social institutions to which one belongs. Admittedly, the ideals are always a bit beyond realization, but Bradley believes that approaching them, even at some distance, accounts for the satisfaction of the ordinary moral person.

There are, as might be imagined, major problems with the grid-based conception of roles. Most obvious are those created by overlapping institutional commitments. The same person may be vice president of a corporation, alderman of a city, and father of two children. What is his station? To what exemplar does he relate? The answer, I think, must recall the import of the literary or fictive element in spatial ethics. Model identities are multidimensional. They are not cardboard paste-ups that reflect only on, for example, fatherhood. A significant part of being a good father is to do well at whatever other roles one plays in society. (It has always bothered me that Ernst Kaltenbrunner, the head of the SS and the administrator of the death camps in Nazi Germany who was executed after the Nuremberg Trials, was regularly described as a good father. It is difficult to imagine that one could be a good father and direct the atrocities that Kaltenbrunner did.)

The spatialist's ethics are dominated by concerns for place that are defined in terms of sets of responsibilities. The evaluation criteria for station occupiers need not be collections of rules or formulas for action. Instead, exemplars provide both motivation and grounds for evaluation. Though rules and formulas might be devised, they are seldom used in practice. All of these features conspire to produce another characteristic of spatial ethics: it is predominantly shame based.

For the spatialist, the primary moral motivation is to measure up—not to be found inadequate to the tasks that define one's identity. Shame avoidance propels spatial ethics. Shame is sometimes confused with guilt, but the two concepts and moral emotions are quite dissimilar, with very different ancestries and lexical histories. Guilt is an economic notion. Its roots lie in the concept of debt. Immoral acts, it was probably imagined, unbalance the social/moral books, creating a debt owed by the offender to either the victim or the society as a whole. In the *Genealogy of Morals*[24] Nietzsche wrote that the idea that a criminal deserves punishment because he or she could have acted differently is a late and subtle form of human judgment. The much older idea depends on the notions of creditor and debtor, notions derived from commerce.

Nietzsche maintains:

> Buying and selling are older even than the beginning of any kind of social forms of organization. It is rather out of the most rudimentary form of personal legal rights that the budding sense of exchange, contract, guilt, right, obligation, settlement, first transferred itself to the coarsest and most elementary social complexes. . . . The eye was now focused on this perspective and forthwith arrived at the great generalization: everything has its price. All things can be paid for, which is the oldest and naivest moral canon of justice.[25]

In effect, Nietzsche argues that the practice of compensation is the prior responsibility practice and also the root of the notion of debt and so of guilt. The legal documents from the ancient Middle East tend to support this assessment, though there is considerable room for doubt about whether the notion of compensation predates the concept of community. In any event, its compensatory foundations suggest that to expiate their offences, offenders must repay or restore, which gives rise to the concept of the fine and the Anglo-Saxon doctrine of wergeld. When the debt to society or to the victim is retired, the original status quo is restored.

The conflation of guilt and debt is evident in the early sacred literature and subsequent translations. *Debitum* in the Lord's Prayer, for example, was rendered in the Old English as *gylt* and then as *geld*. The concept is still preserved in the expression "paying one's debt to society."

Guilt is a threshold notion.[26] It depends on the establishment of rather specific boundaries and limits to behavior, which are usually defined in rules and laws. Guilt occurs because of a transgression, a trespass of those limits. When the line is crossed, one is guilty; otherwise one is innocent. Although crimes may have degrees, guilt does not. You cannot be a little bit guilty, though you can be guilty of a lesser charge.

Guilt is a minimum-level-of-acceptable-behavior-maintenance notion. Guilt-based moralities tend to focus on the basic requirements for being moral. Such moralities tend to be rule dominated. They are not, in Urmson's terms, aspirational level moralities.[27] Guilt avoidance is accomplished simply by playing within the rules and obeying the laws, a strategy that usually that places minimal demands or constraints on one's behavior. In a guilt-based moral system a person will feel guilty for having acted in a cowardly manner when the rules require that everyone share the burden of the community's defense but will not feel guilty for not behaving heroically. Guilt feelings can be most devastating when they arise from the knowledge that one has not behaved in even the minimally appropriate ways.

There is a peculiar psychology that relates to guilt. Erik Erikson[28] reports that among guilt-oriented persons the dominant view is that a human life is a string of discrete actions each of which can be more or less isolated and evaluated against appropriate rules of conduct. A person's life is a set of events ordered on a linear path like the frames of a motion picture film run at a steady speed from beginning to end. The moral evaluator is like the editor of the film, cutting out certain frames and holding them up for scrutiny. The therapy for the guilt ridden that emerges from this metaphysics is a subtraction or deletion process: bad actions are subtracted, and right actions are encouraged as substitutes for them in future instances. A price is paid for violations, but identities are not particularly threatened. In the guilt scheme a clear distinction is drawn between what a person is and what a person does. Relatively stable identities through time are essential to any creditor/debtor system.

As Morris has noted,[29] guilt is an auditory notion; it is associated with hearing and speaking. The ritual of confession is a product of a guilt morality. People who feel guilty tend to feel compelled to communicate their misdeed. They want to speak and be heard. Thus a significant amount of the language that relates to guilt has auditory overtones: recanting, retracting, confessing, repenting, and nagging.

Although Nietzsche claims that guilt is the rudimentary moral concept, shame seems to me more primitive. It even has a natural expression, where guilt does not. Humans who are ashamed blush. Charles Darwin wrote that blushing is the most human and most peculiar of all of our expressions. Mark Twain commented that "Man is the only animal that blushes. Or needs to."[30]

Our word "shame" apparently derives from the Germanic "skem" and "skam," from the Indo-European root "Kem/Kam" meaning "to cover, veil, or hide." The "s" prefix makes it reflexive, so it meant "to cover or hide oneself." ("Shame" shares this root with the French word "chemise.") Shame, rather than involving transgressions, relates to failure, shortcomings, feelings of inadequacy and inferiority, exposure of weakness, and fault. When one is ashamed, the normal response is to conceal oneself, to try to mask oneself. Shame depends on sight. It relates to the way one sees oneself and wants to be seen by others and to how one thinks one is perceived by others.

The close linking of shame, vision, and identity is dramatically portrayed in *King Lear*, Stanley Cavell maintains.[31] In the first scene of the play, Gloucester, who has built his career on an image of respectability in the eyes of others, acknowledges he has fathered a bastard whom he has not properly recognized. He jokes about it to avoid his shame, but as Taylor notes, "Avoidance of shame is one way of losing self-respect, for it is one way of blurring the values the person is committed to."[32] Gloucester's joking avoidance succeeds only in more deeply implanting his son's sense of illegitimacy and returns to haunt Gloucester when his public mask is torn off. Shakespeare creates a literal association between shame and vision—of avoiding eyes and of having eyes voided, of not letting others see you and of not being able to see them—when Gloucester is blinded and then mocked.

Experiences of shame are characterized by a sensation of the loss or the slipping away of the identity one has tried to maintain and project to others. To be shamed is to be stripped of one's self-image. Hence, only those who hold themselves in some degree of esteem and/or associate themselves with some sort of ideal or model identity can be shamed. Those who do not are unshameable and so beneath contempt.

Especially in the Old Testament, shame is linked with awe. Humans are to stand in awe before God because of their shame. The concept of shame encourages the distinction between the sacred and the profane, the clean and the unclean, the mysterious and the mundane. Yet the modern Christian church and the institutions of our society have maneuvered us away from shame in favor of a litigious approach to morality and salvation. Records are easier to keep. The cost of the shift, though, has been a narrowing of the gulf between the holy and the ordinary. Nietzsche argued that Christianity lacks modesty, that Christians not only dare to speak the name of God, but they have the nerve to do so with a familiar form of address. Despite such influences shame has held a firm place in the moral education and consciousness of many people.

Certain episodes of shame reflect the spatial nature of the way persons identify themselves. Relationships individuate people (partially at least), so people may feel deep personal shame for the actions or appearances of those with whom they are associated, even though they have themselves done nothing shameful. In *Pride and Prejudice*, Elizabeth Bennet feels so ashamed of her family's behavior at the party at Netherfield that she cannot imagine Darcy being attracted to her. "Elizabeth blushed and blushed again with shame. . . . To Elizabeth it appeared that had her family made an agreement to expose themselves as much as they could during the evening, it would have been impossible for them to play their parts with more spirit and finer success."[33]

Shame-based responsibility, because it constantly evaluates the whole person, is a much more rigorous master than guilt. Suffering shame is an identity crisis. Shame anxiety is a feeling of radical isolation, and it is often described as a sense of disappearance of self. Persons who are ashamed report feeling as if they have turned to stone or into lowly animals. Therapy for the shame ridden is therefore more complicated than therapy for persons who feel guilty. Literally, the cure for shame is to become a different person. Isolation of the act or series of acts that provoked the shame may be impossible. In any event, it is usually irrelevant to recovery.[34]

Shame is a visual rather than an auditory concept.[35] The last thing a person who has been shamed or is ashamed wants to do is talk about it. Confession has little to do with shame. In fact, it may be helpful to think of the contrast between guilt and shame in terms of the contrast between the function of words and pictures. When ashamed, one's picture of oneself is disturbingly different from what one wants to project.

A sense of community is a prerequisite to a sense of shame. Shame requires an audience, Gabriele Taylor notes.

> The audience . . . is primarily needed for an explanation of shame: in feeling shame the actor thinks of himself as having become an object of detached observation, and at the core to feel shame is to feel distress at being seen at all. *How* he is seen, whether he thinks of the audience as critical, approving, indifferent, cynical or naive is a distinguishable step and accounts for the different cases of shame.[36]

Consider the small Irish town of Innisfree in the classic film *The Quiet Man*. Sean Thornton (played by John Wayne), an Irish-American prize fighter, returns to his homeland after having killed an opponent in the ring. He asks permission to marry Mary Kate Danaher (Maureen O'Hara). At first the request is denied, but after a number of deceptions in which most of the townspeople participate, Mary Kate's skinflint brother consents. When he learns he has been tricked, however, he withholds her dowry.

Sean does not immediately realize he has been shamed, but that fact is not lost on Mary Kate. She cannot bear to be seen by the townfolk as long as her husband will not fight to recover her dowry from her brother. He will not do so, having sworn not to fight again. She will not consummate the marriage. In desperation she deserts Sean, triggering him, with some urging from friends, to haul her off the train and drag her back to her brother to demand the dowry. What may appear to those outside a shame culture to be an act of misogyny, the humiliation of Mary Kate before the townfolk, is actually a public act of shaming her brother in which she is a more-than-willing participant. The dowry is paid and promptly burned, and a donnybrook erupts that restores the worth and social status of everyone in the community.

Shame, but surely not guilt, can arise with respect to things about oneself that are totally outside one's control. (Elizabeth Bennet's boorish family is one example.) Physical deformities can be major sources of shame, so we spend a lot of time and money to hide them. When the deformity is not maskable, however, shame can provoke deep metaphysical, theological, and moral doubts.

In *Of Human Bondage*, Philip Carey is born with a clubfoot. He is consumed with shame for it and fears his return to school and the taunting of his classmates. He is persuaded by the vicar that if one really believes in God, mountains can be moved. Next to a mountain, what is a clubfoot? So young Philip prayed, "Oh God . . . please make my foot all right on the night before I go back to school."[37]

The foot is not made "all right." Philip's reaction is no longer to only be ashamed of his appearance but to be ashamed for a God that could create a universe in which Philip Carey has a clubfoot and do nothing to make it right.[38] A natural extension of the Philip Carey syndrome is to doubt that life has any meaning, treating the shame caused by a physical deformity as a sign that the universe is ultimately void of significance. Shame, despite its many virtues, is problematic as a ground for moral responsibility. It would seem to have no built-in braking mechanism along that slippery slope of meaninglessness, and that is a major weakness in a shame-based system. Shame not only ostracizes from community those who no longer warrant association, but it can also alienate the shamed from any sense of meaningfulness, especially when the shame is rightly perceived as not in the control of the person who suffers it. Shame is a much more powerful moral weapon than guilt,[39] but on the other hand, to lack shame is to have no concern for self-image, honor, loyalty.

Returning to the spatialist's model-based conception of responsibility, we should say that the exemplar associated with each station sets the highest standard of behavior for it. Falling significantly below the standard is much more than the moral lapse of not living up to rules. The way the spatialist arranges the moral world, such failures must constitute severe threats of being neither the person one thought one was nor the person one represented oneself as being. If Bradley's metaphysical position with respect to individual identity is adopted, then one would be in danger of losing one's identity altogether if one should fail to perform the essential tasks of one's station(s). The primary moral motivation is maintenance of identity. The problem is that the spatialist does not seem to allow for anything like a person without such a station identity. There is no room for a man without a country. Instead, there is a place for everyone and everyone is in a place.

Another great spatialist, Plato, identifies shame as the foundation of law.[40] He credits the fear of shame with saving "us from many great evils, playing a greater role than anything else in procuring for us victory and safety."[41] The sense of shame is the wellspring of moderation, courage, and especially justice. At least in *The Laws*, Plato seems to see shame as the unifier of the virtues. In that he is opposed by Aristotle, a confirmed temporalist, who argues that, "it is incorrect to speak of a sense of shame as being a virtue or excellence for it resembles an emotion more than a characteristic. . . . It is defined as a kind of fear of disrepute, and the effect it produces is very much like that produced by fear of danger."[42]

The effect of shame that Aristotle notes is the one the spatialist wants to achieve: the fear of being uncovered as inadequate, as noted above, dominates the spatialist's moral arsenal. Such a fear can lead in two distinct directions: either the shameful person may cover up too well, stonewall his or her moral shortcomings, and so precipitate a general social failure or, as Plato seems to think more likely, the shame-filled person may be driven to those greater achievements in the position that are necessary to restore social status and esteem.

Shame-based morality, insofar as it stresses the measure of the station occupier against an objective ideal model, has both a private and a public aspect. There is the private sense of inadequacy and the public ostracism, the holding in contempt, the derogation of the shameful for the failure to measure up. In effect, the spatial shame-based ethicist integrates the Kantian private person with the Bradleyian pulse-beat of the system.

6 • Power, Control, and Group Situations: And Then There Were None?

If we know that a group of people has the power to do something, it is natural to think that each of the members of the group, to some degree at least, has the power to do it. Insofar as determinations of moral and legal responsibility are usually thought to be dependent on resolutions of questions regarding what someone has the power to do in a situation, the distribution of power in collective units is an important factor. To have power in a situation is to have certain abilities and capacities in that situation.[1] Hence, to have power in a group is to possess the dispositional property of being able, if one wants, under certain conditions, to move a group to action or inaction. To have power over a group's behavior is not necessarily to have exercised that power or even to know one has it. However, the latter as well as the former may be moral failings for which one can and should be held responsible. Under what conditions is a particular member of a group liable to be held responsible for what the group as a whole did or did not do?

I adopt the position[2] that when a person has power[3] with respect to a particular occurrence or event, there is some intentional action (or actions) that person can perform at the appropriate time that will insure that the event will occur and that there is some intentional action (or actions) that same person can perform that will prevent the event from occurring. This account of power corresponds to what John Martin Fischer calls control.[4]

Fischer identifies two different kinds of control that are relevant to responsibility. Typically, when we speak of someone being in control of a situation, we mean that he or she actually has causal control of it. If I am in control of my car, then I cause it to move in the way it does. If I lose control, the car moves without my causing it to do so. Rather than actual causal control, I will have what Fischer calls "regulative control" if I have the power to both ensure the occurrence of an

71

event and prevent its occurrence. Fischer uses an example of an airline captain whose plane is flying on automatic pilot. The computer turns the plane to the west and the pilot does not intervene, but he has the power to ensure that the plane will turn west. For example, should the computer instruct the plane to turn south, he can switch to manual control and bring it around to the west. By the same token, he can prevent its turning west by overriding the automatic pilot. Fischer explains that "the outcome is here *responsive* to the pilot."[5] It seems correct to say that even when one did not have actual causal control of an event, one could be held responsible for it if one had regulative control. "Moral responsibility requires control (of at least *one* of the two sorts)."[6] Usually we have both types of control, but in many important cases, and especially in cases of omissions, we only have regulative control if we have any control at all. In other situations, such as the Frankfurt-type cases discussed in chapter four, we may have only actual causal control. In all of these circumstances, however, the operative moral principle will be that to be held responsible, a person must have had at least one of the two types of control.

The adoption of this principle explains the asymmetry between responsibility for actions and for omissions that has been mentioned in previous chapters. Fischer writes:

> If the lifeguard is to be morally responsible for failing to save the child, he must have regulative control over the child's being saved. But in order to have regulative control over the child's being saved, he must have the power to ensure that the child is saved, i.e., to cause (in the manner appropriate to control) the child's being saved. Thus, he must be able to save the child. In general, if an agent is to be morally responsible for failing to do X, he must be able to do X. But when an agent does X, he may exhibit direct causal control without having regulative control over the upshot.[7]

Suppose that ten people, all for personal reasons, are riding on a bus. Each has a different destination. They do not know each other. Halfway between Nowhere and Neverwas, in the middle of the desert, the bus driver suffers a massive heart attack and dies. The bus swerves out of control off the road into the desert and finally comes to rest, partially on its side, against a sand dune. One of the passengers is Sister Augusta, a Catholic nun traveling to her convent in California. She is a shy, unassuming person who has devoted her life to the service of God and the care of little children. The passengers, all bruised, some bleeding, make their way out of the bus. Although there is damage to the vehicle, it should be driveable if they can right it, and it could get them to the next town. None of the passengers, however, makes any effort to begin the task. All sit around moaning, some cursing their luck. The sun is getting higher in the sky, the temperature rising to well over 105 degrees.

Obviously none of the passengers can right the bus singlehandedly. Not only would it take most of them to do the job, but it would take some clever jerry-rigging as well. Still, no one makes an effort to get the group organized. They just sit there feeling sorry for themselves. Sister Augusta, after binding up cuts on her own arm, offers some rudimentary medical assistance to the others. She knows that the desert conditions will soon be unbearable and that not only is the road seldom used, but the bus has ended up far from the road and is shielded by dunes. They are not likely to be spotted by anyone driving by.

The question: Is Sister Augusta responsible for the death of two of the older passengers who later in the day collapsed from the heat? Is she responsible for the group's failure to make an effort to right the bus? The most the group did was send one of their number over to the road to wave down any passing motorist. After three fruitless, blistering hours he returned sunburned and dehydrated. No car had passed.

To determine Sister Augusta's power and control in the situation we could first collectivize our analysis of power and control. Doing so would require inclusion of a coordination allowance. The actions of any one passenger, regardless of his or her intention or desire to bring about the bus-righting, will have to be coordinated with the actions of other passengers or the group cannot be said to have power in the situation. In other words, for the passengers to do what they, as a group, have the power to do, each (or most) must have information about what the others are likely to do to contribute to the desired event. How they get that information and how they act on it is a version of the coordination problem for groups, a near cousin to the coordination problem in iterated Prisoner's Dilemma. If a group effort, no matter how feasible, is to be successfully undertaken, group members must come up with some way of letting each other know what each proposes to do in the circumstances. Minimal coordination sets the parameters on the lower end of the actualization of latent collective power.

Insofar as this group did not act together to right the bus, we can arrive at the minimal coordination only by supposition and stipulation. This is easy to do and commonly done. Most reasonable people observing the situation would counterfactualize to quickly determine that sufficient coordination would have been achieved if the members of the group had informed each other of various things, such as their weaknesses and strengths, special knowledge, and experience in related matters, and agreed on a distribution of tasks, the timing for the performance of those tasks, and so forth.[8] Someone should have said, "If you will do this, I'll do that." No one did.

Some subset of the group of ten passengers on the wayward bus, we will stipulate between five and ten of them, has the power to right the bus. In effect, that subset has regulative control with respect to the bus being righted. No individual passenger has the power, and so none has the control. Still that does not mean that no member or each of them as individuals has the power to see to it that the bus is righted. It seems reasonable to expect that the group's power should distribute in some way over its members. The group is, after all, nothing but ten people on a bus. The identity of the group is just that of the aggregated ten people left stranded in the desert. Take away one of the group and it will be a different group. If Sister Augusta never got on the bus, this group would have a different identity.

Although each member is essential to the identity of the group, each member is not indispensable with regard to the activities the group might undertake, even if all ten participate in the activity. The question is whether Sister Augusta has any individual power and/or control in the matter of righting the bus when there is no longer an issue about whether the group has the power to get the job done. This is a different question from the one that might arise if we had said that when a group has collective power, every member has some individual power. That clearly is not the case, for we could always form a second group by adding a randomly selected individual to the first group. It would still be true that the new group has the power to do the task (because the old group did), so this randomly selected individual would have some power as well. For example, if the passengers having the power to right the bus means that each passenger has some power to right the bus, then the passengers plus you (wherever you are) have the power to right the bus, so you have some power in the matter of the bus-righting. That is, of course, silly from a practical point of view, though it might appeal to those who see every human as intimately interrelated to every other in a vast network of moral responsibilities. We are implicated in each other's tasks. After all, if you have the power to do something all by yourself, then the duo of you and I have the power to do it as well. So on this suspect power distribution principle, I should have some power in the doing of it and perhaps some responsibility for its being done. There is something romantically appealing in that notion, even something morally good, something to be encouraged, but nothing of any real help in sorting out the responsibilities of people like the bus passengers who find themselves in specific group activity circumstances. What is important in those cases is whether or not a particular member of a group is dispensable with respect to the matter for which the group, or subgroup, has power and is being held responsible.

Someone is a dispensable member of a group with respect to a certain task if, when all of the members of the group except that person wanted the task to be done,[9] it would be done, even if that person opposed its being done. A person is nondispensable with regard to the task if his or her opposition would alter the outcome. The task would not be done, despite the fact that the other members of the group wanted to do it.

The power distribution principle that actually works in groups, as I developed it elsewhere,[10] may be summarized as: a person has some power with respect to a task if a group of which that person is a nondispensable member has collective power with respect to the task.

We may imagine that with respect to the bus-righting, among the passengers there are both dispensable and nondispensable people, though uncovering no-mological grounds for drawing these distinctions may be difficult. To make it easy, let us say that there is a very old man from Kansas, an Eastern European emigre who speaks broken English, riding on the bus to visit his grandchildren in Winnemucca, Nevada. No matter what he wants to do, the outcome will not be affected because of the way the others regard him. He is also too weak to provide physical assistance. That leaves nine. What of them?

Although none of the remaining passengers is as impotent as the old man, most will be unsuccessful if they make individual appeals to the group to try to right the bus. A pall of defeatism covers the lot. Is each, then, dispensable in the situation? Even though there are no individually powerful members with clear regulative control, none who are able alone to convince the group to try to make the effort, that does not mean that there are no nondispensable members of the group with respect to the whole matter of bus-righting. We can expose this if we suppose that if some of the passengers had wanted to right the bus, they would have been able to convince those in the subgroup needed to do the job to lend a hand. The requisite subgroup members would have joined in, even if they personally would have preferred to sit in the burning sands awaiting either rescue or their Maker.

In effect, there could be a critical mass of passengers who, if only they started trying to right the bus, would draw to the task enough of the others to do the job. Who would be included in that critical mass? If the old man from Kansas were to make the effort, the others might think it altogether futile, since he has no persuasive power and commands no respect in the circumstances. Excluding the old man, however, the critical mass might be six or seven passengers, or it could be as few as two or three. There is no formula for such things.

The emerging dynamics of the group may be such that if the right three members make the effort at the right moment, the necessary number to get the job done will join them. We might imagine a scenario in which Sister Augusta decides to inspect the prospects of righting the bus and is joined by two others. These three attract the remaining passengers, and the task is successfully accomplished. Such a scenario makes crucial assumptions about the effect on others that the efforts of a nun would have. If a number of the passengers are Catholic, Sister Augusta's power could be significantly greater than if they are all atheists. Let us assume that only one other member of the group is a Catholic and that most of the remaining members would be suspicious of his joining the nun in her crazy attempt to right the bus. They might think that because he fears he is near death, he does not want to offend a representative of his religion, no matter how harebrained her scheme. Still, if at least one other passenger joins them, the others will reconsider and participate, perhaps reluctantly. The point is, there is a critical mass of members of a group that has collective power with respect to most matters in which the group has collective power. It follows that each member of that critical mass subgroup has some individual power and regulative control in the circumstances.

In very random groups it is likely that the critical mass subgroup in question could be composed of any persons in the group. Where strong influences exist because of a group member's station or role outside the group (if, for example, one of them is a member of the clergy, an engineer, etc.), the subgroup will almost always have to include that person. Hence Sister Augusta, owing to her station in the general society, may be an nondispensable member of the critical mass subgroup. She could exclude herself from that group by becoming hysterical, irrational, or fanatical. But she remained calm, and so clearly had some individual regulative control in the circumstances. Each of the others has some power as well, because each could be a nondispensable member of the subgroup that could begin the bus-righting.

Suppose that if Sister Augusta plus any three passengers started to right the bus, the required number of others would join in the effort. Each member of the group except the old man is a potential part of that critical mass and so will have some individual power. Suppose that in addition to Sister Augusta, two passengers decide to make the effort. The others still think it is futile. But if one other passenger joins the subgroup, the balance will be tipped and the effort will be made by all. A passenger from Walla Walla comes over to the subgroup. He and the other three (including Sister Augusta) will be nondispensable members of the group with respect to the bus-righting because for each person in the critical mass it will be true that if all four want to try to right the bus, the effort will be made; if only three of them want to right the bus and the fourth member does not, then the effort will not be made. But in the situation as described, any three of the members of the critical mass may be replaced by any other three from the larger group of passengers. Therefore, what is true of the power and regulative control of any one passenger (the man from Walla Walla, for example) is true of every other passenger, except the old man from Kansas and Sister Augusta; her presence in the subgroup is required if it is to be efficacious. (There is another scenario in which she may be a dissenter, while the critical mass forms around others and the job is done, but that is not the story of the dynamics offered here.) As is usually the case, sociological conditions of station, place, and respect limit substitutivity in the critical mass. The film *Twelve Angry Men* provides a classic scenario in which the sheer weight of critical reasoning skills determines the nondispensable membership of the critical mass. The weight of numbers may sometimes be the crucial factor in determining the critical mass for a group, while on other occasions factors of social position, intellect, and training will be operative. Influence often translates into power in a group.

Peter Morriss writes:

The connection between power and responsibility is . . . essentially nega-tive: you can deny all responsibility by demonstrating lack of power. You can do this . . . by proving that you couldn't have done the crime. Or you can do this by showing that you couldn't have prevented the catastrophe. In either case, power is a necessary (but not sufficient) condition for blame: if you didn't have the power, you are blameless.[11]

In summary, if a person such as the old man from Kansas is powerless in a situation, that person cannot be said to have any regulative control in the cir-cumstances and so bears no responsibility for what was done or not done by the group of which that person just happened to be a member. Insofar as most group members are not impotent with respect to matters of group activity or inactivity, each bears a share of the responsibility for the outcome. As a rule, those in the group with influence due to social position bear individual responsibility for the collective actions or omissions of the group, even though they had no individual power to effect the outcome.

This sort of analysis identifies the basis for attributions of responsibility to members of groups, but it leaves unanswered a question that moral philosophers consider central: the question of whether the individual knew or should have known that he or she had influence, power, or regulative control in the circum-stances such that the desirable outcome could have been realized. The analysis I have provided may tell us that Sister Augusta could have done something that would have been efficacious with regard to the bus-righting, but should she have been aware of her power?

I think she should have. A person has a moral responsibility to understand the station he or she occupies in society at large and in more restricted groups. People turn to religious personages in time of trouble, which places a responsibility burden on them that is greater than that of ordinary people. If an engineer or an automobile mechanic were in the group of passengers, the power equation would be different and the assessment of responsibility altered. If one of the passengers were a doctor who, for fear of future malpractice suits, did not take the lead in providing medical care to the injured, we would surely judge him or her morally deficient. If some of the passengers were to die as a result, the moral responsibility for their deaths would surely be assigned primarily to the doctor, even though the doctor could not have done the job alone.

It is possible that individuals may have no idea of their power in any particular group or set of circumstances into which the group may be thrust. In such cases it may not make sense to say that they should have known that if they did X, the group would respond in the desirable way. People may not know their individual powers and have had no way of finding out about them. Still, there is a rational person test that can be applied. Simply, any rational person in the circumstances should recognize the reasonable course of action and try to communicate it to the group. If the person is unable to persuade the group or enough of the members to create the critical mass to accomplish the task, at least the person has tried and, in the process, learned the limits of his or her power. I think of Piggy in *The Lord of the Flies*, a boy who realized more clearly than the others what the situation required. He tried desperately to convince the other boys on the island of the proper way for the group to organize. However, he lacked the powers of persuasion, the authority and the brute force necessary to bring about the outcome he desired, and the results were tragic. Attempts like Piggy's may serve to exclude one from a share of the individual moral responsibility for the group's actions or inaction. Individual moral responsibility for collective actions or omissions may not be assessed because of group association alone, but "I would have been but one against the many" is not a morally exculpating plea either.

7 · The Responsibility
of Inactive Fictive Groups
for Great Social Problems

Important global social problems like hunger relief and environmental protection cannot be solved by individuals acting as individuals. Individuals are virtually impotent with respect to any of these problems, despite the best of intentions. Norman Care makes a noble effort to motivate what he calls "shared-fate individualism"[1] by using the sad facts of world destitution and the gross disparity in quality of life experienced throughout the human community. But his service-oriented moral prescription looks hopelessly romantic in the face of the realities. It is one thing to say that we ought to make career choices to serve others rather than ourselves, but quite another to identify any real impact that choice will have on the problems. Larry May points out[2] that those who do make individual efforts often become justifiably frustrated in the face of the enormity of the problems and soon drop all pretense of being personally responsible.

Moral theory, however, should not abandon the global matters, even if they seem unmanageable to the favored subject of Western moralists, the isolated individual actor. Some philosophers, such as May, argue that it makes sense to hold "loosely structured groups"[3] responsible for the harms they (as a group) might have prevented if they did not act to solve the problems. Members, then, are to be held responsible for group inaction where group action was required.

The causal relationship between the groups in question and the problems needs clarification. The group's inaction probably was not the cause of the problem in the first place, though we will allow that in some cases it might have been a contributory factor. Usually group inaction either exacerbates the problem or leaves it unresolved. Consider world hunger. Is the relevant loosely structured group (presumably, the affluent of the world) the cause of the problem by virtue of that group's inattention to it? That simplistic explanation overlooks myriad other causes. Furthermore, there seems to be a moral difference between an omission that causes harm and one that does not relieve an already existing harm. That distinction is crucial in the way we think of responsibility assignments in "Bad Samaritan" cases, and such cases seem to be paradigmatic of the great social problems.

Saying that a group that never actually formed and so never performed any concerted action (or inaction) is responsible for anything will seem vacuous unless somehow the group responsibility devolves to or is shared by the individual members of that fictive group. If individuals are not "clutched" in some way, the exercise of holding fictive groups responsible appears pointless. In this they are quite different from our bus passengers of the previous chapter.

Loosely structured groups are not fictive in at least one sense. They are bunches of real people, but what defines them as a group for moral purposes? Imagination and point of view make a group of stars into a constellation. Have we any better criterion here? We can assemble in our imaginations all sorts of groups and collectivities of people, but what limits are to be imposed on such gatherings when we make responsibility ascriptions? What sort of defenses are open to a person trying to avoid inclusion in the blamed group if the crucial property that draws one in is having omitted or failed to do something?

"All those that didn't do x are responsible for y" may be a simple causal claim such as "All those not buying grapes are responsible for the grape surplus." But moral responsibility ascriptions are more than causal claims. They involve fault and entail such social responses as punishment and blame. Suppose the non-grapebuyers are held morally responsible for the surplus and that a nongrapebuyer feels unjustly included in the sanctioned group. He or she may be allergic to grapes or hold religious views forbidding the eating of grapes. Morality would normally allow him or her to justify not buying grapes and thereby escape the group being held responsible.

Before further examining the problems with holding so-called loosely structured groups responsible for their inaction in the global problem cases, I will assemble a few reminders about the responsibility for omissions. As noted in the previous chapter, I agree with John Martin Fischer[4] that there is a basic asymmetry between moral responsibility for what one does and moral responsibility for what one omits or fails to do. It is a basic principle of moral responsibility, accepted by moralists of almost every stripe, that a person cannot be held morally responsible for failing to do something he or she could not have done. (One can, of course, be held responsible for doing something one could not have avoided doing, as discussed in chapter five.)

Fischer, as noted in the previous chapter, persuasively argues that moral responsibility generally links up with control. Consider the following case: Levi the

Levite is walking down one side of a road somewhere in the Middle East. Across the road, in obvious distress, lies Sam. Levi has a first-aid kit with him, but decides not to go to the trouble of providing aid and succor to Sam. He walks on down the road, and poor Sam dies. Levi never learns that the road is heavily mined and that he could not have crossed it without being blown to bits. Even if he had tried, he couldn't have provided aid to Sam, so should he be held morally responsible for not providing it?

The fact that Levi could not have provided aid to Sam must be given great weight. I would go so far as to say that it justifies our *not* holding him responsible for his failure to give aid. Ought implies can, and he couldn't. We may, of course, hold Levi morally responsible for his failure to *try* to provide aid to Sam. He could have tried, though trying probably would have cost him dearly, perhaps his life. Still, his failure to even try reveals a character fault for which he should be blamed. But this shift to what he tried or did not try to do illustrates the usual practice where moral responsibility for omissions is concerned: redescribing the case from one in which the action cannot be done to one in which something can be done—for example *trying* to do what cannot actually be done. We adjust the specification until we locate the doable, then assign responsibility.

In cases of omission, facts external to the person determine the content of the responsibility ascription. Following Fischer, the crucial factual issue in such cases is the extent of the person's regulative control of the event for which he or she is being held morally responsible. Claims about the responsibility of loosely structured groups for what they do not do must amount to claims about the regulative control possessed by such groups in specific circumstances or with respect to certain events.

Consider again Levi and Sam on the road in the Middle East. Does Levi have regulative control over Sam's receiving aid? He cannot, in the circumstances, ensure that Sam will receive aid. Nor, we may assume, can he prevent it, though it is only necessary that Levi lack one of these abilities for it to be out of his regulative control. Levi, then, cannot be held morally responsible for failing to give aid to Sam.

To apply this standard to fictive groups that fail to act to solve the great social problems, we need to ask whether they have regulative control with respect to those problems. Do they have the power *both* to ensure and to prevent the events for which they might be held responsible? How could we establish that they do? I haven't any idea. The exercise would be extraordinarily imaginative. Suppose we think of settling responsibility for the world hunger problem on Upper- and Middle-Class People from the Western Industrial Democracies (UMCPWIDs). Let us stipulate, as I think is true, that the target group is not the actual cause (or

even a major contributing cause) of the hunger for which it is being held responsible. The UMCPWIDs didn't cause it. Weather, indigenous political problems,
and the like were the real culprits. To be held morally responsible for it, however,
the UMCPWIDs must be in a position to override the actual causal factors and
either perpetuate the hunger or relieve it. And how is so nebulous a group as the
UMCPWIDs to do anything like what is required? It makes little sense to say
that they *can* unless they are transformed radically. But transformed into what?
The UMCPWIDs must be turned into a corporation-like entity (or entities) in
the fullest sense of the term, with vast powers on the global scene. But is such a
corporate entity actually formable? What would it look like? How would it function? As these questions become more and more intractable, the sense of the
original responsibility ascription fades. In their disorganized states, fictive inactive groups certainly do not have the requisite control for moral responsibility.
Inaction is all one can expect from a group gathered only in the moralist's imagination.

We might shift our focus to the capacity of individuals to organize effective
groups. If an individual has such a capacity, then he or she would have regulative
control over the forming of that group. Hence, as discussed in the previous chapter, such an individual can be said to be individually responsible for his or her
failure to exercise that capacity and form the group in the circumstances. Matters
have shifted from the Field of Collectivity Dreams to the Field of Individual
Dreams. Build it and they will get involved!

The responsibility focus shifts to the nonformation of a decision-structural
unit. But how do we tell whether any particular group of people could have been
organized? Virginia Held provided a reasonable-person test.[5] Simply, if it is obvious to a reasonable person that the harm can be prevented by constituting an
otherwise random collection of people into a decision-making and acting consortium, then a group that does not organize in the situation is responsible, not for
the harm, but for not organizing. Larry May tries to delineate when it is reasonable to attribute to an assembly of people the ability to develop "a mechanism of
co-ordination in a short enough time period."[6] His argument is persuasive in cases in which a number of people on a beach might have organized to save a
drowning child. But are the great social issues simply inflated versions of these
cases? Could some group, if only they would organize, control an African famine
in the way the sunbathers could rescue the child?

It may or may not appear to the reasonable person that a certain group of
people, if organized, could prevent widespread starvation. How do we apply the
reasonable person test in these cases? And further, how do we determine that a
person with the necessary leadership attributes was in the position to effect the

requisite organization? Who is in the group that should be organized? And what of the matter of timeliness? If nothing happens on the grand scale, how are we to ascertain that something might have happened if only _____?

Consider the following story: By coincidence of their individual schedules, six people happen to arrive at a particular street corner at 4:30 P.M. At precisely that moment a strong gust of wind tips over a trash can and garbage litters the corner and starts to spread down the block. The wind is distributing the garbage in such a way that none of the six acting alone could hope to retrieve all of the trash and replace it in the can. If anyone even tried to do so, he or she would surely risk life and limb in the traffic. However, if each were to pick up a portion of the litter, the job could be effectively and efficiently accomplished with little risk or serious inconvenience to anyone. Five of the pedestrians do not think twice about the matter and hurry off. One, Suzy Spotless, picks up some of the trash, perhaps even a sixth of it, then goes about her business. Should the gang of six be held responsible for the spread of the trash? If they are, that would seem to imply that as long as there is a way to refer to a unit of people, that unit or collection may be the target of responsibility ascriptions.

The story of the people on the street corner reveals something else. Suppose we ask whether Suzy Spotless is or is not a member of the targeted group. May suggests that insofar as a group never really organizes, membership in it is determined by the property for which the group is being held responsible: its inaction.[7] But in this case Suzy did what she would have been expected to do had the group formed, yet she is still a part of the group held responsible for the litter by virtue of the fact that, in the circumstances, her picking up a sixth of the trash was not the right thing to do. She did not attempt to organize those on the street corner to do the job she could not accomplish on her own. Her independent actions do not immunize her from sharing the group responsibility for the litter. Those who try singly to do the right thing in circumstances where only a collective effort stands any real chance of succeeding deserve little or no moral credit and cannot escape collective responsibility for the harm. In Suzy's case, it does not matter that she has no leadership capacity.

A vivid example of this principle with respect to poverty in the Third World occurred when Michael Palin, ex-member of the "Monty Python" cast, journeyed around the world for the BBC. In Bombay he was beset by beggars. He refused their pleas on the grounds that whatever he might afford to give one or two would do little or no good with respect to the real problem. He obviously felt a bit uneasy morally about refusing the beggars, but he shouldn't have. Only a vast collective effort could hope to adequately respond to poverty and its attendant ills in Bombay and other Third World locations.

But should Palin be held morally responsible for not organizing a collective that is able to make a significant dent in the problem? I suspect not. He may not have the persuasive abilities of a Bob Geldof. [Aside: Had Geldof not organized Band Aid and Live Aid, should we hold him doubly responsible as, in May's terms, he was "doubly necessary?"[8] I think people like Geldof act in supererogatory ways when they organize others to respond to the world's great social problems.] More importantly, unlike the people on the street corner or the passengers on the bus in the previous chapter, it is not at all clear what group is to be organized. The UMCPWIDs again? Why? Perhaps the beggars should be organized to combat the problem themselves. Perhaps the world's thirty richest people should be organized to heap effective donations on the Third World's poor. In cases of this sort, what is the appropriate unformed, fictive group? Who would really have regulative control were they, counter to fact, organized?

This gets so incredibly complicated that we are likely to be wrapped up in an academic dispute over possible world scenarios so far into the future that any hope of actually making a positive contribution to solving the social problems will be utterly lost. After all, what would be the point of holding fictive groups responsible if it isn't to provoke otherwise inactive people to do the right thing in the first place? Rather than beat around those bushes, it would seem to make some practical sense to focus on already existing entities that have the resources and the power to effect the changes we think morality recommends. I propose to do so in chapter nine.

8 · Hobbes and the Hobbits: A Short Excursion into British Literary Foundations for a Lesson in Political Responsibility

Over and above all of the things said of it in debates on contractarianism,[1] Hobbes's *Leviathan* is a myth of civilization, an alternative to the Judeo-Christian vision of human nature that has dominated Western thought. St. Augustine writes, "The human race, and the world it inhabits, . . . sprang from the creative act of God, and was as perfect as its creator. But, by an original sin, mankind became separated from the source of its happiness and peace."[2]

Hobbes envisioned no paradise from which human beings had fallen, no gloriously happy natural life forever lost. Hobbes's myth emphasized our imperfections, our littleness—our hobbitness. The world "contains the materials for the satisfaction" of all of our desires (except the desire for immortality), yet in nature, Hobbes was convinced, each of us would live a solitary life in dismal fear. Humans are rational and self-interested. Prudence is our guide and felicity our goal. ("Felicity" is Hobbes's term for success in obtaining what we desire.)

But the object of my desires may be also the object of yours. We are, after all, basically alike. Each of us can be, and often is, a distinct impediment to the other's felicity.

> To have cultivated a garden is to have issued an invitation to all others to take it by force, for it is against the common view of felicity to weary oneself with making what can be acquired by less arduous means.[3]

In the Hobbesian perspective, competition is our natural state. We are enemies in a state of war.

> There is no place for industry . . . no culture of the earth; no navigation . . . , no commodious building . . . , no knowledge of the face of the earth; no

85

account of time; no arts; no letters; no society, and, what is worst of all, continual fear and danger of violent death; and the life of man solitary, poor, nasty, brutish, and short.[4]

The felicity of each of us depends upon much more than individual choices and actions. One's success or failure is intricately interwoven with the choices and actions of many other people over which one may have little influence or control. How can one ever insure one's felicity? It is as if we are always playing Prisoner's Dilemma-type games with each other in which self-interest counsels us not to cooperate with the other player in achieving a mutually beneficial outcome if, given the average of the payoffs, one can do better by not cooperating. As long as both players have the same possibilities, neither will act cooperatively and neither will benefit. The more rationally we try to act, the more likely we are to produce the result no one wanted.

Hobbes believed that the solution to this dilemma must come from practical rationality even though it was also the cause of the problem. The task is to make it prudent for people to choose to act in ways that are likely to be optimal for all, even if not maximal for any particular person. Hobbes argued that the most collectively rational thing humans can do is agree on rules of conduct that are likely to maintain the conditions for communal prosperity, which he saw as an aggregate of individual prosperity, and a power with sufficient force to coerce almost everyone to observe them. To do that, Hobbes believed, we need a special kind of agreement, a social covenant that will create and empower a sovereign to set and enforce the rules of the activities and institutions in and through which we each try to achieve our own conceptions of felicity. In effect, the sovereign requires us to keep our contracts with each other and to cooperate at every opportunity rather than take advantage of each other. And if someone does not cooperate? The sovereign punishes or even kills the offender.

Hobbes describes the sovereign as "that great Leviathan, or rather, to speak more reverently, that mortal god to which we owe . . . our peace and defense."[5] The social contract we make with each other forms the sovereign, and all rights we had in nature transfer to that entity. The relationship between subjects and sovereign is not contractual. The sovereign, for Hobbes, is "an artificial (person) who represents or 'bears the person' of each of those who, by agreeing among themselves to do so, creates him and authorizes all his actions."[6] Hobbes's sovereign is an office and however that office is filled (whether by a single person, as in a monarchy, or a body of persons, as in a democracy), it must have the absolute right to enjoy the support of its subjects. Hobbes admits that his theory is indifferent to the type of sovereign. What is important is that the sovereign must be indivisible and have absolute power.

I suggest that the underlying mythic conception of Hobbesian political theory has its origins in British Celtic lore and that it emerges in the Arthurian traditions that dominate much of English literary and philosophical thinking about the responsibility relationships between subjects and sovereign.

The Arthurian legends focus on a British warlord who probably fought against invading Saxons at the Battle of Badon in 518 A.D. and reportedly died in combat against Mordred at Camlan 21 years later. The familiar stories of King Arthur and his court—of gallant knights and beautiful ladies—are based on the tales of the Celtic oral tradition.

It is characteristic of those Celtic stories that important events occur near springs, fords, forest clearings, or large trees. These sacred sites are defended by a king (or knight) who is regularly challenged to fight. If the challenger prevails, the defense of the place falls to him. It was winner take all: all goods, all titles and the wife and daughters of the loser. Why must a warrior/king stand constantly at the ready against all challengers, and why does the successful challenger inherit the task? Although the sites were believed to be sacred and so warranted protection, their defenses actually were occasions to test the power, vigor, and martial skill of the guardian, who Frazer called "The King of the Wood." "The post which he held by this precarious tenure carried with it the title of King; but surely no crowned head ever lay uneasier, or was visited by more evil dreams, than his. For year in year out, in summer and winter, in fair weather and in foul, he had to keep his lonely watch, and whenever he snatched a troubled slumber it was at the peril of his life."[7]

Why should the strength and prowess of the defender/king be so important? The Celts apparently believed that the power of the sovereign, as demonstrated by victory over challengers or in conjunction with the protection of the sacred spot, was the wellspring of the people's good fortune and the fruitfulness of their crops. The challengers were not so much punk kids out to make reputations as true believers on missions to insure that the king was in full vigor, and they were prepared to die in the effort. The prosperity of the community was the foremost, desperate concern in the whole bloody business. The Celts believed that a land ruled by a weak king, one who had lost physical strength and prowess and/or sexual potency, magically transformed into Terre Gaste, the Wasteland.

Crop failures, drought, animals' deaths, and the like were attributed to the king's having become unable to defend the sacred location. The strongest young warrior would be trained and sent to challenge the king. Presumably he would prevail and become king himself, and the prosperity of the villagers would be magically restored. The political theorists in the Celtic villages soon must have raised a crucial question: Why wait for matters to deteriorate, for plagues and pestilence to beset the community, when a continual flow of challengers should insure prosperity?"

It was not long before the kings devised an alternative scheme. They invented a different type of kingship: the fixed-period reign ending with a challenge, which evolved into a tournament for challengers scheduled once a year, usually on New Year's Day. The champion, who might well be the incumbent, served as king and guardian of the sacred site for the next year.[8]

Apparently in some districts it was believed that a one-year term limitation ought to be put on the office to insure the potency and combat readiness of the defender. They established a rite of annual kingship culminated, or, rather, termi-nated on New Year's Day, by the death of the king, either by fire or beheading. Stories depicting this method of insuring the strength of the monarch abound in Celtic lore. In the *High History of the Holy Grail*,[9] for example, Lancelot is riding in a barren land and finds a ruined city. The townsfolk are gathered in a great hall where a handsome young king carrying a large axe approaches Lancelot and asks that Lancelot cut the king's head off. The king's year of sovereignty is over and his death is required to restore the land to prosperity. Lancelot severs the head of the young king. The same motif is later adopted in the great medieval poem *Sir Gawain and the Green Knight*.

A maimed king (Celtic tales are overpopulated with them) disabled by the dolorous stroke, symbolically a wound through the thighs, was incapable of ward-ing off those forces that destroy the security and stability of the community. Simply, impotency of the monarch defeats communal prosperity. "Neither peas nor wheat were sown, no children were born, marriages did not take place, plants and trees did not turn green and birds and animals did not reproduce so long as the king was maimed."[10]

Thomas Malory's stories of the Arthurian court utilize the magical link be-tween the sovereign's strength and the community's prosperity. Sexual prowess, in particular, is a crucial element of his tales. The events surrounding the concep-tion of Arthur at Tintagel, for example, were commonplace for most of the heroes of Camelot. Arthur, like Galahad and Mordred, was conceived illegiti-mately in a union engulfed in violence, lust, and trickery. He was a product of the king's rape of the wife of his enemy, an affair that required an assist from sorcery, and he was legitimized only by the murder of his mother's husband. Unlike his father, King Pendragon, Arthur did not dominate his court with displays of his sexual and military power, and though we would probably applaud his "civilizing" of Camelot, the Celtic political theorists would have seen his conversion to law and Christian morality as the explanation of the degeneration of his reign. Not incidentally, Arthur's only offspring (by his witchy half-sister, Morgan) was his archenemy Mordred. His marriage to Guinevere was without issue, and she was wooed away from him by his friend and greatest knight, Lancelot. As the plot progresses, Arthur drifts into the background, while his pantheon of knights grabs the spotlight. Arthur spends the better part of his time creating rules that emasculate the very force that founded his authority. Lancelot's sexuality and martial talents dominate Arthur who, rather than rousing to reestablish his potency by a supreme act of passion, is rendered pathetic by a morality antithetical to his Celtic culture. Today we applaud the sentiments about justice, law, and rights attributed to Arthur, but the Celts would have interpreted these notions as the pathetic admonitions of a maimed (at least symbolically) king. No Celt would be surprised that Camelot would soon be destroyed. (John Boorman's film, *Excalibur*, nicely portrays this shift in Arthur and its ramifications for the community.)

In the times of the Anglo-Saxons, the kings' need to maintain the appearance of physical power fostered the use of surrogates, king's thanes, to do the dirty work for which the king ultimately secured the credit. In *Beowulf* the monster Grendel personifies evil, and its destruction would be the king's responsibility. But the king is unfit for the task. The king's thane, Beowulf, is dispatched, and his conquests are counted as if they were those of his king.

Malory penned his famous version of Camelot, *Le Morte d'Arthur*, during the War of the Roses, a period which witnessed another renaissance of the Celtic concept of sovereignty. This one was personified in the heroic figure of Henry Tudor, who was pictured as riding tall in the saddle from out of the dark Celtic mountains of Wales to challenge a maimed king, Richard III, for the throne of England on Bosworth Field.

The Tudors had a meager claim to the throne, so a golden lie was created to cement their authority. The Tudor historians Polydore Vergil[11] and Thomas More[12] were enlisted to manufacture what has come to be known as "the Tudor myth" justifying Henry's claim to the throne. The Tudor myth interpreted the War of the Roses as God's punishment, a magical barrenness visited on the country for the deposition of Richard II. Richard III was seen as God's scourge, visiting just punishment on all those associated with the demise of Richard II and the subsequent betrayal and mass murder in the royal family.[13] The Tudor mythmaking was not the least deterred by the fact that there was little or no fit between the Celtic pattern and what was actually occurring in England at the time. The general population was rapidly gaining wealth; feudalism had died; mercantilism was driving the economy; and news of family feuds over who was wearing the crown was less interesting to the average person than the price quotes on wool in Chipping Camden. Hardly the Wasteland associated with a maimed king! Still, Richard III's reign was portrayed as a bloody tyranny and the Tudors as the founders of a new golden age.

Sir Thomas More, from whom Shakespeare took much of his characterization of Richard III, writes:

> Richard was ill-featured of limbs, crookbacked, his left shoulder much higher than his right. . . . He was malicious, wrathful, and envious from before his birth, ever forward. . . . His mother could not be delivered of him uncut. He came into the world with feet forward—as men be borne out of it. . . . He was close and secret, a deep dissembler, lowly of countenance, arrogant of heart, outwardly companionable where he inwardly hated, not hesitating to kiss whom he thought to kill, pitiless and cruel. Friend and 'foe' were to him indifferent; where his advantage grew, he spared no man's death whose life withstood his purpose.[14]

Other historians suggest that the evidence supports only a few of More's claims—even those about Richard's physical appearance are suspected by some. In any event, in Shakespeare's hands the Richard III of the Tudor myth was cast as one of the monumental figures of the stage. He is the sometimes comical instrument of both good and evil, fated to prepare the way for the Tudors by acts of murder, mayhem, and butchery—the most pivotal quasi-mythical king since Arthur. In him the maimed king of the Celtic legends becomes a demonic Machiavelli. Despite his deformities, Richard III is established as a worthy adversary for the Tudor savior of England.[15]

In some versions of the Tudorized history, the crown itself passed from the maimed king, slaughtered while in search of a horse, to the Tudor line via a bush in which it had become entangled, recalling the Celtic sacred grove of the challenge kings and the Arthurian tradition.

The Tudor myth characterized Bosworth Field as a great moral battleground like Camlan, where Arthur and Mordred met, where good and evil battled and the prosperity of the people hung in the balance. The difference was that though Arthur won at Camlan, he was old and fatally wounded and could rule no more. Borne off to the Isle of Avalon, he became the "once and future king." In case anyone missed the point the Tudors wanted made, Henry VIII (Henry Tudor's second son) had an eighteen-foot-diameter round table (that may date from the time of Edward I) repainted with a Tudor Rose in the center and a portrait of King Arthur at the top. It was hung in the ancient city of Winchester. The portrait of Arthur, however, is actually painted in the image of Henry VIII himself. The Tudors claimed to be direct descendants of Arthur. Had he not died young, the successor to Henry Tudor would not have been the notorious Henry VIII but his older brother, who had been purposefully named Arthur.

The days of the Tudors, however, passed into an era that featured that least of Celtic sovereignty conceptions: the divine right of kings. The successors to the Tudors, the Stuart kings, proclaimed their divine rights to supersede the law, but displayed the statesmanship of what Macaulay called "nervous, driveling idiots." Although Charles I was undeniably a "rickety child," he grew up to be highminded. Unhappily, his mind was seldom on his duties, his judgment was characteristically poor, and his manner was tactless. It seemed that divine right had placed the crown on less-than-royal brows. But the Celtic gods of Britain work in strange ways. Suddenly a religiously founded concept caught fire and blazed across the land from pulpit to pulpit: the distinctively protestant dogma of the priesthood of all believers, of perfect equality before God. When that flame was set to political kindling, it burst into the hottest political concepts of the day: natural rights, equality, government by consent of the governed.

But these ideas did not constitute a new vision of the responsibility of the people in relation to their leaders. Instead they represented a renaissance of the Celtic-Arthurian political mythology. Its spokesman through the Civil War, the Cromwellian Protectorate, and the Restoration was, of course, Thomas Hobbes.

The Celticness of *Leviathan* emerges from beneath a layer of seventeenth century political theory. The prosperity of the people is directly dependent on the might of the sovereign. Hobbes made the sovereign not just one of the people, the dominant knight in tournament challenge, but a creation of the people collectively, an artificial person, a colossus of authority and strength. That may well have been due to the impact of the protestant doctrines on his thinking. To illustrate his view, Hobbes approved as the frontispiece of his masterpiece a drawing of a gigantic monarch composed of the figures of his subjects.

I think Hobbes saw the Celtic light in the forest glade: the people must bear the responsibility for sustaining and insuring the power and authority of their ruler. The grooming of challengers was replaced with the social contract. But the Celtic belief that community welfare dominates private privilege and is necessary for individual prosperity is a centerpiece of his theory. Hobbes certainly knew that the independent members of the community were not especially strong or wise or courageous, yet when they are molded into a sovereign force, they can exemplify those characteristics in monstrous proportions. Hence, I believe the Leviathan may be seen as an offspring of the Celtic virile king concept.

In our century the Celtic conception of the ultimate responsibility of the ordinary people for their own social welfare and security reappears in *The Lord of the Rings*, Tolkien's fantasy of elves, dwarfs, magicians, and Hobbits. Hobbits! Hobbes! It is a tempting idea, but Tolkien himself scotched it. He wrote in a letter to R. W. Burchfield of the *Oxford English Dictionary* staff in September 1970, "I submit for your consideration the following definition of Hobbit: One of an imaginary people, a small variety of the human race, that gave themselves this name (meaning 'hole-dweller') but were called by others halflings, since they were half the height of normal men."[16] In a letter to Roger Lancelyn Green in January, 1971 he added, "The only English word that influenced the invention was 'hole.' "[17]

Tolkien claimed in a number of places, including the preface to the *Lord of the Rings*, that his trilogy was not to be interpreted as an allegory of the times, though "the darkness of those days had some effect on it." He did tell Sir Stanley Unwin, "You can, if you like, make the Ring into an allegory of the inevitable fate that waits all attempts to defeat evil power by power."[18] But the moral of the tale, he maintained, is not to be derived from any allegorical analysis. It is in the story itself. Still, Tolkien felt it necessary to clarify his aims in a number of letters.

> This is a tale about a war cast in terms of a good side, and a bad side, beauty against ruthless ugliness, tyranny against sovereignty, moderated freedom with consent against compulsion that has long lost any object save mere power. [to Naomi Mitchison]

> Every romance that takes things seriously must have a warp of fear and horror. . . . Yet . . . mere mundane hobbits can cope with such things. . . . [In fact] there is no horror conceivable that such creatures cannot surmount with the refusal of their nature and reason at the last pinch to compromise or submit. [to Sir Stanley Unwin]

> The Enemy, or those who have become like him, go in for 'machinery'— with destructive and evil effects—because 'magicians', who have become chiefly concerned to use *magic* for their own power, would do so. . . . Of course another factor then comes in, a moral one. The tyrants lose sight of objects, become cruel and like smashing, hurting, and defiling as such. . . . Against that, only the concerted courage of Hobbits may prevail. [to Naomi Mitchison][19]

Tolkien's Hobbits are remarkably like Hobbes's conception of ordinary citizens in the civil state.

Hobbits are an unobtrusive but very ancient people. . . . They love peace and quiet and good tilled earth. . . . At no time had Hobbits been war-like . . . they had, of course, been obliged to fight to maintain themselves in a hard world.[20]

In *The Lord of the Rings*, men represent the knightly style of heroism of King Arthur and Lancelot. The Hobbits, on the other hand, represent the kind of courage exhibited by common folk who rise to heroism in crisis. Hobbit heroism is motivated by loyalty, love of community, and friendship. Humility restrains Hobbits from rashness, the excess of courage that is usually the root cause of the downfall of the Arthurian knights.

Perhaps the Hobbits' most important characteristic is their devotion to social responsibility. The theme of Tolkien's trilogy is that no matter what the super forces try to do to stop evil, they will fail, they will be subverted, they will render each other impotent. Only the efforts of common folk can insure the conditions for social felicity. The Celtic theme of citizen responsibility for the fruits of pow-erful sovereignty is evident, along with other Celtic conceptions, throughout the *Ring* trilogy. Detailed illustrations would be too involved, but readers will remem-ber, as examples, that Gandalf enters Theoden's court and finds the king ill and cures him, drives out Wormtongue, and brings fertility back to the land. The basic plot is constructed in the seasonal manner of the Celtic tales. The quest from Rivendell begins in the dead of winter and is achieved in spring. At the end of the year the cycle is completed back at the Shire. Frodo's progress is from the natural fertility of the Shire to the most desolated part of Middle Earth. And Frodo and Sam's great quest does not end at "The Crack of Doom." They return to the Shire and thereby restore the land to its former fertility.

Tolkien uses Celtic themes and incorporates the same basic responsibility message that is a central tenet of British literature and political philosophy: citizens ultimately bear the responsibility for the effectiveness of government. Sovereigns must be powerful, but power in the sovereign's hands not only cor-rupts, but it also dissipates the sovereign. Ordinary people are required to act, sometimes heroically, just to protect their own safety and security. (This also is one of the primary themes of Robert Graves's monumental works on the Julio-Claudian Roman Emperors.[21])

Tolkien wrote to Auden, "I saw the value of Hobbits . . . in providing subjects for ennoblement and heroes more praiseworthy than the professionals. . . . *The Lord of the Rings* really falls in the same class as . . . Beowulf and the Shakespear-ean historical tragedies."[22]

Failure of the people to monitor their sovereign allows the business of government to fall into the hands of those using authority for personal gain. Mobilizing the people in a democracy is a difficult task. Bureaucracies sometimes grow into monsters, like Grendel, that make a habit of invading the homes of the citizens and making off with property and lives. We may feel powerless in the face of a big government, but it is to just such a disenchanted population that the Celtic-Arthurian-Hobbesian-Hobbit myth speaks. It tells us that insuring the strength and the commitment of our leaders to the tasks of good government is the continuing responsibility of all of us—we the people. Just as the ordinary people had to continually test the strength of the Celtic king and the Hobbits had to destroy the evil ruling ring, so it is with us, the ordinary people, that the responsibility for the prosperity of our communities ultimately rests. If our society drifts into an uncompetitive position in world economic and political markets, if our leaders line their own pockets at our expense, if the security of our homes and persons is regularly and seriously threatened, whose fault is it?

9 · The Wasteland: Whose Responsibility?

It is characteristic of the stories of the British Celtic tradition, as discussed in the previous chapter, that pivotal events occur near springs, fords, forest clearings or special trees. These sacred sites were defended by a king or knight who could be challenged in order to test his ability to protect the special place. And why is the spot guarded? Not just because it is sacred, but because the prosperity of the people depends on the strength and the resolve of the defender to protect the sacred springs and forests, or so the Celts believed. If the defender, Frazer's "King of the Wood,"[1] loses virility, if the place is no longer safe, the land is magically transformed into Terre Gaste, the Wasteland of which T. S. Eliot wrote. The Celtic legends forged a link between environmental protection and long-term communal prosperity. The link lies in the responsibility shouldered by the defender to guard the sacred place and the responsibility of the people to insure that the appropriate defender was on the spot.

Celtic mythology is invigorating, sometimes brutal, and certainly pagan. Still, the Celtic doctrine of the protection of sacred places and the threat of magical barrenness if they are not protected speaks across millennia and worldviews. The Celts were nature worshippers; hence they had deep religious as well as economic reasons to guard the environment. But, more importantly for us, they understood the need to locate responsibility for environmental protection with those who are most likely to have a positive effect on that goal. Although the people bore the responsibility of insuring that the defender remained capable of his task—grooming and sending challengers to test the vigor of the defender—the defender held the ultimate responsibility for preventing the onset of the Wasteland.[2] Should he fail the defender was beheaded.

One of the major problems with conceptualizing responsibility for environmental protection is identifying roles in the first place. Specifically, when we talk

95

of caring for the environment we naturally talk about what everyone ought to do: recycling, picking up litter, and so on. That's all very nice, and it certainly gives people a sense of participation in the effort, but if we really want to prevent the Wasteland from becoming the human habitat of the future, we need a moral and metaphysical theory that lays the responsibility where it can produce long-term good. The idea that primary environmental protection ought to be shouldered by each and every one of us is another example of the kind of nonsense produced by atomistic individualism. It tends to leave caring individuals frustrated after early bursts of energy and enthusiasm. It also leaves the job undone, often barely started. The problem is not that individuals have no role to play; it is that environmental problems, like so many great problems, cannot be solved until a proper division of labor is settled.

In the spring of 1989, a week or so after the *Exxon Valdez* piled into a reef and befouled the waters and shores of Prince William Sound with eleven million gallons of oil, a Wall Street analyst of some reputation was interviewed on national television (CNN). He maintained that disasters of this sort are bound to occur in the industry and should be understood as a cost the society must absorb for its oil-based economy. He went on to argue that neither Exxon nor individuals on the tanker or in the company should be held responsible for the incident. In effect, he claimed that no person, natural or corporate, ought to be held liable for damages. It seemed to him that Exxon was making a magnanimous gesture by voluntarily cleaning up the damaged region. The startled reaction of the other discussants left a few awkward moments of silent airtime before someone attempted a rejoinder.

When I first heard this view expressed, I, like many others, was shocked. Here was another free-enterpriser defending big business as it desecrates the earth. Responding to his position, however, is not as simple as it sounds. In the first place, we ought not to be much concerned with events like the *Exxon Valdez* spill. Dramatic though they are, they really are not major environment protection problems. Control of such spills, insofar as accidents can ever be controlled, will be a matter of technological improvement and government regulation. Tankers with stronger hulls must be employed and crews better trained. Once that has been said, there is not too much more to the issue. In any event, the Prince William Sound oil disaster should be of far less interest to us than such concerns as global warming, air pollution, and the general degradation of the water supply; these are the truly difficult problems of responsibility in environmental matters. To deal with them in a responsible and effective fashion, we must be prepared to dynamite some of the most cherished and firmly placed cornerstones of the political liberalism that has dominated Western academic discussion of moral responsibility for centuries. I am prepared to tolerate that sort of desecration to bring these environmental problems under control.

There are enormous difficulties in motivating responsibility ascriptions with respect to the environment. One reason, no doubt, is that traditional theories of ownership, such as Locke's, exclude waste. Hence, it is hard to get people to accept ownership of things they throw away, flush away, or spill. Though the ownership of waste would make a useful study, that is not my interest. Instead, I will argue that establishing the grounds for holding us, an aggregate of individual natural persons, responsible for full-scale environmental protection is virtually impossible from within the liberal individualist tradition. In other words, I will contend that no sensible responsibility relationship can exist from which individual responsibility for environmental protection can be derived and to which we as individuals are party.

In the first place, environmental protection, for moral purposes, cannot be based on any relationship that might be imagined between us, collectively or individually, and other species. Consider what I have elsewhere called the "input conditions of responsibility-ascription."[3] Pincoffs's formula for responsibility, mentioned in chapter two, exposes them: A imputes C to B on account of D, in light of E, and in the absence of F.

You may recall that C is an event or condition or state of affairs, usually an unpleasant one. If the event is the oil spill on Prince William Sound, the question is whether A [you or I] can impute it to Exxon (B^1) or the tanker captain (B^2) or both, etc. D is an activity or action performed by B, and E is the set of role requirements that establish B's relationship to A and to the event. F is the defense, excuses or justifications B could offer. Pincoffs's formula is for responsibility ascription, so C is his focus—an untoward event. But if the concern is responsibility assignment, then we need to look primarily at the relationship between A and B, what I will call the responsibility relationship, and at E, the role requirements. In short, our interest should not be in nailing the party liable for any particular oil spill, it should be in establishing the assignment of responsibility for general environmental protection itself. In terms of the Celtic traditions, we should not be concerned primarily with pinpointing and then beheading the particular lax defender, but in determining who the defenders should be and what their duties are. In effect, we need to uncover the requirements for being a responsible party in long-term environmental matters. Who or what can play the part of B when environmental protection is the task?

Insofar as we are talking of moral matters, B must be a person. It makes no moral sense to hold sea otters or whales, for example, responsible for whatever they might do to mess up the ecosystem. Strictly speaking, we should probably say that only those persons who stand in a responsibility relationship to each other can ascribe responsibility to each other. That, however, is a long way from actual practice. I do not stand in any responsibility relationship with Jim Bakker, but I ascribe blame to him for his misdeeds. A (in Pincoffs's formula) need not be linked to B in a relationship that generates responsibilities for B in order for A to sensibly ascribe responsibility to B for some C, failure to meet them. But for that ascription to make sense, it must be the case that B does have a responsibility to do something that would have prevented C. For B to have such a responsibility, there must be a party, P, with whom B has a relationship that defines roles and duties. The problem for environmental protection is to identify the appropriate parties, B and P.

No one is responsible to the sea otters for their protection. Is anyone responsible to anyone else for the protection of the sea otters? Laws are in place protecting elements of the environment, so violators theoretically owe the state an obligation on which they have defaulted. But is it a moral obligation? Is the state a person and hence a suitable party to the relationship? The preponderance of thinkers in the Western liberal tradition would be reluctant to say it is.

Typical of the discussion of enviromental responsibility is the view that protection of the environment is owed to future generations. Of course we should protect it for ourselves as well, but in either case these are difficult claims to understand. Protect it for what? For our possible enjoyment? For someone else's possible enjoyment? How many of us are ever going to visit the shores of Prince William Sound? It's not on my vacation wish list. It surely is not likely to be enjoyed by the millions and millions of people living on the Indian subcontinent or in Africa. There is a bothersome WASPiness about protectionism based on possible future enjoyment of existing people. At least future generations are safer candidates, as we do not know what their interests will be or how they may need to use the environment. Many people talk as if we ought to leave it to them in good repair. But why?

It seems to me that environmental protection as a long-term project depends on persons existing now being in a responsibility relationship with the generations that will (or may) exist in the remote future. Yet it is very difficult to see how any relationship deep enough to support responsibility assignments can exist between any persons existing today and distant generations. I reject as grossly sentimental the view that we have a responsibility to protect the environment because it contains living things that have rights. Again, a responsibility to whom? And with respect to what role requirements? Though I admit to certain negative feelings about some birds, I have nothing against flora and fauna. I would rather they continued living than not, and I support organizations who work to protect them. But it is a matter of charity, not obligation, especially in such cases as the sea otters.

Returning then to the possibility that a moral responsibility relationship with respect to the environment exists between people now living and future generations, we should note that traditional liberal individualist theories utterly fail to provide the basis for such a relationship. Consider the big two of that tradition: Hobbes and Locke. Any attempt to create the relationship must account for the asymmetry in power to harm between those persons now in existence and future generations. As the environmentalists remind us, we can certainly make those in the future worse off, but they will never be able to reciprocate. They can tarnish our reputations, but that is hardly comparable to the messes in which we can force them to live. We, individually and in the aggregate, can materially hurt or help them. They can neither hurt nor help us.

For Hobbes, as Barry notes, "morality offers convenient articles of peace."[4] But insofar as Hobbes's view depends on the relative equality of the parties to the social contract in their ability to harm each other, Hobbesian responsibility relations cannot be established between us and future generations. Moral obligations for Hobbes depend on mutual risks of harm. We have no Hobbesian reasons to respect whatever interests in the environment future generations may have. Lockean entitlement protection hardly fares better in motivating a responsibility relationship across generations. That is no surprise, for Locke's property theory is in no small measure responsible for our carelessness with the environment. For Locke, and more recently Nozick:

> Provided an individual has come by a good justly, he may justly dispose of it any way he likes. . . . Since we have a right to dispose of our property as we wish, subsequent generations could not charge us with injustice if we were to consume whatever we could in our lifetimes and direct that what was left should be destroyed at our deaths.[5]

Or we can destroy it as we go along and owe nothing to those in the future.

I have no recipes for the proper use and care of the environment. That is not my interest here. Instead, I want to locate the stewardship obligations in a responsibility relationship that makes sense and not in mystical extensions of the traditional views. As should already be obvious, I believe that our concept of responsibility assignment embodies Michael Walzer's position that obligations to others depend on actual relationships with them.[6] "Actual relations" does not, of course, mean equality in the ability to cause each other harm. I, for example, have such a relationship with my children and with my students. But how can any of us have an actual relationship with generations of people who will not be born until we are long dead? The answer is that there are persons that exist now that can have actual relations with the generations of the future. They are corporations or corporation-like entities.[7]

The major reason that atomistic individualism has such problems with future generation relations (and this is evident in both liberal politics and libertarian economics) is that it treats corporation-like entities merely as things, legal fictions, shorthands for aggregations of natural persons. They have no moral standing and so cannot enter into obligation-generating relationships; only their members can.

I have shown elsewhere[8] that the actions of corporations can be understood as redescriptions of the actions of humans. Corporate Internal Decision Structures provide the licenses for such redescription. Corporations can do a number of things that are not sensibly reduced to the actions of those associated with them: they can join cartels, manufacture automobiles, enter bankruptcy, and set the price of goods and services. Corporation-like entities manifest intentionality and make decisions, have rights and duties in law, carry on nonlegal relationships with other corporations and with human persons—a major portion of the spectrum of activities and relationships we associate with persons. They are historical entities with births, lives, and deaths. They flourish and decline, succeed and fail. Roger Scruton has pointed out that they can "even be the leading characters in a drama, as in Wagner's *Die Meistersinger*.[9] I shall argue that not only can corporation-like entities be persons from the point of view of morality, but they are also essential elements of the moral world. Robert Solomon hints at this when he writes that "business is a social practice not an activity of isolated individuals."[10] He goes on to say that business can only take place in "a culture with an established set of procedures and expectations" that are not open to tinkering by individual human beings.[11] The maintenance of the business culture is, according to Solomon, a prerequisite for the prosperity of a nation and, he both implies and states, of the happiness, in the Aristotelian sense, of the human members of the society. The corporate culture's existence and character are clearly central to Solomon's conception of the good life. The business culture is also not, he assures, the product of an invisible hand operating for our benefit unbeknownst to or unintended by any of us.

Suppose that corporation-like entities were what the atomistic individualists say they are: aggregations, mere fictions of law and commerce. In such a world, we may assume, individuals can contract to assign responsibilities, and they can also enter into noncontractual relations with each other based on affection and companionship in which responsibility assignments will play some role. But none of these responsibilities will endure much beyond the death of one or both of the parties. No wonder we feel impotent as individuals with respect to the protection of the environment! Not only is there bloody little any one of us can do to make a real difference when we live, but we cannot ensure that what we do will survive us. And we will never enter into the actual personal responsibility relationship with future generations that is necessary to ground an obligation in us not to do them harm by despoiling their environment.

As Roger Scruton notes, "The care for future generations must be entrusted to persons who will exist when they exist: and if there are no such persons surrounding me, how can I have that care except as a helpless anxiety?"[12]

But surrounding me, intermingling with my very identity, are exactly the sort of persons who will exist (or are likely to exist) when future generations are the existing generations. The responsibility relationships to future generations can be sensibly articulated through corporation-like entities. The maintenance of the environment in order to protect those generations from the Wasteland is a reasonable responsibility of such entities. Indeed, they are the best bearers of it, and through each of our identity-dependency relations with those corporation-like entities we share in the obligation.

The atomistic individualists cheat themselves out of participation in meaningful long-range responsibility relationships. Their purposes in living must be drastically limited, which no doubt accounts for their typical cynicism about most everything over the long haul. It is no wonder that they put what hope they have in invisible hands.

The springs, forests, and waterways of our planet cannot long withstand the treatment they have received from both corporate and natural persons. Environmental protection now is essential to the prosperity of those who will live in the future. But only corporation-like entities can be sensibly assigned responsibility for that protection. Individual human persons participate in the task only through their corporate associations. There seems to me to be a close analogy between our role in environmental protection and that which the ordinary Celt played with respect to the defender of the sacred spot.

10 · Exorcising the Demon of Cultural Relativism

We are often told that individuals and multinational corporations find themselves in moral quandaries when they have to decide what set of principles and rules they ought to play by when working or doing business in a foreign country. Presumably this issue arises when the inhabitants of the foreign (or host) country hold a radically different set of moral beliefs than we do in the industrial Western democracies or when at least some of their moral beliefs are significantly different from ours. The standard example is that of bribery: the individual or corporation defends the practice of bribing foreign government officials and agents of foreign customers in order to garner contracts and facilitate services by arguing that bribery is acceptable or even expected in the host country. We may, with Norman Bowie, refer to this as the "When in Rome, do as the Romans do" principle.[1] As Bowie notes, application of this principle (call it the R-principle) does not necessarily reveal a moral disagreement.

Often factual matters differentiate cultures with respect to what may at first blush seem to be moral disagreements. For example, there is nothing morally wrong with marketing infant formula in our country, but in countries where the water is not safe to drink, one ought not market it to those who must mix it with unsafe water. People in our culture and in the other country, let us suppose, firmly agree with the moral principle that innocents are not to be harmed, so there is no real moral disagreement between us. Still, the application of that principle leads to different results in very different situations. Therefore questions of the infant formula sort are not very interesting. If all apparent disagreements could be dissolved by uncovering common moral doctrines and relevant factual differences, the moral responsibility problems of multinational corporations and people living in foreign cultures would cease to be of serious concern. But some moral theorists and, presumably, a number of corporate executives maintain that something like the R-principle has moral status in cases quite different from the infant formula type.

Does the R-principle really have moral weight when the moral differences between cultures are not attributable to environmental or other factual matters? Suppose that there is no disagreement between two cultures with respect to what sorts of actions constitute bribery. A genuine moral disagreement might be one in which culture A holds that bribery is impermissible and B holds that it is morally permissible under the same set of factual descriptions. A person or corporation whose home is in A but lives in or does business in both cultures is confronted with the option of bribing in culture B. (It is not clear whether the R-principle requires or only advises bribery in B.) A number of philosophers seem to think that a method needs to be devised to guide those from our culture who find themselves in such circumstances. Bowie argues that if the moral principle of B is justified but that of A is not, or both are justified, then one has a moral responsibility to act in accordance with B's moral principle.[2] That sounds fine, but how are we to determine whether the moral principles of a culture are justified or not? We would need a method of evaluating moral principles that is independent of any culture. If we had such an independent moral point of view, we would have no need to raise questions about the R-principle in the first place.

Bowie thinks we do have something like an independent set of moral principles, at least for corporations. He assigns that role to what he calls "the morality of the marketplace." He then recommends that multinational corporations heed the "morality of the marketplace" wherever on the globe they operate. In the process of doing so, he expects that they will improve the morality of host countries by advancing the cause of democracy and human rights.

I suspect Bowie is right when he claims that the morality of the marketplace approaches a universal morality. However, I will argue that the morality of the marketplace, if it is a morality, is at least a part of a universal morality. In other words, radically different *moral* principles do not exist if by "radically different" we mean that the principles in question would demand incompatible behavior in the same situation. Bowie may worry that he cannot escape Rorty's ethnocentrism[3] unless he can independently justify the morality of the marketplace, so he goes on to argue in favor of capitalism. To do so is unnecessary, I think, and beside the point. All Bowie needs to show is that the morality of the marketplace is a part of our morality, in order to grasp, with Rorty, the ethnocentric horn of the dilemma. But for reasons that are not exactly Rorty's, that argument is not suspiciously antiliberal. We must start from our own morality, and we need not apologize for ending there. Furthermore, we can exorcise the demon of cultural relativism without having to distinguish between essential and accidental aspects of a morality and without having to endorse the R-principle, even in a limited number of cases.

Attacks on radical relativism have been made with respect to alternative logics, the Sapir-Whorf hypothesis, and so on. Some of the most persuasive have taken as their point of departure Donald Davidson's well-known argument that not many of the beliefs of a culture can be false: "The reason for this is that a belief is identified by its location in a pattern of beliefs; it is this pattern that determines the subject matter of the belief, what the belief is about."[4] Davidson's point is that if more than a few of our beliefs about some subject can be false, it would be possible for us to conceive of someone such that almost all of that person's beliefs about that subject are false. Davidson notes, however, that "false beliefs tend to undermine the identification of the subject matter."[5] Simply, if we were to admit to the possibility that someone (or some culture) could hold beliefs about a subject that were mostly false, we would have to conclude that we had misidentified the subject of those beliefs.

Suppose the subject matter in question has to do with the way people ought to behave when doing business. Further, let us stipulate that we hold a number of beliefs about what people are morally responsible for doing in those circumstances and that members of another culture hold beliefs that are incompatible with ours. What must we conclude? Because we cannot hold that most of our beliefs are false and the same must be said of their beliefs, then either we must have been wrong that their beliefs were about what people are morally responsible for doing (moral beliefs) or we misunderstood at what features of the circumstances their moral beliefs were directed. In the latter case we should expect to discover our error regarding what the members of the other culture are talking about and then revise our original judgment that radical disagreement exists between us. In the former case we must conclude that their beliefs are not moral ones. David Cooper has seen the outcome of this argument: "We can only identify another's beliefs as moral beliefs about X if there is a massive degree of agreement between his and our beliefs. Hence, there is no chance of radical moral diversity."[6]

Such a strategy against the relativist, however, will fail if, rather than distinguishing moral beliefs and judgments from others in terms of content, we identify moral judgments as those having certain formal features such as that popular Kantian favorite, universalizability. It will certainly be conceivable that the people of culture B might make universalizable judgments about responsibility that are radically different from, that is, incompatible with, the judgments of people in culture A.

Although the formalistic position has had many advocates, it has been the target of devastating criticism in recent years. Philippa Foot has argued that formal features do not mark off moral judgments from others.[7] For Foot, judgments are moral if they express principles that connect to issues of human welfare, happiness, and the like. But Foot's approach, though it offers an escape from formalistic criteria, as Cooper notes, does not escape the suspicion that it is but an exercise in stipulation. "Attractive as the stipulation that moral principles *must* display a concern for welfare, happiness, etc., might be, to the extent that it remains a stipulation, the formalist can remain unimpressed."[8] The Davidsonian approach will, as it happens, arrive at the same destination as Foot, but in doing so it avoids the appearance of arbitrary stipulation.

Imagine that the people of culture B have not developed any geometrical concepts that are even roughly equivalent to the familiar forms of Euclidian geometry. Instead of square, triangle, circle, and so on, they use the notion of "blob." "Blob" is not a univocal term. Within different contexts it takes on different meanings. They talk about "forming a blob," "the angles of a blob," and whether a blob of one sort would be preferable to that of another. We can interpret what they say when they talk of blobs in imprecise, though correct, geometric expressions. Under such conditions we would be right in claiming that they have a geometry of a sort.

What cannot be imagined is that the people of culture B have replaced all geometric concepts with, for example, aesthetic ones, that in the place of our beliefs about geometry they have substituted aesthetic beliefs. Aesthetics cannot be their geometry. Lacking geometric concepts and beliefs, they simply have no geometry. Aesthetics is not an alternative geometry. It does not stand to geometry as Riemannian triangles do to Euclidean ones. (It is certainly not relevant to our interpretation of what they are claiming that our aesthetic concepts and our geometric ones can be used in discourse about the same objects.)

Analogously, that a concept or belief is a moral one is for it to fit in a system of moral beliefs that, to a large degree, resembles our system of moral beliefs. In fact, we cannot identify a member of culture B's beliefs about certain types of behavior (say bribery or cannibalism) as moral beliefs if a subset of the beliefs of culture B are not our moral beliefs. If b (a person of culture B) reports that he believes that bribery of public officials to secure his (or his company's) goals is his moral responsibility or that, at least, it is morally permissible, we first need to ascertain whether b and we use the term "bribery" in reference to the same sort of activity. We do. The next, and natural, move is to determine what force "moral responsibility" has when b uses the term to express his belief. That he is prepared to universalize his judgment is not relevant to our problem, for, as suggested above, such formal criteria have proved unreliable marks of the moral.

Before continuing, I want to clarify certain points. First, I do not claim that it is a criterion of a culture's having a morality that its members believe that people ought not to engage in bribery. (I have elsewhere discussed different types of truncated moralities and will not reiterate that discussion here.[9]) No specific moral belief is essential to a culture's having a morality, that is, genuine moral beliefs. That b's beliefs about the moral responsibility to bribe or the permissibility of bribery are radically different from our own neither proves that b has no morality nor that b's moral principles are incompatible with ours. All it shows is that when b says that bribery is his responsibility or that it is permissible, he is not expressing one of his moral beliefs.

Second, behavioral criteria are not sufficient to distinguish moral from nonmoral beliefs. There are at least three reasons why. Suppose b tells us that he approves of bribery. He thinks it should be legal, and he neither objects to nor refuses to do business with anyone whom he suspects of attempting bribery. Does his approval of bribery arise from moral considerations? Perhaps he has religious views that encourage acts of bribery (as do most other members of culture B). From behavioral clues alone we are not likely to be able to determine that his attitudes are moral ones. But even if we could identify solely on behavioral grounds when he was exhibiting his moral attitudes, we will not likely, on the same grounds, be able to tell what moral beliefs b actually holds. Does b really believe that bribery is his moral responsibility rather than morally wrong, or is it something other than bribery as we understand it that he thinks is his moral responsibility or is morally permissible? To answer such a question, we need to know more than that b exhibits certain attitudes. We have to ascertain the object of those attitudes, which is unlikely to be a simple matter of observation. To borrow an example from both John Searle[10] and David Cooper,[11] let us suppose that the people in culture B disapprove of the keeping of promises or contracts. That seems hard to imagine, for we should first have to suppose that they engage in, or at least have the concepts of, promising and contracting. It is hard to see how they could have the concept of contract or promise and not believe that the parties are obligated with respect to them, yet it is not simply a matter of definition that "promise keeping must be morally approved." Still, if the evidence seems to support the conclusion that members of B disapprove of what we identify in their activities as contracting and promising, we should first question whether we have properly identified the practice they disapprove of. It may be some other feature of the practices that regularly are associated with those activities. Perhaps they disapprove of the shaking of hands or of the typical linguistic form in which the promise is couched. Perhaps we have utterly failed to under-stand their social life.

The force of the Davidsonian approach is that radical moral disagreement is not possible between cultures. However, that certainly does not rule out the possibility of a considerable divergence of opinion with respect to specific issues. After all, a range of viewpoints exists in our culture about abortion, euthanasia, and myriad other issues. Our morality has not pronounced the final sentence with respect to these areas of controversy. Contrast these with a concept about which no reasonable dispute is brewing, like murder. A primary reason we have the concept of murder is to mark off as unjustifiable certain kinds of homicides. Perpetrators of homicides that are correctly described as murders perform deeds that are indisputably morally wrong. "Murder is wrong" is necessarily true, unin-formative, and certainly not a matter of debate. "Euthanasia is wrong" is quite another story. That assertion is clearly debatable. One form of argument in sup-port of it identifies euthanasia with murder, another draws an analogy between it and murder, and so forth. The moral status of euthanasia is not resolved, but we would be wrong to conclude that because Steven and I disagree over whether euthanasia is permissible, we must have different moralities. Our disagreement is more likely to be an indicator that we share a basic morality. Were we to be engaged in a heated debate over whether murder is wrong (I do not mean a debate over whether a particular homicide really is a murder), then whichever of us is maintaining that murder is *not* wrong cannot be expressing moral beliefs. One might imagine trying to teach a child that murder is wrong and getting into an argument with the child over whether or not it really is wrong. The disagree-ment would not signal that the child has a radically different morality, only that it has not yet learned its lessons in morality. From within the scope of morality there is, however, considerable space for disagreement. Bribery, I suspect, is more like euthanasia than murder.

A visitor from our culture might question an official in a host country about an attempted bribe by saying something like, "Bribery is wrong," and hear in re-sponse, "No it's not, it's just a normal cost of doing business, a cementing of goodwill and friendship between seller and buyer." This is a genuine disagree-ment, but it does not signal different moralities. That, however, does not mean it will be resolved. Will the moral question of euthanasia be resolved? It is in principle resolvable; that is, the term "bribery" might come to name a moral concept as "murder" does, but it is characteristic of morality that there are re-markably few such concepts. As things now stand, a judgment like "Bribery is morally wrong. It cannot be your moral responsibility to do it" is not a matter of moral bedrock. It must be supported, and such support on moral grounds comes either by appeal to existing concepts or principles within our morality or by allegation that the consequences in human affairs of the practice of bribery are morally relevant.

But from where does this concept of moral relevance arise? A consequence is morally relevant only if it is generally recognized to be so and, as the Davidsonian approach entails, if there is no agreement between members of different cultures on the moral relevance of a number of factors arising from any practice (that it produces or involves harming of innocents, causes suffering, enslaves, etc.), it would be a mistake to say that both have a morality. It is unintelligible to claim that judgments that do not reflect our general agreement about those factors are moral judgments. Hence, if we are correct in interpreting b as maintaining that bribery is a moral responsibility, we must treat our difference with b as a dispute over the application of morality.

Bowie claims that if the morality of a host country is "in violation of the moral norms of the marketplace, then the people have a moral obligation to follow the norms of the marketplace."[12] His reasons for this recommendation are difficult to fathom. He tells us that systematic violation of marketplace norms would be self-defeating. One might wonder if this is a formalistic criterion of moral action: that it should not be self-defeating. But surely it would be a morally happy situation were certain practices self-defeating: those that are morally wrong. So, the fact that doing something in a certain way defeats the purpose of doing it cannot be, by itself, a moral reason for not doing it in that way. Bowie advises following marketplace morality as against that of a host country because to do so is to "provide something approaching a universal morality."[13] Hence, by sticking to the "morality" of the marketplace, Westerners (whether individuals or corporations) become missionaries for true morality. Bowie rightly notes that to make this a palatable claim he needs to justify the morality of the marketplace. To do so he offers what he calls the "contribution to democracy argument."[14] Democracy is supposed to embody the recognition of fundamental human rights, namely those created and protected in a true morality. What we have in Bowie's argument, then, is an appeal to the concept of fundamental human rights as a characteristic of genuine morality or in other words, a stipulation about the content of moral principles with respect to which neither the formalist nor the Davidsonian need be impressed.

The appeal to the morality of the marketplace and then the defense that such a morality maintains rights reveals that the whole issue of competing radically different moralities is a nonstarter. Why not just start with rights protection? How is it justified independent of the fact that we believe it to be so?

A culture that has no interest in protecting human rights (a Confucian culture, for example) may still have a morality, but its beliefs cannot contradict all our moral beliefs. Hence, a basis for an argument and a possibility for conversion on the issue of rights protection would exist between us. The norms of the marketplace might provide the teaching situation to expand the moral beliefs of the other culture. However, the members of the other culture may, quite apart from the marketplace, convince us that the protection of individual human rights is not that morally important. Continued trade and other relationships with China, for example, could lead to such a reevaluation of what those in the United States believe to be morally basic.

The R-principle has no moral status, even if it does have legal status. When local customs stand in opposition to Western moral principles, then the excuse (or is it a justification?) that "I was only doing what they do" will be morally unacceptable. If I lived in Saudi Arabia, would it be my moral responsibility to subjugate women? Do Saudi men have such a responsibility because that is a part of their culture? If I were dealing in South Africa in the 1980s, should I act in accord with its system of apartheid? To take up the practices of a tribe of cannibal headhunters because one happens to be in their community is immoral because those practices are immoral, no matter who adopts them. That is not to say that we may not come to understand and appreciate why people in other cultures act as they do. We may uncover hitherto hidden sociological, geographic, climatic, historic explanations for their customs. But none of those accounts will make their behavior any more moral or any less immoral, though they make it more intelligible. If a Western person would be acting immorally if he or she intentionally killed people, dismembered them, and ate their flesh in Milwaukee, he or she would be acting immorally if he or she did so in the company of a jungle tribe. And so would be the members of the tribe, regardless of their traditions. In fact, those currently supporting changes in Western practices and traditions make clear that the mere existence of a practice in a culture is no guarantee of moral status. Slavery was morally wrong in our culture, even when it was widely practiced. The mistreatment of minorities and women is wrong, despite the fact that it is widespread and has deep historical roots. In short, if we have moral reasons for opposing certain practices in our own culture, we have the same moral reasons for opposing the practices in any other culture and in any other historical epoch. That does not mean that members of one culture will have the same set of moral responsibilities as those of another. Responsibilities depend in large measure on what I called in chapter five the spatial structure of a community. Obviously communities that do not have comparable or convertible structures

will not have comparable responsibility sets. However, if the responsibilities derive from general moral principles (such as not killing innocent people) rather
than being solely tied to tasks or stations, they cannot be incompatible from one
culture to another.

An interesting related question, but one that has nothing to do with the basic
claims of cultural relativism, is whether certain tasks or stations in a society are
immoral by virtue of the responsibilities associated with them and so never justified in a culture. To fall in such a category, the tasks of a station would have to be
tasks that could not be performed without violating basic moral principles. A
culture in which a large number (I have no idea where the line ought to be
drawn) of such stations existed would be immoral and so lacking in moral justification for its existence. The Columbian cocaine cartel and the Mafia leap to
mind as examples. The culture of the Ik tribe in Uganda may now, as suggested
by Turnbull,[15] also qualify. In any event, it is not the case that a visitor in another
culture has a moral responsibility to act in a way that is common to his or her
counterparts in that culture if they are acting in ways that cannot be justified
according to the principles, or extensions of the principles, of our morality. But
then, the natives in that culture have no moral responsibility to act that way
either.

11 · Moral Responsibility and Heroism

Nobody has any heroes anymore. Where have all the heroes gone? During the 1988 presidential debates, both candidates were asked to name their heroes. Michael Dukakis hemmed and hawed for what seemed like many minutes before citing his immigrant parents. George Bush was equally unprepared, though he finally remembered he had seen the movie *Stand and Deliver* and so put forth Jaime Escalante and all those nameless others who work for the betterment of the deprived to make this a "kinder, gentler nation." The general audience response was respectful but puzzled.

In 1982 Ronald Reagan seized a heroic moment, interrupting his State of the Union address with praise for Lenny Skutnik. And who was Lenny Skutnik? Who now remembers him? In January of that year, Lenny, a government employee on his way home from work, dove into the freezing Potomac River to rescue a woman who had survived the crash of an Air Florida plane. Lenny was the country's hero for a few weeks (or was it 15 minutes?) and then returned to his mundane life. Was Lenny Skutnik just an ordinary person who on one extraordinary occasion did something heroic? Or did he do what anyone else would have had a moral responsibility to do under the circumstances? Did he simply do his moral duty?

What makes a hero or a heroine? It is interesting to note how dramatically the heroes and heroines of popular culture have changed over the last four decades. The fifties was the decade of the cowboy. In 1958 alone, fifty-four western feature films were made and eight of the top ten television shows were westerns. The western hero embodied the values of rugged, conquering individualism that dominate the stories of the winning of the American West. Those same values were said to exemplify the American war effort in the forties. Dwight Eisenhower, former Supreme Commander of the Allied Forces in Europe, was president then,

111

and his executive leadership qualities (perceived if not actual) were personified in movie gunslinger after movie gunslinger. Ordinary people in those films were commonly portrayed as weak and cowardly, in dire need of firm direction and examples of courage. The fifties western hero not only had to fight off the bad guys, he usually had to do it alone. Community members took refuge in homes or behind storefronts or went about their business almost oblivious to the conflict being fought out in the local barroom or on their muddy streets. The battle won, the preserver of their liberty was unable to enjoy the spoils. He had made the town safe for its citizens, for democracy and free enterprise, but not for himself. Like MacArthur's old soldier, he had to fade away, ride off into the sunset.

John Kennedy's presidential Inaugural Address, famous for its proclamation of a new decade, a new generation, a new community, prepared, unlike the citizens of the western towns, to "bear any burden, meet any hardship, support any friend, oppose any foe to assure the survival and the success of liberty," turned out to be the same old cowboy hat. Ironically, it was shot down in a Texas town. The New Frontier collapsed into the Vietnam War. The traditional western hero lost his reason to be and was supplanted by the outlaw and the savage, revengeful anti-hero in a string of films made in Spain by Italians. They starred Clint Eastwood as a man with no name.

The popular-culture hero of the sixties did not emerge to cult status until the last half of the decade, and he certainly did not wear cowboy hat and boots. The country had been drawn into the jungles of Vietnam. (And despite the hopes of those who supported the Persian Gulf War against Iraq, Americans cannot forget the debacle.) Everything American, as Francis Coppola tried to show in *Apocalypse, Now*, was shipped up the Mekong—everything from refrigerators and surf-boards to Playboy Playmates—and it all just disappeared. Martin Luther King and Robert Kennedy were assassinated, and hope virtually faded from the scene. Then pacifism swept over the culture with its new hero: Jesus Christ, superstar.

The Jesus Movement was the antithesis of the political leadership of the late '60s and early '70s. It was genuinely countercultural. Johnson and Nixon fought and lost an unpopular war; Jesus, the "conciliatory romantic hero . . . of the era,"[1] was the personification of love and peace. Then American political leaders turned into nice guys like Gerald Ford, the compassionate, bumbling pardoner, and Jimmy Carter, the born-again Christian whose "Human Rights Credo was laughed at in the global community"[2] and scoffed at in Washington. The virtues of the Christian spirit seemed to translate into a vacuum of leadership that was filled in popular culture by the super hero, the masked avenger, the adventurer out to right wrongs and fight for truth, justice, and the American Way. On film we got Superman and Rambo and Luke Skywalker. In politics we got Ronald

Reagan, the shoot-from-the-hip ex-cowboy actor who was beaten in the 1976 primaries because he was perceived as too dangerous to be president.

The origins of the popular super heroes seem to be in the comic books of the Depression, but their resurrection in the '80s carried them to new and more spectacular heights. There are at least two distinct types of super heroes. One type is superior to humans; Superman is the archetype. These super heroes do not come from earth or if they do, "they are 'semi-aliens' like Captain Marvel and Wonderwoman. . . . They are with us, but not of us."[3] Their weaknesses, if they have any, are not human weaknesses. The laws of nature do not even restrain them. The super heroes of the second type are more like demigods. They are human, mortal, and vulnerable. When cut, they bleed but they seldom get cut, despite being involved in one certain-death situation after another. They always escape to continue their crusades. Because their superiority to us is only one of degree, they may have psychological problems and other human foibles. They cannot leap tall buildings in a single bound, but they seem to spend a lot of time scaling buildings. The paradigm of this type is, of course, Batman. Remember that Clark Kent is only Superman's assumed name—part of his disguise. Batman's real name is Bruce Wayne.

The super hero, complete with extra special effects, supplanted the all-too-human westerner, who had been reduced to a self-doubting, impotent, ordinary guy shaken by anxiety. The substitution, however, was morally expensive. The super heroes represent the advertised moral values of America, but ordinary people cannot hope to emulate them. The super heroes cannot serve as models. Their virtual indestructibility makes their risk taking far less death defying than human heroism typically requires. Super heroes may be entertaining and even didactic, but they are not morally heroic. They also teach little or nothing about shouldering responsibility when things get difficult. The super hero craze may reflect a cultural loss of faith in the idea that mere mortals can rise to and sustain themselves on heroic levels.

What does one have to do to be a moral hero? I think there are four necessary conditions for heroism. First, heroic acts must be performed in order to achieve morally desirable ends. That requirement allows us to distinguish real heroes from sports stars and other celebrities. Although winning for the home team or the old alma mater is desirable, it is not morally desirable. Morality is usually indifferent to whether the Spurs or the Lakers win. The outcome of World War II, however, was not a matter of moral indifference. Eisenhower, Bradley, Patton, MacArthur, and the rest may be heroes, in part, because how the war ended mattered morally. The outcome of the American Civil War was also of moral import, and that may explain why U. S. Grant, despite disreputable personal traits, is a hero of the war and Robert E. Lee, whose personal traits were beyond reproach, was not. One can be a hero in a losing cause, but not in an immoral cause. Rommel, for example, was a brilliant general, but not until he associated himself with the plot to assassinate Hitler did he achieve something of the heroic.

A war might start with clear-cut, morally desirable aims, but its moral evaluation may shift due to its prosecution so that its outcome becomes a matter of moral indifference. Consider the Trojan War. It started with the violation of the Greek guest-friendship rules when Paris kidnapped his host's beautiful wife. The Greeks were morally justified in mounting a campaign against the Trojans. However, because of the sacrifice of Iphegenia and the Greek conduct of the war once they finally arrived on the plains of Ilium, culminating with Achilles's desecration of the body of Hector, the Greeks lost the moral high ground. They finally won—not by heroic deeds, but by trickery. So the first condition of morally heroic deeds is that their ends must be unambiguously morally desirable.

The second condition is that a heroic act must be undertaken with full knowledge that one's life is at risk. Knowing sacrifice of self-preservation is crucial. It would be odd to honor people as heroes if they never knew or anticipated the risk they were running; some sort of epistemic condition is needed. Only if Lenny Skutnik understood that he could very likely die in his attempts to save the passenger does the deed take on an heroic character. If he did not or could not make an assessment of his deadly danger, or if he were Superman and knew the danger was minimal, he is no hero. Superman may always be a bit concerned that the victim he is rescuing is carrying a hunk of Kryptonite, but he knows the chances are remote.

This self-sacrifice condition is noted by a number of philosophers, including John Rawls,[4] who identifies heroic deeds as good acts that would be moral obligations except for the cost run by the hero. Heroic deeds, then, are not just benevolent acts of helping others or of acting in ways to achieve good ends. They must involve risk of life and limb. Insofar as many moralists, especially since the advent of the centrality of the individual in the social contract theories of Hobbes and Locke, believe that morality cannot require acts against self-preservation, heroic deeds should not be morally obligatory. They seem to be actions it is good to do, but not bad not to do—deeds one cannot be held morally responsible for not doing.

Knowingly risking one's life is not necessarily heroic, even though such a deed may be greatly admired by the more timid. There must be a major difference between heroism and what may be called "deep play" (a term, that is, I believe, owed to Bentham). Deep play is any activity in which the stakes are so high that it is irrational for anyone to engage in it. The marginal utility of what one might win is far outweighed by the disutility of what one stands to lose. The rush created by the realization that their lives are on the line may be part of the reason deep players play. But they are not acting heroically when they ride the wild surf at Weimea or climb Mt. Everest or take a naked plunge into the icy waters of a river in the dead of winter. In short, risking self-preservation is a mark of the hero, but not a sufficient one.

Further, the risk taking, not the loss, is crucial. A loss, even a loss of life, may occur, but that will be tragic and not necessarily heroic. Consider another case following the crash of the Air Florida plane into the Potomac. An unidentified passenger of the doomed plane passed the lifeline from a hovering helicopter to four other people. By the time the helicopter returned again, he had been swallowed up by the icy waters, gone forever, and forever anonymous. Had he taken the line himself and been saved, no one would have thought him a moral slacker. It was not his death that made him a hero. It was his willingness to pass the rope even though he was aware of the terrible risk he ran himself. If actually suffering the loss were crucial, there would be no living heroes.

Suppose, counter to fact, that when this passenger first attempted to pass the rope to another passenger he had been swept down the river and none of the group was saved. Would he still have been a hero? The utilitarians have always held that a person's intentions are irrelevant to the moral worth of his or her actions. Results are what count. That view seems to be consistent with ordinary intuitions when a person is performing a morally obligatory act. In the case of heroic deeds, however, it seems much more important to know what the person intended. That is never more important than when a failure occurs. A hero must have the proper moral intentions when he or she undertakes the deed at the risk of self-preservation. But what is the appropriate intention? Generally speaking, it must be to benefit others. After all, if the man in the Potomac had let go of the rope in order to retrieve his fur coat and was swept to his death, his act would have been foolish, not heroic. Thus, a fourth condition: The hero's intention to help others must be proportional to his or her sacrifice.

There are problems with this altruistic requirement. For example, the hero's intentions might be construed to mean that he or she preferred to do the deed. If the act were the one that the hero preferred to do in the circumstances, then he or she wanted to do it. If the hero wanted to do the helping deed at the risk of self-preservation, then many philosophers (usually from within the Kantian tradition) will claim the hero did not really act for the good of those being saved. Heroism will lose moral significance if heroes just do what they want to do.

Most heroic acts, however, are fairly spontaneous. With few exceptions, people do not go about looking for situations in which to be heroic. (The exceptions would be the comic book super heroes and the knights errant of Arthurian legend.) Heroic moments happen with little time for contemplative decision making or examination of intentions. Heroic deeds may reveal character more than isolatable intentions. Character, however, is not an accidental property of a person. As Aristotle maintained, it is the product of intentional choices that have become ingrained habits of acting.[5] Heroism, in fact, may be one of the better manifestations of character. Still, intentions do play a role, if not a major one, in evaluating the heroic. You cannot be heroic if your self-sacrifice is only for your own pleasure.

Most moral thinkers, as J. O. Urmson noted in his famous paper "Saints and Heroes,"[6] recognize only a threefold classification of actions from the moral point of view: Some acts are obligatory; some are of no concern to morality; the rest are forbidden. Kant writes that the moral law (the categorical imperative) asserts an obligation that: "either commands or prohibits; it sets forth as a duty the commission or omission of an action. An act that is neither commanded nor forbidden is merely permissible, since there is no law to limit one's freedom (moral title) to perform it, and so no duty with regard to the action. An action of this kind is called morally indifferent."[7]

Heroic deeds certainly are not morally indifferent. "Hero" is surely a term of favorable moral evaluation. Heroes are exalted, held up to us as examples. We give heroes awards, build monuments to them, name cities in their honor. But heroic deeds are not obligatory, hence the so-called great moral theories seem to have no theoretical niche for them. It cannot be your responsibility to be heroic like it is your responsibility to keep your contracts. Heroism seems to be a matter of choice; in that case, morality should be indifferent to it. But it is not! So either heroism will have to be subsumed into moral responsibility or moral duty (but then all of us could be obligated at least on some occasions to act heroically) or the way philosophers have categorized human actions for moral evaluative purposes will have to be modified.

Kant and a number of other moral theorists who have followed in his train distinguished between types of duties. Perfect duties are negative duties, duties of omission, for example, duties not to commit suicide, not to act out of carnal lust, not to lie, and so on. We are always morally constrained with respect to these obligations. To transgress them is vice. Imperfect duties, for Kant, are duties of virtue. They go beyond the formal principles of action and command the adoption of a purpose, not just the performing or the refraining from specific actions. Hence, they leave considerable room for choice in determining the actions one will take to meet the commanded end. The when and the how are left to each of us. If there is a moral law commanding us to make benefiting others one of our ends, it will not be violated if we do not benefit others on this or that occasion when we might have done so. You will not have failed your moral responsibility if today, when approached by a beggar, you refuse to give.

The problem with this sort of thinking is that as one gets older the realm of choice (the opportunity to decline to perform the actions) must become narrower and narrower. The actions become less and less optional. If one is near death and has not yet acted to achieve the morally commanded purpose, they must become mandatory. Luck in finding occasions to perform imperfect duties could also enter into the picture. Should a person who, owing to the sheltered nature of his or her existence, has never had the opportunity to perform actions to benefit others, seek out objects of charity? Is that then a perfect moral duty?

Benevolence seems to be a solid candidate for a Kantian imperfect duty of virtue. And benevolence as a moral purpose can be satisfied with occasional charitable donations. Clearly, heroism, of the sort demonstrated by Lenny Skutnik would also satisfy the benevolence duty, but intuitively there seems to be a vast moral difference between giving a donation to the needy and risking one's life in a rescue attempt. Furthermore, Kant notes that "to provide oneself with such comforts as are necessary merely to enjoy life . . . is a duty to oneself. . . . How far should we expend our means in practicing benevolence? Surely not to the extent that we ourselves would finally come to need the charity of others."[8] Heroism, however, requires that one put one's very life at risk, and that violates one of Kant's perfect duties to oneself: "The first of man's duties to himself as an animal being is to preserve himself in his animal nature."[9] In the Casuistical Questions related to his examination of this perfect duty, Kant asks, "Is it murder to hurl oneself to certain death (like Curtius) in order to save one's country?—or is voluntary martyrdom, offering oneself as a sacrifice for the welfare of the whole human race, also to be considered an act of heroism."[10] Presumably that voluntary martyrdom would be permissible. Unfortunately Kant never answers his questions. He seems to hold heroism in high moral regard, but, given the bulk of his thinking on virtue, does not seem to regard it as a higher duty than the preservation of oneself.

Despite appearances, one can never be in a conflict of moral duties, according to Kant, as between performing an heroic act and preserving one's own life and limb.

> A conflict of duties and obligations is inconceivable (*obligationes non collidunter*). For the concepts of duty and obligation as such express the objective practical necessity of certain actions, and two conflicting rules cannot both be necessary at the same time: if it is our duty to act according to one

of these rules, then to act according to the opposite one is not our duty and is even contrary to duty.[11]

Apparent conflicts between the perfect duty to preserve one's life and an act of heroism risking that life to benefit others may arise because they are the products of two different grounds of obligation. Kant maintains that not the stronger obligation but the stronger ground of obligation takes precedence. The ground of the obligation of self-preservation is apparently stronger than benevolence (although Kant's own casuistical questions cast doubt on whether it is so in all heroic cases.) In any event, as a perfect duty, transgression of self-preservation is vice and guilt, while transgression of an imperfect duty is "mere lack of moral worth," "want of virtue," "lack of moral strength." It seems fair to Kant to say that heroism in itself is not a moral responsibility, though it may be one way of achieving an end which is an imperfect duty. But that end is, arguably, not superior to the perfect duty of self-preservation, transgression of which is always risked by the performance of heroic deeds.

The utilitarians have a simpler answer. They ignore all distinctions between responsibilities and heroic acts, because for them, an action that will produce more good than any other action in the circumstances is one's moral responsibility in those circumstances. Bentham writes, "Of an action that is conformable to the principle of utility one may always say . . . that it is one that ought to be done, . . . that it is right it should be done, . . . that it is a right action; at least that it is not a wrong action."[12] Further, if it is the only action in the circumstances that conforms to the principle of utility, if it is the only morally right thing to do, then one has a moral responsibility to do it. Still further, it would seem that if there are two or more actions that conform to the principle of utility but to varying degrees (that is they maximize general utility to a greater or lesser extent), then the action that increases general utility to the greater extent, *ceteris paribus*, is a moral responsibility. According to Bentham, good Samaritans like Lenny Skutnik, despite their personal risk taking, may be doing no more than meeting their moral responsibilities. Sometimes, by doing what you ought, you die. (*Necesse est et ut eam; non ut vivam.*) Often you run great risks.

The utilitarian approach to self-sacrifice, as so many writers have pointed out, shakes our intuitions even if the numbers increase on the side of those benefited by the hero's death. Ivan Karamazov challenges his pious brother Alyosha, "Imagine that you are creating a fabric of human destiny with the object of making them happy in the end . . . but that it was essential and inevitable to torture to death only one tiny baby, . . . to found that edifice on its unavenged tears, would you consent to be the architect on those conditions?"[13]

Well, why not? For the utilitarian, the baby has a duty under those conditions to die and should do so willingly, as in an Aztec sacrifice.

Removing the special moral status of heroism destroys important distinctions and shadings in the way we color our lives. Ethics should not be monochromatic when the moral world of the ordinary person is so colorful. More than numbers count and not all good acts are duties. In fact, if self-sacrifice to benefit others is always a moral responsibility, there is no point in praising those who do it. Still, Christopher New has written: "Heroes often deflect praise with the disclaimer 'I was only doing my duty.' I conclude that they are, though modest, right."[14]

Not everyone can act heroically, because many of us do not have the talents or the abilities to do so. That is a pretty basic fact about us. Those who might be called "modified duty theorists" argue that although ordinary people do not have responsibilities to be heroic, heroism is the moral responsibility of those who can act heroically. Capacity determines responsibility. If you cannot swim, you have no duty to rescue a drowning person. But if you can, and you attempt no rescue, you are guilty of moral failure.

This version of reading heroism out of morality ignores another basic fact, the same one the utilitarians often ignore: the stakes in heroism are life and death. Capacity or not, this is not just another set of responsibilities. We do not give out Medals of Honor to soldiers who just did their duty, nor do we court-martial those who do not perform heroically in the face of certain death.

Sidney Hook notes that "a democratic community must be eternally on guard against" heroes.[15] Heroes may sincerely believe that they accept democratic principles, but there are two features of democracy that ultimately block or frustrate heroes. One is its basic commitment to the principle of majority rule, and the second is the slow pace of democratic action. Throughout history, majority rule has been notorious for visiting disasters on minorities. The dynamics of democratic group decision making also generally insure conservative responses, rife with compromise—not the stuff of heroism. There is a wonderful scene in the Mel Brooks film *Blazing Saddles* in which the hero begs the townsfolk to give him twenty-four hours to come up with a plan to defeat the bad guys. They answer back in unison, "No!" Not only is the hero likely to be in the minority as a person of action, he or she is sure to grow impatient with the fussing and fuming of the townspeople. There is a Chinese proverb that says, "The hero is a public misfortune." Perhaps that is why we prefer the fifteen-minute real-life heroes to those with sustained careers. You will never read a book or article about how Lenny Skutnik had an extramarital affair with a movie star or fathered children out of wedlock or regularly got roaring drunk and relieved himself in his neighbor's bushes.

In times of national crisis, however, democracies must find heroes to lead them. "In a troubled world, no democratic community can survive for long unless it entrusts its leaders with great powers."[16] But Nietzsche's detested common folk must reclaim their community from the hero once he or she is no longer necessary or they will become the hero's abject subjects and the hero will, in Nietzschean parlance, become as contemptuous of them as when he or she first set eyes on them.

We stand in a nasty political ambivalence vis-à-vis our heroes. They are sometimes necessary, but they are also threats to the commonweal. It is probably a good thing for democracy in America that we really have so few heroes, if any, and their roles are played now by celebrities. The difference, as Daniel Boorstin has said, is that we no longer look for God's purposes in our leaders, we look for their press agents. "A celebrity is a person who is known for his well-knownness."[17] Heroes are distinguished by their achievements at risk of self-preservation, celebrities by their images or trademarks. Celebrities are made, usually by the media; heroes are self-made.

If heroes are not needed in politics, are they also dispensable in morality? Urmson says they are.[18] He argues that heroic actions, though worthy of abundant moral praise, are beyond responsibility and so not necessary to a basic morality. For him morality has two realms: the realm of responsibility and duty—that which must be done or avoided, and a higher realm where we can assess actions as good and commend them to others but where the morality is one of aspiration, not requirement. In the first realm, morality can be stated in rules and principles; in the second, models. Urmson believes that a society can survive with only the first level of morality and it will be neither brutish nor short. Without the second level, however, it will be impoverished. The morality expressed, and even the way it is expressed, in the Hebrew Book of Covenant is of the basic level, while the admonitions of the Sermon on the Mount express the aspirations of the second.

Urmson's vision of the two levels is appealing, but there are difficulties. If heroes are moral models, then the rest of us would seem to be moral failures for not at least trying to be like them. That would, however, make heroic behavior our moral duty, and so the two levels would collapse into responsibility. Yet it makes little sense to hold heroes up as paradigms of human virtue unless we have some responsibility or moral obligation to emulate them. (It may also be a serious misreading of the Christian message to think that the Sermon on the Mount does not impose duties to "Go and do thou likewise.")

The two realms idea is salvageable, however, if we think that the moral use of the heroic models does not commit us to saying that we have responsibilities to act in ways exactly similar to heroes. Instead, moral models can be used to point at the virtues that they manifest. The dominant virtue of heroism is courage.

Aristotle identifies courage as one of the cardinal, though complex, virtues. He writes, "The brave man is as dauntless as a man may be . . . while he will fear even the things that are not beyond human strength, he will face them as he ought . . . for honor's sake; for this is the end of virtue . . . courage is noble."[19] Courage, Aristotle maintains, is the mean flanked by the extremes of recklessness and cowardice. It is always put to the service of furthering moral goals. Courageous persons are not deep players in that courage is never solely practiced for its own sake. Imagine a soldier in battle. Were he purely rational, he would surely look for some way to escape the fray. But he decides not to run; he decides instead to expose himself to the risk of almost certain death. If he does so just to show how brave he is, he is a deep player, not courageous. If he does so primarily because of the external goal, the hope of victory in a moral cause, he is courageous. He may even be a hero.

We are not a moral model-conscious society. We teach rules, not lives. The turn towards litigation in the last thirty years has produced cowardly rule followers who maintain only minimum standards of moral behavior. The virtue of courage that the emulation of heroes could infuse into our culture has been replaced with an ethics of laws and loopholes in which the standard advice is to check with your attorney to see if you are exposed to lawsuit before volunteering for anything. Courage has lost ground to security. Yet without courageous acts throughout society, we are in jeopardy of losing the security our ancestors courageously gained. Maybe we are so impressed with the brave deeds of people like Lenny Skutnik because we know that most of us would have calculated the legal liabilities and the physical risks and never ventured into the Potomac.

Poor Lenny Skutnik was introduced in his hometown as the man who sat with Nancy Reagan during the State of the Union Address, not as the hero of the Potomac. His brief status as a celebrity overshadowed his role as a moral model.

The loss of shame as a primary moral emotion in our society, and with it the loss of the sense of community, makes the achievement of an aspirational level in our morality extraordinarily difficult. Abstractions in moralistic prose have never had much of an effect on the human race. Ideals must be exemplified, principles made incarnate. That is surely one of the great lessons of the Christian scriptures. In the end, it does not matter whether the heroes we try to replicate are real or fictional. What matters is that the heroes held before our collective consciousness are emulatable personifications of the virtues on which the flourishing of a good society depends.

12 · The Burke of a Mill

To burke: To murder someone by suffocation so as to leave the body intact and suitable for dissection. To suppress quietly and unceremoniously.

The Burke for whom the verb is named was William, an infamous wholesaler of cadavers to the surgeons of early nineteenth-century Edinburgh. He, or at least a wax model of him, now occupies a place in Madame Tussaud's Chamber of Horrors. The verb was not created to honor Edmund, the famous philosopher-politician of the latter half of the eighteenth century. His image is not in the wax museum. The Mill to be burked is not the famous John Stuart, but his somewhat less famous father, James. (For the record, neither Mill is honored with a wax effigy in Tussaud's.)

I shall construct a series of arguments that are not dependent upon or derivative of Edmund Burke's account of representation, though they were provoked and inspired by Burke. I find these arguments persuasive against a Millian delegate theory. I hope to provide some strong reasons for adopting a position on legislative responsibility that is clearly Burkean and which may also lend some credibility to a possible interpretation of Burke's most controversial views on government.

In the *Second Treatise of Government* John Locke describes a legislature as a "fiduciary power to act for certain ends."[1] He maintains that insofar as the government is representative, legislators should in some way be bound to the will of their constituents. His reason for holding this view is, paradoxically I think, based on the principle that no one has the power to place himself or herself under the "Absolute Will and arbitrary Dominion of another."[2] This law of self-preservation dictates, Locke seems to think, that legislators act only as agents of the "Power of the People," representing the people by making their will present

122

in the legislative process, and that they are to be held accountable to the people as any fiduciary would normally be held accountable to his principal. Locke adds, "The Community perpetually retains a Supreme Power of saving themselves from the attempts and designs of any Body, even of their legislators, whenever they shall be so foolish, or so wicked as to lay and carry on designs against the Liberties and Properties of the Subject."[3] This fiduciary relationship is the cornerstone, for Locke, of the doctrine of the supremacy of the legislative branch of government. If the legislature is directly accountable to the electorate and the right of self-preservation for each citizen is inalienable and nonnegotiable, then each citizen theoretically maintains control of his or her preservation by controlling his or her lawmaker so long as the legislature is the supreme government power. (This, of course, is pure fiction because the theory of popular sovereignty is also conjoined with a majority rule principle. Hence, not every citizen has control of his legislator. Only those in the majority do. This point is not lost on Burke.) The supremacy of the legislature for Locke is provisional, dependent upon its continued incorporation of the ends, if not the will, of the people in the matters it legislates.

It would be an injustice to Locke to characterize the fiduciary relationship he has in mind as bound agency as many of the populists would prefer it, rather than free agency. The power of the legislator and the scope of his or her actions clearly are to be limited by the ends of the people, but it is instructive that Locke uses the notion of trust to characterize the relationship, implying a form of free agency. What Locke intended with respect to type of agency cannot be determined. Locke does not comment on the subject of instructions. Nonetheless, from what Locke says about removal it seems that he would not have treated the legislator as bound on particular issues to the instructions of the majority of his constituents. The ends of the people set the parameters on legislative behavior, but Locke does not give the people the effective power to dictate specific legislative actions.

In his *Essay on Government*,[4] James Mill restates the Benthamite's creed that the only true end of government is the attainment of the greatest happiness of the greatest number of people. He then goes on to argue that only a fully representative system can achieve that end. Obviously government cannot be democratic in the classical sense, Mill allows, because "the people as a body cannot perform the business of government for themselves." Hence the "goodness of government" depends upon "the right constitution of checks" that assures the identification of the people's happiness with the legislator's decisions. The legislator "must have an identity of interest with the community." How is that identity to be insured? "If things were so arranged that, in his capacity of representative, it would be impossible for him to do himself so much good by misgovernment as he would do himself harm in his capacity of member of the community, the object would be accomplished."[5] The legislator, for Mill, has two aspects, that of the representative who wields a certain amount of power, and that of the common citizen who is liable to be the victim of the misuse of legislative power (even his or her own). The power placed in the legislature is essential to guard against usurpations and other forms of malfeasance that might be practiced by the executive or the judiciary. There is a critical point beyond which that power should not be limited, for limiting it to prevent legislative misgovernment is likely also to weaken it and thus destroy its capacity to check other governmental activities. If the amount of legislative power should not be diminished, Mill reasons, the only way to insure the utilitarian ends of government is to limit the duration of the period of time any one person can exercise that power. "The smaller the period of time during which any man retains his capacity of representative, as compared with the time in which he is simply a member of the community, the more difficult it will be to compensate the sacrifice of the interests of the longer period by the profits of misgovernment during the shorter."[6] Most current term limitation advocates in America are probably blissfully unaware that the underlying arguments for their campaign have such a pedigree.

Mill recognized that limiting the duration of legislative service is inadequate to fully insure that the greatest happiness of the majority will be promoted. There must be "a conformity between the conduct of the representatives and the will of those who appoint them."[7] That will only achieve the desired end if those doing the appointing, the electors, are themselves representatives of the people. What could be more representative than full enfranchisement and a mandated legislator?

Millian legislators are to view themselves as delegates or ambassadors of their electors. Should they stray from the path of representing the will of the electors, they can expect to be turned out of office. Either they promote the interests of the majority of the electors as the majority understands their own interests or they will have to seek another line of work. De facto, Millian delegates bind themselves to the instructions of their constituents. They willfully accept mandate. They represent the majority by translating its will into legislative votes. The whole system in its pure form may be appealing; it is unfortunate that it is morally flawed.

One flaw in any pure delegate theory of representation is, as Burke noted, that it robs legislators of their judgment. It makes each legislator's capacity for rational decision making subservient to the "collective will" of the majority of his or her constituents. Hence, it obligates legislators to sacrifice their autonomy, something many philosophers regard as a basic condition of moral responsibility and moral citizenship. According to some philosophers, Robert Paul Wolff, for example,[8] freely sacrificing autonomy is tantamount to intentionally failing to meet a fundamental moral responsibility. Such a view is Kantian. "Man . . . is subject only to his own, yet universal, legislation, and . . . is only bound to act in accordance with his own will, which is, however, designed by nature to be a will giving universal laws."[9]

The principle of autonomy is the cornerstone of the Kantian concept of the kingdom of ends. Kant probably, and Wolff without doubt, would regard the Millian delegate doctrine as heteronomous and hence as an affront to the moral dignity of the legislators.

I will not rehearse the familiar Kantian (or Wolffian) arguments for the moral necessity of autonomy. Pressed too hard, as Wolff did in his famous book on anarchy, they appear to erode the very basis of government itself. In a state of anarchy representation is not an issue. Wolff's insistence that all "political obedience is heteronomy of the will" is too extravagant an indictment upon which to attack Mill. It simply has not been shown that autonomy and authority are exclusive notions. Wolff recognizes that in a direct or perfect democracy in which a single negative vote constitutes a veto, autonomy and political authority would be compatible.[10] That particular system, however, is an artificial construct set up as a straw man for Wolff's anarchistic arguments and is certainly not of interest here. It is clear that the delegate-legislators are supposed to be heteronomously obedient to the will of the electorate. They are expected to follow the instructions of the majority of their constituents, to regard their own judgment and will as secondary to that of the electors, and hence to preserve popular democracy. Having noted that, I do not wish to pursue the difficulties in pressing the autonomy obligation against the delegate theory. It is too much of a double-edged sword to be effective. I will simply note in passing that though the Kantian autonomy argument owes much to Rousseau, Rousseau adopts a deputy theory of representation. Rousseau does seek to preserve the moral liberty of each citizen, even at the cost of some autonomy for the legislator. Insofar as Rousseau's legislators are also sovereign and have moral obligations to conform their wills to the general will in order to be free, his deputy theory may escape the Wolffian criticism by having it, as it were, both ways.

Burke expressed his theory of representation in his famous speech to the electors of Bristol on November 3, 1771. Bristol was a popular constituency, not a rotten borough, and had a long tradition of instructing its representatives in Parliament. Henry Cruger, the other member elected that day, had preceded Burke to the podium and had assured the electors that he would, following custom, regard all of their instructions as authoritative over his votes. Burke began by clarifying an important distinction. He agreed that in all cases he would prefer the interests of the Bristol electors over his own interests. However, preference of interests was not to be confused with sacrificing judgment to instructions. "Your representative owes you, not his industry only, but his judgment; and he betrays, instead of serving you, if he sacrifices it to your opinion."[11] Underlying this distinction is Burke's most fundamental conception of government as a matter of judgment rather than of will. Justice, for Burke, is a substantive, not a procedural issue. Amicable resolution of a clash of wills is no guarantee of the moral defensibility of the political actions that are undertaken.

The authoritative instructions (Cruger's) view directs the legislator to ignore his or her own convictions, judgments, and dictates of conscience when they are not identical to the opinions of the constituents. Such a doctrine obviously robs legislators of their autonomy in the very enterprise in which they most need to exercise rational skills. The process of representative legislation is a deliberative process, a matter "of reason and judgment" that proceeds by discussion and decision making. Burke argues, "What sort of reason is that in which the determination precedes the discussion, in which one set of men deliberate and another decide . . . ?"[12]

Burke's comments draw attention to a basic though often ignored difference between the delegate and trustee theories: as suggested above, the delegate theory assumes that government is primarily, if not solely, a matter of will and interests, while the trustee theory presupposes that successful and morally justifiable government must be a matter of judgment and wisdom. If Burke is right in his analysis of government, if there is truth to be found in political or moral-politico matters, then moral wisdom and what may be called, after Hilary Putnam, moral skill,[13] is the virtue of good government service. Robbing government officials of their exercise of judgment not only offends their dignity, it also does a disservice to the governed by allowing opinion to supplant reasoned decision making concerning morally acceptable political means and ends. If government is nothing but a matter of battering out compromises between conflicting interests and wills, then the delegate theory is the more attractive of the two, for the will of the people will be given prominence, the legislative process conceived as the distillery of the general will on all political matters.

There is little reason to enter again into the dispute about whether or not moral issues, and hence most political issues, are resolvable on substantive rather than procedural grounds. As I have written elsewhere,[14] I think that by and large they are. If moral resolutions of political matters are to be found, if there are morally right answers even in hard cases, then we are morally obligated to discover them. Therefore, the dispute on representation reduces to a question of the moral justification of the principle that morally correct governmental decisions are to be preferred to decisions that happen to be reached by democratic means. How can such a principle be morally justified?

In a parliamentary speech, Burke argued against a bill that would have actualized the Millian solution by making elections more frequent.[15] The electors' opinions are, he often allowed, to be given frequent and serious consideration. They are to be regarded as data to be sifted and computed in decision making, but, Burke maintained, contrary to the Millian expectation, frequent elections will not necessarily combat legislative corruption. Also, Burke slyly pointed out, there is no denying that the electors are themselves corruptible. They are easily confused or seduced by politicians to misinterpret their own interests. He might also have suggested that rather than fighting corruption, term limitations encourage grasping politicians to get as much as they can for themselves during their stay in office, unconstrained by having to face the electorate for a reelection bid. Rather than furthering the purposes of the Millian delegate conception, term limitation could have the effect of making control of the legislator by the electorate less likely.

As suggested earlier, some might regard the principle of autonomy as providing the strongest argument against the delegate theory. However, there is another way to consider the issue that also conveniently sidesteps Kantian commitments while focusing on the legislator and not on a theory of government, a way that concentrates on some of our basic convictions about the relationship between intentionality and responsibility. Mackie's "straight rule" as discussed in chapter one maintains that a person can be held responsible for only and for all of that person's intentional acts.[16] All of my subsequent revisions kept intact the notion that one may be held morally responsible for those aspects of one's behavior and one's actions for which there are true descriptions of what one did that say that one did those things intentionally. William Wollaston captured the basic idea when he wrote: "That act, which may be denominated morally good or evil, must be the act of a being capable of distinguishing, choosing, and acting. . . . Because in proper speaking no act at all can be ascribed to that which is not endued with these capacities."[17]

Consider whether the votes of a delegate-legislator are properly ascribed as acts of that person. Two features of intentionality are crucial. Although intentionality clearly is a causal notion, it is an intensional one. It does not mark off a class of events, and attributions of intentionality in regard to any event are referentially or semantically opaque with respect to other possible true descriptions of the same event.

Assuming that a particular legislator, call her L, is a Millian delegate of her constituents and that she cast a "nay" vote on a tax reform bill, the following should be true descriptions of what occurred:

- L's body moved in some way (she pushed the "nay" button, or said "nay," or raised her hand).
- L intended to push the "nay" button or say "nay."
- L's intention, however, was *not* (or at least was *not necessarily*) to vote against the tax reform bill.
- L's intention was to represent the opinion of the majority of her constituents on this matter. Hence: L intentionally pushed the "nay" button; L intentionally registered the opinion of her constituents; *but*
- L did not intentionally vote against the tax reform bill.
- L's intention was not to vote against tax reform, it was to faithfully register the opinion of her constituents, even though to do so she intentionally pressed the "nay" button.

On Mackie's straight rule, we should say that our legislator can be held morally responsible only for those aspects of the event of her pushing the "nay" button redescribed in true sentences that say she did those things intentionally. Wollaston again makes this point:

> For that, which . . . has not the opportunity or the liberty of choosing for itself, and acting accordingly from an internal principle, acts . . . under a necessity *ab extra*. . . . But that, which acts thus, is in reality only an instrument in the hand of something which imposes the necessity, and cannot properly be said *to act*, but *to be acted*. The act must be the act of an agent: therefore not of his instrument. A being under the above-mentioned inabilities, as to the morality of its acts, . . . can be but a machine [in our case, a voting machine]: to which no language or philosophy ever ascribed . . . *mores*.[18]

The semantic opacity of intentionality ascriptions should, according to the straight rule, shield the delegate from moral responsibility for the other aspects of the event when, for example, it is redescribed as a vote against tax reform. What L did intentionally was to register the vote of her electors. She may not at all share their views and even if she does, her delegatory act is not properly described as intentionally voting against tax reform. The delegate ought then to be held responsible only for the perfect translation of the poll of her constituency into a registered response on the question before the assembly. This seems rather straightforward, but of course it is not. Even though we seem to be able to drive an intentionality wedge between different descriptions of the delegate's actions, the gap created is forced closed by application of other principles of responsibility exposed in chapter one.

The simple straight rule of responsibility may capture many of our intuitions about the relationship between intentionality and responsibility, but as noted in chapter one, we at times hold people morally responsible for the unintended aspects of their actions or the unintended effects they produce. For example, we generally hold people responsible for their acts of negligence. Hence, if a person knows or should know that doing something will result in an untoward event and even if he or she did not directly intend to bring about that result, if he or she still performs the causally efficacious antecedent act and the event does occur, he or she may be said to have collaterally or obliquely intended that untoward outcome and so, *ceteris paribus*, can be held morally responsible for it. If delegate L is relatively certain that if she votes as instructed by her constituents the result will be the passage of a measure that cannot be morally justified because it will have seriously untoward effects, and if she still votes as instructed, she can be said to have obliquely intended that result and be held morally responsible for its occurrence. If we do hold her morally responsible, however, we countermand the principles that underlie the delegate theory. Our holding her responsible implies that if L knows or should know that voting as instructed will have untoward results, and if she votes as instructed, she is morally liable for those results. Therefore she should not vote as instructed. Furthermore, it suggests that L ought to investigate the probable results of her casting a "yea" or "nay" vote on any particular issue, regardless of the poll of her constituents. If L does investigate probable outcome, she likely knows more of the situation than her electors. That could provide grounds for treating her as more responsible for the untoward outcome than her constituents, because she would seem to be negligent (if not wicked) should she follow instructions and vote in a way that will be likely to produce morally unacceptable results. If, on the other hand, L steadfastly avoids investigating the probable results of her votes, she would be regarded as thoughtless at best, and more likely, as negligent for acting out of self-imposed ignorance. The delegate is captured by responsibility for the untoward outcome, regardless of her intentions when pressing the "nay" button. "I was just voting the wishes of the people in my district" has a hollow ring to it.

It may be argued along lines suggested by Mackie[19] that the delegate-legislators ought not be held accountable for the untoward outcome of voting as instructed, but only for their negligence in not voting in a different way when they knew or should have known those results would occur. This kind of argument can be quite persuasive in the case of dangerous or drunken driving that causes death. One should probably be held responsible for negligent driving, whether or not it causes death, rather than for causing the unintended death. Otherwise, as Mackie writes, "mere chance may make a great difference in the treatment of two people who are equally negligent, . . . but it just happens that someone gets in the way of one but not of the other."[20] The negligence of delegate-legislators, however, is not so easily divorced from the untoward outcome of their voting as instructed when they know that doing so will probably have those effects. The negligence of the delegate-legislator is built into that concept of representation. To be a delegate is to allow oneself to be negligent and to refuse to let one's knowledge or well-founded belief that voting as instructed will have a morally unacceptable outcome affect one's pushing of the voting buttons.

The gap necessary to protect the moral status of the delegate-legislator is also closed by yet another common revision of the straight rule of responsibility. The delegate conception of representation is a kind of two-agent performance. It is not an action in which the represented is present in the act of representation except, of course, in a symbolic way. Actually, it is easier to think of the action of the representative as provoked, accused, or stimulated by the action(s) of the represented and thereby as a two-person performance. (The delegate is like the corporate agent whose actions are stimulated by corporate executive actions and who is therefore only an extension of the corporation.) Of course the majority of the constituents is not a single person, but it may be treated as an aggregated collective or sum-individual whose collective action conjoined with that of the legislator constitutes the delegate vote. In a perfect delegate system, one might imagine that the two-agent performance will be such that the delegate's action is always a rather automatic and hence perfectly predictable response to the constituents' action. Normally we would regard the responsibility for the delegate's action, voting against the tax reform bill, for example, to fall back on the sum-individual, that is, the electorate, by reason of collateral or oblique intention of second effects. However, we also recognize in matters of agency that if the second agent, the delegate, should have known or did know that the outcome would be morally unacceptable, and if the agent could have done something other than he or she did, and that act would have had a morally acceptable outcome, then the agent must share the responsibility. Indeed, he or she may be held primarily accountable for the event caused.

This sort of analysis may at first appeal to the delegate theorist. As Mackie suggests,[21] the only catch is that historically, the more automatic the response of the second agent, the more the responsibility is to be transferred back to the first agent. This will not really help the delegate theorist whose reason for arguing that legislators ought to commit themselves to automatically responding to the instructions of the majority of their constituents is that the desired automatism is not the case. And insofar as legislators do have the choice of voting as instructed or voting according to their own convictions no matter what the theorist tells them they should do, responsibility should be shared or even fall more heavily upon the legislators than upon their constituencies. We need only remind ourselves that the more automatic the representative's actions become, the less of a moral agent he or she becomes, the more of an instrument, the more of a means only to the ends of others. (And it might well be asked whether willfully enslaving oneself in such a fashion can ever be morally justified. Is this another form of the tyranny of the majority?)

A crucial mistake often invades would-be Burkean accounts of the trustee legislator and appears to strengthen defenses of the delegate theory: failing to distinguish between what I will call legislative style and legislative focus. Burke talks in his speech to the Bristol electors (and elsewhere) as if the trustee must always focus his legislative activity on the interests of the society at large and away from his borough. "Parliament is a *deliberative assembly* of *one* nation, with one interest, that of the whole—where not local purposes, not local prejudices, ought to guide, but the general good. . . . You choose a member, indeed; but when you have chosen him he is not a member of Bristol, but he is a member of *Parliament*."[22] However, Burkean trusteeship is not incompatible with an almost exclusive district focus, and the local district is not the only focus that may compete for the attention of the trustees. For example, the interests of ethnic or racial groups that comprise only a minority of the persons in a district may sometimes be legitimately regarded by legislators as their primary focus.

The real issue that underlies the confusion of style with focus hides in the Burkean concept of representation itself. It is usually assumed by political theorists that the representative must represent some persons or group of persons or the legislator is not representing at all. (Some would say that is contained in the very notion of representation.[23]) But that assumption is dependent upon the theory of government as a clash of wills rather than as an attempt to make and carry out judgments for society about the good and just (the will/wisdom dispute mentioned earlier).

Burke, who takes the side of wisdom over will, nonetheless recognizes that "representative" would be a misnomer unless the legislator represented something. Insofar as legislators do not (or ought not) uncritically adopt the opinions of their constituents or anyone else per se, Burke argues that they are to be seen as representing interests. By "interests" he means abstracted types of human endeavor, such as the farming interests, the mercantile interests, and the banking interests. Hence, he argues that representation crisscrosses boroughs. And he thereby scandalizes modern popular democrats by talking about virtual as opposed to actual representation. The idea is that, for example, the interests of the blacks of Birmingham, Alabama, may be virtually represented by a senator from Michigan though not actually represented by him. Virtual representation, as Hanna Pitkin observed,[24] has the virtue of always, tautologically, being good representation. If the senator does virtually represent the interests of blacks, then he indeed represents those interests. If he does not represent those interests, he does not virtually represent them either. Actual representation of the interests of the majority of people in the district may vary in quality. But here the distinction between focus and style must be most clearly drawn. Focus is a substantive question; style is not and for Burke, representation is a matter of substance, of content. It ought to be the representation of what Pitkin calls "unattached interests,"[25] not people. The interests represented by any legislator constitute his or her focus, and insofar as representing such interests does not compromise the autonomy of the legislator by making him or her subservient to the will of others, no question of style is involved. The argument that the trustee theory is not a theory of representation must define representation only in terms of wills, wishes, and opinions—in terms of people, and that is the real bone of contention.

The Burkean conception of government by judgment can only be successful if the powers of legislation are in the hands of those best suited to make well-reasoned and morally justifiable decisions. It may appear odd to the casual reader of Burke to find that many contemporary legislators embrace the Burkean conception of representation. *The Official Guidebook for Ohio Legislators*, for example, quotes Burke's Bristol speech with approval and adds that, "The pressures of the legislative arena, the need for rapid decisions, the difficulties the legislator is likely to encounter when sampling the views of his constituents, and the technicalities associated with proposals he must consider, require him to rely extensively on his own perception of the merits of the matter under consideration."[26] Practical concerns aside, the adoption of a Burkean position by proclaimed democrats is difficult to reconcile. After all, Burke's representation doctrine is known to be only a corollary to his championing of a natural aristocracy as the only way to insure good government.

The natural aristocracy doctrine is clearly consistent with the commitment to the autonomy of the legislator and for Burke, the wisdom necessary to legislate could only reside in the traditional landed aristocracy of his time.[27] If the natural aristocracy doctrine as Burke understood it necessarily entails trusteeship, then we ought to put aside the earlier arguments endorsing it against the delegate theory, despite their persuasiveness. For surely elitism, especially as defined in terms of inherited wealth, is morally suspect. Even Rawls, however, has shown that trusteeship need not be unjust.[28] Of course we must forego the commitment to a ruling elite of the leisure-class despite Burke's eloquence when describing its virtues. That does not mean, however, that we should not insist that legislative offices be placed in the hands of those in the society who have superior political wisdom, decision-making abilities, and practical and moral reasoning capacities rather than in the hands of those whose only claim to the office is their popularity with the masses.[29]

Trusteeship in itself does not deny the principle of fair opportunity, but if the trustee is to be a good legislator according to the Burkean ideal, then that principle will be denied. Wisdom and good judgment are not characteristics of all persons, so some people will be excluded from legislative positions if those characteristics are treated as qualifications for office. Even when all persons of like ability, regardless of social rank, are included in the class of potential trustees, the principle of fair opportunity is denied. But as Rawls points out:

> To be consistent with the priority of fair opportunity over the difference principle it is not enough to argue . . . that the whole of society including the least favored benefit. . . . We must also claim that the attempt to eliminate these inequalities would so interfere with the social system and the operations of the economy that in the long run anyway the opportunities of the disadvantaged would be even more limited.[30]

Burke argues only that the natural aristocracy benefits the whole of society. But he could have argued, within Rawls's framework, that the relevant condition is also met. Again, however, the argument must be based on the more fundamental commitment to the wisdom-over-will conception of legislative government.

13 · Law's Concept of Personhood: The Corporate and the Human Person

A legal person may be described as any entity that is a subject of a right or as any entity recognized in law as supporting such capacities as instituting and/or defending judicial proceedings. Legal personhood is always something conferred, never merely the result of the act or acts of parties. Nor is it an inborn quality of humans. In fact, legal personhood raises those on whom it is conferred from whatever natural associations they may have enjoyed with other entities to membership in a society.

The idea of a legal person (indeed the term person itself) comes from the Romans. The Latin *persona* was originally limited to the theater, *dramatis persona*. Roman law appropriated the term to refer to anything that could *act* on either side of a legal dispute. In Roman law it was clearly understood that all legal persons are artifacts of the law itself. It was no concern of the law that legal persons may have an existence prior to or outside of the legal sphere. The biological status of a subject was not relevant, so it was not necessary to draw a clear distinction between real and artificial juristic persons. All were creations of law.[1] Coke characterized this view as based on the position that a legal person exists only because of the acts and considerations of the law.

Roman law may be profitably thought of as identifying legal personhood with legal status. Status is not a question of fact so much as it is a matter of legal principle. That is, the characteristics an entity must possess to have legal status are fixed by law, not given outside of it.

There is, of course, a significant difference between Roman law and the English common law on the interpretation of legal status. In English law, status is conferred, as a matter of public law, only on exceptions to normality. Hence "the attribution of status implies a legal classification of exceptions to the normal man."[2] It might be conferred on married women, illegitimate children, bank-

134

rupts, convicts, mental incompetents, and so on. In English law, Graveson writes, "status . . . is . . . applicable to any body in fact capable of sustaining any degree of legal personality."[3] Its roots lie in Norman land tenure and in the wergeld-based codes of the Anglo-Saxons.

Status should be kept distinct from legal capacity, the possession of legal power. The farmer is a legal state of being, the latter a state of doing. "Capacity" refers to the legally permitted abilities one has to affect one's own rights and those of others. Status determines one's legal condition in the community. The terms have been used to define each other. Bentham, for example, claims that to have legal status is to have certain capacities, rights, and duties. Austin defines it as "an aggregate of rights or duties with capacities residing in the individual as a member of a class."[4]

In Roman law, on the other hand, to have legal status was, *eo ipso*, to be a normal legal person, an empowered citizen. Status distinguished the Roman law of persons from the law of things and embedded it in private law.

Applied to corporate entities, the Roman conception of the legal person produces the Fiction (or the grant or concession) theory. In the introduction to a leading contemporary text in corporation law the specter of the Roman persona thrives:

> Saying that corporations are persons serves as a useful shorthand for the fact that the law recognizes them as distinct legal entities endowed with separate legal characteristics that are often identical to those of natural persons . . . [a] corporation is merely a "fiction," a creation of the intellect, and thus . . . dependent for its recognition by the law on some act by the state.[5]

Justice Marshall in the *Dartmouth* case provided perhaps the most famous American statement of the Fiction theory: "A corporation is an artificial being, invisible, intangible, and existing only in contemplation of law."[6]

Roman law recognized two types of organizations. One, a *societas*, was governed by contract and its assets were owned by the contractors. The other, a *universitas*, was a legal entity separate from its members, capable of holding property and of possessing distinct rights and obligations. Personhood was conferred on the *universitas*, not the *societas*.[7] It is important to note, however, that it is elemental to the Fiction theory and to Roman law that legal personhood was always conceived as a privilege and not a matter of right. (This has crucial implications for the understanding of corporate responsibility.)

In 57 B.C. the *lex Julia de collegia* authorized corporations, but to be granted incorporation and so personhood, an association had to show that it would be "helpful to the state or beneficial to the public."[8] The suggestion, not worked out in Roman jurisprudence to my knowledge, is that corporations are extensions of the state. In fact, all legal persons *qua* legal persons must be extensions of the state. In the corporate cases this is clear and has produced interesting legal results. Corporations, according to the Fiction theory, can do only what the state permits them to do. So as George Ellard notes, all of their actions are "in effect acts of government, corporate officers being ultimately accountable to the state."[9] The Fiction theory must hold the state responsible for the supervision of the acts of corporations. That was accomplished within the charter-granting process in which the acts of the corporation were strictly limited to those described in the articles of incorporation. Any other activity in the name of the corporation was *ultra vires* and so not actually attributable to the corporate body. In the Fiction theory, then, corporations are law-abiding by definition. The same can be said of all legal persons. Hence, the status problem of outlawry arises.

Canon law treated corporate entities on the basic Roman model. They were *persona ficta* in an even more literal sense than they were in Roman law. Holdsworth identifies Innocent IV as the first pope to create the designation.[10] He was, apparently, responding to the difficulty of preserving the tenets of the law while dealing with ecclesiastical bodies such as monasteries. In the eyes of the law, monasteries were comprised of dead persons, yet they had vast property holdings. Abbots regularly had to obtain enforcement of the rights of their orders to property. Pope Innocent IV therefore endowed himself with the power to create artificial persons that possessed property and other rights. The property in question, however, belonged to no abbot or specific collection of monks, to no human person(s). Its ownership lay completely in the "hands" of the *persona ficta*. Monks and abbots were treated as guardians entrusted with the maintenance of the property. This canon law conception of the corporation migrated into English law during the Tudor period.

By 1615 Coke had written in *Sutton's Hospital*[11] that for there to be valid corporations there must be "a lawful authority of incorporation." He meant in effect, that there must be a sanctioning body empowered to create, sustain, and monitor artificial persons. Holdsworth argued that the reasons for the criminalization of conspiracy are virtually the same as "those which make it necessary to regulate the activities of groups . . . who may acquire great power by organizing in corporate form."[12] The *ultra vires* doctrine embedded in the Fiction theory solves the control problem and probably explains why the Roman conception survived in corporate law so much longer than it did with respect to human persons. The Enlightenment liberals could see it, at least at first, as a protection for the individual against the power of organizations. But that was to misconstrue its tenets and when they realized that the Lockeans found a replacement more in keeping with their individualism.

In effect, the Fiction theory of legal personhood is grandly totalitarian, at least in its extreme forms. All rights, privileges, and duties are ultimately conferred by and through a central civil authority. In the corporate sphere the activities of freely associated humans are severely restricted, and the interests and wills of organizations are either interpreted as extensions of the state and always lawful or as reducible to the actions and attributes of the human membership. The question of the legitimacy of the conferring authority, however, is a major stumbling block. I am reminded of the scene in *Monty Python's Quest for the Holy Grail* in which two peasants question Arthur about how he got to be king. They are told about the Lady of the Lake presenting the sword Excalibur to Arthur, but they are unpersuaded that such an aquatic ceremony could create supreme political authority. Arthur then gives away the real source of his power by threatening the lives of the peasants with the sword. So much for the Fiction theory!

The nineteenth-century liberals foisted on the law the contractual theory of the corporation which "interprets the corporate form as but a convenient summarizing device for the limited rights and duties of the private parties who contractually create [it]."[13] Sovereign authority vis-à-vis corporations is thereby limited to its authority over any other contractual relations between consenting adults. In American law this conception of corporate legal personhood had its heyday in the 1880s. If the contract theory can be said to have any virtue at all (even in its own time it surely did not reflect much of corporate life or the role of corporations in society), it is that it separated corporations from the state. It removed their status as special creations of the state and placed their establishment and operation in the hands of private individuals.

In legal history the major rival of the Fiction theory is the Reality theory. The basic premise of the Reality theory is that the law does not invent its subjects, it recognizes the nonlegal existence of persons. The most influential versions of the Reality theory were put forth by Gierke,[14] Figgis,[15] Maitland,[16] and Freund.[17] When applied to human persons, the Reality theory draws few detractors, for it simply asserts that extralegal considerations regarding personhood dominate the issue of whether any human ought to be treated as a legal person. The law's task is to capture the players in the social game as its subjects. It does not create those players, though it attempts to regulate their play.

Gierke and the other Realists did not restrict the theory to human persons. In fact, humans were hardly their primary interest. For the Realist, corporations are persons regardless of the law's attitude towards them. They meet the conditions of personhood that are applied to any natural entity seeking admission to the legal sphere. In fact, they are natural persons. (This point is clarified by Ellard's distinction, borrowed from Pollock and Maitland, between natural and physical persons. "Often large classes of physical persons—Jews, monks, serfs in medieval England, minors and mental incompetents in the United States—are not deemed natural persons by the law."[18]) Law, according to the Reality theory, recognizes persons, but it doesn't create them. Law merely determines which societal facts are in conformity with its requirements. De facto personhood precedes de jure personhood.

I have argued in chapter seven and elsewhere[19] in support of the view that corporations are intentional systems and that they manifest the ability to do such things as make decisions, act responsibly, enter into both contractual and noncontractual relationships with other persons, and so forth. They may be blamed or credited for what they do in their own right. And, as I will show in chapter sixteen, they can be punished.

Corporations, as I have argued,[20] satisfy conditions for individuation and identity over time that do not depend on a steady-state membership of human individuals. A corporation may remain the same entity through time despite radical changes of personnel. In fact, corporations do a better job of avoiding the paradoxes of identity than do human persons.

Roger Scruton identified three properties that are typically set forth in the philosophical literature as essential to what it is to be a human person.[21] Following Scruton, they are: unity and duration as an animal, rational agency, and self-awareness. The puzzles and paradoxes of personal identity arise because philosophers suppose that these three features mark out three ways of individuating persons. A human is that particular person because he or she is that specific animal, a body enduring through an uninterrupted biological life. He or she is that rational agent (rather than any other) because there is a continuity of beliefs and projects or a stream of consciousness with which that agent is identified. He or she is that certain self because his or her identity through time is, in Kant's idiom, "'original', presupposed by awareness and determined by nothing knowable."[22] The puzzles of personal identity arise because of the philosophical failure to establish any necessary connections between these three features of human personhood. For example, rational agents may be conceived of as enduring despite body transfers, as Locke's stories were meant to show. Self-awareness need not be linked to having any particular stream of consciousness, let alone any particular body.

The human personal identity quandary has been the subject of a vast literature. It is periodically solved and unsolved. It can be ignored in this context because the difficulties that have rendered human personal identity through time problematic do not ensnare the corporate person. Scruton comments that the discussion of the problems of human personal identity and individuation reveals "the corporate person to be composed of metaphysically problematic parts, but if you divide things finely enough, everything is composed of problematic parts."[23]

The crucial point is that in the case of corporations, we do not have to be concerned with the possible paradoxes arising from the conflict between physical/bodily identity and rational agency identity because corporations are not members of a natural kind, at least not in the way discussed by Locke that generates some of the classical puzzle cases. Also, no one is claiming that corporations are self-aware in any way that would satisfy the Kantian condition.

Gierke and Bradley would probably disagree with the view that corporations are not natural (or even self-aware) in the same way that humans are. That is a weakness of their positions. Gierke argues that corporations are organic, that they have life processes. Bradley writes (albeit about community), "It is an organism and a moral organism; and it is conscious self-realization."[24] Hauriou's position is much closer to the mark.[25] He maintains that corporations are institutions, not organisms. Scruton clarifies Hauriou's distinction: "Institutions are characterized by procedures and roles which exist independently of those who make use of them; they have a longevity conferred by the principle of succession to office and this longevity is something which, in the nature of things, is not shared by an organism."[26] Hauriou maintains that corporate personality exists only in those institutions in which there is a corporate will. By corporate will he means something akin to my analysis, in "The Corporation as a Moral Person,"[27] of corporate intentionality that is not reducible to the intentional actions of the human persons within the corporation. In short, it is the presence of what I have called a Corporate Internal Decision Structure (a CID structure) that accounts for the personality of the corporation. Such a structure contains the organizational relationships and lines of internal authority and responsibility as well as the rules by which corporate policy is recognized and implemented. It is important to note that the CID structure not only forms the personality of the corporation, it determines its identity as well. It is constitutive of the corporation. A corporation is that particular one because it has that particular CID structure. Hence, within the CID Structure the three features, the tension among which produces the infamous puzzles of human personal identity, are unified or eliminated, leaving only problems of identity over time that plague all entities as Locke, Hume, and scores of other philosophers have shown. One only needs to ruminate a few minutes on Hume's discussion of the identity of a ship to appreciate the way solutions may be managed for the problem of corporate identities.

A ship, of which a considerable part has been chang'd by frequent repara-
tions, is still consider'd as the same; nor does the difference of the materials
hinder us from ascribing an identity to it. The common end, in which
the parts conspire, is the same under all their variations, and affords an
easy transition of the imagination from one situation of the body to another.[28]

A corporation's CID structure provides its "common end" and the organizational
edifice in which its members "conspire." The point is that corporate personality should not be cast in doubt just because it does not mirror human personality
and so is not prone to the same perplexities of personal identity as the human
variety.

Furthermore, it would be a grand mistake to identify a corporation's personality with some amalgam of the personalities of the humans employed by it. In fact,
a corporation might not have any humans working within it and yet possess an
individuatable personality and manifest rational agency and so qualify for legal
personhood according to the Reality theory. Consider the following scenario
adapted from a tale told by Meir Dan-Cohen:

An entrepreneur started and directed a manufacturing business. After a
number of financially profitable years, he was bought out by a syndicate.
The syndicate built up the company and then it issued shares for public
purchase. As the number of shareholders increased and shares were traded
on the market, a professional management team was installed and control
of the corporation passed to them. Throughout these periods of its existence
the company was active politically and culturally in its community. After a
period of time the company decided to buy up its own shares. In fact, it
bought up all of the outstanding stock in the company. As its capital was
mostly self-generated and its management self-perpetuating, this move oc-
casioned no significant change in operations at the company. The management team then decided to completely automate all aspects of the company's operations. In effect, it became both ownerless and fully-automated.
However, it continued to manufacture its product, its legal status did not
change, and it continued to act in the community as it had in the past.
Finally, the management team decided that because the operations were
already computer-run, and very efficiently and profitably at that, computers
could also handle all of the management decision-making as well. By and
large, reliance on the computers had made the human managers redundant.
Through a process of not filling positions upon retirement, the company

became totally computerized. "All the management functions, and all the decision-making processes, were ably programmed and delegated to the computers." [Herb Simon would be proud!] The company went on manufacturing and reinvesting its profits. It continued to support community causes and cultural events and backed political candidates committed to increasing the Constitutional rights of corporations. Hardly anyone who dealt with the corporation realized it had converted to computerization on so grand a scale.[29]

This totally computerized corporation was still capable of litigating its grievances and defending its rights. Although its end state was hardly identical to its beginning state, it is not difficult to uncover a "common end in which the parts conspire." Nor is it difficult to find a historical thread that provides sufficient evidence for us to call it the same corporation and so for it to be responsible and liable for its actions in its previous stages of existence. Its CID structure was not radically altered despite the absence of humans in decision-making positions. For legal and moral purposes, it remained the same person through time.

The Reality theory of legal personhood states that there is a moral reality to the entities recognized as persons in the law. Corporations, at least those with CID structures, are moral persons and so warrant that legal status. In fact, were they to be denied it, the moral offense would be tantamount to denying legal personhood on racial, religious, or sexual grounds to a fully competent human.

The American legal system has been steadily advancing toward its own version of the Reality theory since 1886 and the *Santa Clara* case.[30] The Reality theory does not seem to have played a role in American jurisprudence before *Santa Clara*. In fact, Horwitz has persuasively argued that the Reality theory was "nowhere to be found in American legal thought when the case was decided."[31] He further shows that it was a decade later before the theory actually absorbed the case, but by then the theory was getting its biggest American boost, not from the law, but from big business, which saw itself legitimized by the theory. Nonetheless, *Santa Clara* applied the equal protection clause of the Fourteenth Amendment to corporations, and it did so in full knowledge of the fact that "the language of the amendment was written to protect persons."[32] *Hale v. Henkel*[33] solidified the position of the Reality theory in 1905. In *Hale* it was decided that the search and seizure provisions of the Fourth Amendment apply to corporations. In 1978 *Bellotti*[34] applied the freedom of speech provisions of the First Amendment to corporations. The storm of protest from the old-line liberal individualists was deafening. Typical are the remarks of John Flynn:

Bellotti ... leads to the inexorable conclusion that any state regulation in-
terfering with the functioning of the undefined marketplace of ideas violates the First Amendment without regard to the implicit impact of the
expansion of the meaning of corporate personhood on the political life of
society, the balance between individualism and collectivism, and the long-
term consequences of the decision for other state and federal regulation of
corporations.[35]

What was the impact on society? There are strong reasons supporting the view
that the recognition of the reality of the corporate person in law is more of a
boon than a disaster for human persons. These reasons are not, however, even
remotely legalistic.

In *The Asymmetric Society*[36] James Coleman argues that before the legal recognition of corporate persons, society was conceived by its members as a rigid differ-
entiation of persons in fixed positions. Bestowing legal personhood on corporations produced a structural change of enormous sociological magnitude: "It is as
if there has been extensive immigration over this period, not of persons from
Europe or Asia or Africa or South America, but of men from Mars—a race of
persons unknown in history. And this new race of persons has come to crowd out
natural persons from various points in the social structure."[37] Human persons,
Coleman maintains, were freed from the fixed estates of the older social order
because the structural stability of society was provided by corporate entities. In
effect, humans can now roam over the stations created and maintained by corporations and in fact, a single human can simultaneously occupy several positions
in the structure of society. Positions may be freely changed and exchanged. Corporations, in Coleman's account, are responsible for the significant increase in
human personal freedom. This may not turn out to be the blessing that the Enlightenment liberal would, on first reading, suppose. The Enlightenment goal,
echoed confidently in the nineteenth century by Sir Henry Maine, was to con-
vert social relations, including the law, from status to contract. The rise of the
modern corporation has succeeded in bringing that about for human persons.
But, as Hobbes had to admit (and many modern-day liberal individualists try to
ignore), contractual relations require a stable social structure. Corporate entities
now provide the requisite fixed elements of the edifice. Humans are no longer
relevant parts of the structure. They are occupants of the places, or stations,
within it. They are free in that their places in the institutions of society are ne-
gotiable matters of contract, and their whole existence is not inexorably linked
to a specific role generally dominated by another human in a superior role. The

market for humans and their talents is open. The structure exists independent of the particular humans who have the choice to contract for their services where and when they desire.

Humans are now economically and sociologically freer than ever before in history. They are also "irrelevant in a fundamental sense."[38] Anyone can be replaced at any time. The positions endure. What is lost in a purely contractual account of human/corporate relations is the concept of membership and the noncontractual obligations created by membership. There is, however, nothing intrinsic to legal corporate personhood that requires such a polarization of the human and corporate person. In fact, the concerns revealed by the sociological analysis are remediable in the metaphysics of corporate personhood.

Rather than counterpoise humans and corporate actors from within the Enlightenment liberal bias, another perspective recommends itself. Writers such as Rousseau, Burke, Hegel, and Bradley suggest that in the state of nature or, if you will, behind the Rawlsian veil of ignorance, humans are only potential persons. According to the Reality theory they would not qualify for legal personhood. To achieve full personhood a human must associate with corporate institutions that forge relationships between their members and between their members and the larger corporate units, and through those units to culture, civilization, and past and future generations. To be a full-fledged human moral person is to find a place (or places) in the structure of corporate entities.

For Rousseau, civil union is essential, not only for civil liberty and rights, but for the moral freedom, "which alone makes man the master of himself."[39] Though for Rousseau individual humans can exist outside the corporate union of the state, they cannot achieve completeness as moral persons in its absence. The corporate entity converts humans into moral entities. Bradley makes a stronger claim because he denies that talk of individuals outside of corporate-like relations makes sense. "What we call the individual man is what he is because of and by virtue of community . . . communities are thus not mere names but something real."[40] For Bradley, the child at birth is born into "a living world . . .which has a true individuality of its own."[41] That perspective, of course, is Hegelian.

Hegel maintains that "the corporation is the second ethical root of the state."[42] The family is the first, but the corporation is the "one planted in civil society."[43] The corporation is "like a second family for its members."[44] Corporations form the stable basis on which the family can flourish, because they assure the family's livelihood and provide the focus for the assessment of worth for family members employed by them. Corporate membership and rank is the only external mark a human individual needs of "evidence he is somebody."

Unless he is a member of an authorized corporation an individual is without rank and dignity, his isolation reduces his business to mere seeking, and his livelihood and satisfaction become insecure. . . . In civil society it is only something common to particular persons which really exists, i.e. something legally constituted and recognized. Hence he cannot achieve for himself a way of life proper to his class and less idiosyncratic.[45]

The term "livelihood" is aptly chosen. Livelihood was *not* first defined in the *Oxford English Dictionary* as "means of living, maintenance, sustenance." It was originally "course of life, . . . kind or manner of life." Corporations provide not only the means to earn the funds necessary to sustain one's lifestyle, but they also create, maintain, and define the lifestyles that are in fact lived. In effect, corporate membership is required for moral personhood (Rousseau) and for the sense of worth and identity of the individual human (Hegel).

If one isolates and abstracts the human person from the corporate relations that define and determine his/her identity and worth as is required by the liberal individualists, the characteristics needed to generate the notions of duty, responsibility, and rights are lost. In the absence of associations, value has no foundation. The Hegelian argument for the necessity of corporate entities to the moral life brings to mind Aristotle's dictum that to live the good life one must live in a great city.

To secure his position, even within his own system, Hegel would have to show that there is an internal relation between human and corporate personalities, "that something essential to the first must be obtained through the second."[46] Hegel would probably have called that something *Bildung*. Scruton glosses it in terms of "non-contractual obligations." I have suggested its roots lie in the concept of livelihood. Corporate persons are crucial to the linkage between the past and future that is required in any robust conception of rational agency. Scruton's way of putting this should suffice:

[The] relation to the unborn and the dead is necessary for the fulfillment of the rational agent . . . for it forms the premise of self-justification. The individual is justified by the knowledge that he did right by those who survive him, whom he never will know, and who promised him nothing; and equally by those who preceded him and bequeathed to him unknowingly their store of trust.[47]

The protection of obligations to both the past and the future has always been a central task of law, perhaps because it is so crucial to our understanding of place and culture and so of moral personhood itself. The endurance of corporate persons, a prospect that terrorized the Enlightenment liberals, insures the projection of moral and cultural responsibilities in both temporal directions. Corporate juristic personhood acknowledges in law what "is necessary to the ecology of rational agency."[48]

14 · Better Off Unborn?

No person shall maintain a cause of action or receive an award of damages on behalf of himself based on the claim that but for the negligent conduct of another he would have been aborted.

—Minnesota statute 145.424

The tort of wrongful life allows a child to sue the health-care provider whose negligent actions were major causes in the mother's decision not to have an abortion. It makes the claim that the child would be better off unborn.

I have a personal interest in the development of the legal concept of wrongful life and its related application of principles of responsibility. I was born with a rare condition that was always fatal within a few months of birth. An immigrant Jewish doctor, having just escaped Nazi persecution with the aid of the Belgian underground, arrived in New York City within weeks of my birth. He was informed of my hopeless case by one of his relatives who happened to be my mother's obstetrician. Special permission was secured for him to try a radical operative procedure he had been working on in Europe. While a late winter blizzard raged, he was driven up the Hudson Valley to the hospital where he conducted the surgery. Obviously, he was successful and because of his procedure, treatment of that condition is now routine.

I often wonder if I would never have been born had prenatal diagnosis been available to my parents back at the dark beginnings of World War II and had a landmark abortion case already been decided in the manner of *Roe v. Wade*. In that famous 1973 decision the Supreme Court reasoned that a "fundamental component of the Fourteenth Amendment is the right to privacy that includes the right to choose whether to conceive a child or to terminate a pregnancy."[1] If that brave doctor had not been smuggled out of Belgium, if my life had been only a few months of pain, would I have been better off unborn?

Tort law has always been driven by technological change. Developments in medical technology have been allied with dramatic movements in constitutional law. Like so many other significant legal movements, the wrongful life tort first appeared in an odd, out-of-the-way little case. In *Zepeda v. Zepeda*[2] (Illinois, 1963) a son brought a tort action against his father for causing him to be born illegitimate. The father had seduced (or induced) the plaintiff's mother into adulterous sexual intercourse by promising to marry her. He was married to someone else at the time and chose to remain so after the affair. Young Zepeda claimed that he was owed compensation for the deprivation of his right to be a legitimate child, to have a normal home, to inherit from his father and his paternal ancestors, and for being stigmatized as a bastard. The appellate court of Illinois refused to recognize a cause of action in *Zepeda* for the explicit reason that if they did, the courts would be overwhelmed with similar cases. They advised that the whole matter of wrongful life be placed in the hands of the legislatures.

Zepeda was not really a wrongful life suit. Today we might classify his case under the tort of dissatisfied life. But *Zepeda* was important because it saw matters in terms of a child's cause of action, addressing the issue of the liability of an individual to the child whose very existence is attributable to that individual's wrongful or negligent actions.

As noted in chapter five, Shakespeare wrote about the same issue in *King Lear*. Gloucester fathers an illegitimate son, Edmund, whom he does not legitimize. In the process of pursuing compensation for his dissatisfied life, Edmund provides a model for the popular meaning of "bastard." He deceitfully turns his father against his other and legitimate son, then betrays the old man to his enemies, knowing full well they will torture him and pluck out his eyes.

Wrongful life is distinct from the more widely recognized tort of wrongful birth, which depends upon the same set of facts. Wrongful birth is a parent's cause of action brought for damages for the birth of an unexpected or defective child. Compensation is sought only to cover the expenses of child rearing and care. The parents must support their claim that except for the physician's negligence, they would not have conceived the child or they would have terminated the pregnancy. Although pro-life groups may be stirred, such a suit does not run to questions of the value of life itself. Wrongful life, however, is quite another story.

The Supreme Court decision that fuels wrongful life is, of course, *Roe v. Wade* when it is interpreted as implying that anyone who negligently deprives parents of the right to terminate a pregnancy should be held responsible for the natural consequences of that deprivation. To provide the factual grounds for the negligence claim, medical science had to make significant advancements in prenatal and preconception testing, and it has done so. Genetic testing can now determine if would-be parents whose backgrounds indicate the presence of genetic defects have a high probability of bearing a defective child. After conception the testing shifts to the fetus. Amniocentesis and ultrasonography are used to detect fetal abnormalities.[3]

The wonders of modern medical science have brought with them terrible responsibilities both for making decisions and for bearing the consequences of those decisions. The wrongful life tort is the avenging angel that may make more true than ever the old quip that God did not make a perfect world, so he created the plaintiff's bar.

The history of wrongful life cases is short. Cases tend to fall into three categories: preconception injuries, genetic counseling mistakes, and postconception injuries. In *Gleitman v. Cosgrove*[4] (1967) the New Jersey Supreme Court dismissed the child's claim that the physician failed to inform his parents of the danger of rubella. This failure to inform, it was argued, caused the parents *not* to abort. Although the court recognized a causal connection, they barred recovery on the grounds that public policy favors the sanctity of human life.

In *Berman v. Allen*[5], (1979) the New Jersey Supreme Court reversed itself (at least in part) when it allowed the parents to recover in a Down's syndrome case, though the court did not accept the child's claim. The first case in which the child's full-blown independent cause of action was upheld was *Park v. Chessin*[6] (New York, 1978). The *Park* case focused on genetic counseling. Mrs. Park had given birth to a child with polycystic kidney disease. It lived only five hours. Relying on Dr. Chassin's advice that the chances of a repetition were practically nil, she conceived another child who was born with the disease and died in two and a half years.

Two years later the California Court of Appeals upheld an infant's wrongful life claim in the case of *Curlender v. Bio-Science Laboratories*.[7] It was shown that the laboratories negligently performed tests to determine whether the parents were carriers of Tay-Sachs disease. The child, Shauna Curlender, was born with Tay-Sachs, a progressive, degenerative disease of the nervous system that is always fatal. Children with this disease suffer blindness, deafness, seizures, paralysis, and mental retardation and die in two to four years. The court ruled, "The reality of the 'wrongful-life' concept is that such a plaintiff both *exists* and *suffers*, due to the negligence of others . . . and the certainty of genetic impairment is no longer a mystery."[8]

In 1982 the California Supreme Court, agreeing with the decision in *Curlender*, decided that a cause of action for wrongful life is entirely legitimate. The case was *Turpin v. Sortini*,[9] in which the parents of Joy Turpin relied on the erroneous assurance of their doctor that an older sister's severe hearing impairment was not hereditary. Joy was born totally deaf. In reviewing the case, the Fifth District Court of Appeals expressed the belief that legislatures, and not the courts, ought to decide the acceptability of wrongful life suits.

In *Harbeson v. Parke-Davis, Inc.*,[10] a 1983 case in Washington state, the plaintiff claimed that his mother took Dilantin as prescribed by her doctor with the assurance that it would have no ill affects on her pregnancy and that it had in fact caused growth deficiencies and mental retardation. Though the court did not allow general damages, it did find for the child and awarded special damages to cover medical expenses incurred in caring for the child.

When the courts have denied the child's cause of action, it has been on any of seven different grounds:

1. The value of human life makes existence in any form preferable to nonexistence;
2. The defective child's damages cannot be measured because the court cannot compute the difference between life in a defective condition and nonexistence;
3. The health-care provider's actions are not the proximate cause of the child's defects;
4. The wrongful life issue should be left to the legislatures as a public policy matter;
5. A child does not have rights not to be born or to be born a whole functioning human being;
6. Recognition of wrongful life as a cause of action will start a flood of claims; and
7. An excessive economic burden will be placed on the shoulders of the medical profession.

Some of these judicial reasons are more persuasive than others. There is little of philosophical interest in the position that the matter should be left to the legislatures, but I tend to argue because wrongful life is, in the first instance, a social policy issue. It is altogether proper that legislative bodies wrestle with its philosophical implications and expose the responsibilities embedded in the doctrine that is reflected in the cause of action. A number of state legislatures have risen to the task.

The concern that claimants will surge forth to flood the courts if the action in wrongful life is recognized as legitimate may be a practical problem, but it is theoretically irrelevant. If wrongful life is a genuine cause for compensation, then the courts should be open to all who have responsible claims. The matter of dumping another heavy financial burden on the medical profession (particularly obstetricians) may be troublesome from economic and other points of view, but it is hard to see why it should take precedence over the more deeply theoretical concerns expressed in the remaining grounds the courts have used to deny wrongful life suits.

Three of those grounds are especially important. Any one of the three, if accepted, would constitute a sufficient reason to recommend against allowing wrongful life suits. They are: the claim that the assessing of damages in wrongful life suits is not possible; the claim that the tort would reverse the great tradition in law that always presumes in favor of existing human life; and the claim that a child has no right not to be born or to be born a fully functioning, nondefective human being.

The first claim puts forth the argument that wrongful life lies outside the boundaries of tort law. In tort cases the defendant must owe a duty of care, must bear a responsibility for a certain level of care for and diligence in the treatment of the plaintiff. There seems to be little dispute over whether or not the health-care provider has such a responsibility to the unborn child. In *Curlender* the court noted that "no authority has suggested that public policy considerations negate the existence of such a duty."[11] It is generally recognized that a doctor has a professional responsibility to a woman under his or her care, both before and after conception, to detect risk of genetic disorders and to disclose information to the prospective parents if a genetic risk is detected. The latter responsibility should exist even if the doctor has personal moral views against abortion and recognizes that abortion is the parent's only alternative to giving birth to a defective child. But can the doctor be said to have a responsibility to the child, then unborn, perhaps not even conceived? Here the courts have done a little sidestep and adopted the doctrine of "conditional prospective liability." Simply, the doctor's responsibility to the child is conditioned on the fetus's being born alive. Because harm can be foreseen if the child is born alive, there is good reason to impose a duty owed to the child by the doctor. That duty, however, does not include preventing the child from coming into existence. After disclosure that matter rests, in accord with *Roe v. Wade*, with the parents. The duty to disclose is not the duty to dispose.

The doctor's basic duty is established in law, but the burden falls on the child (the lawyer representing the child's interests) to show that there was a breach of that duty. How is that to be shown? The child must prove that a causal relationship existed between the doctor's failure to properly inform the parents of the risks and their failure to prevent conception or to terminate the pregnancy. To accomplish that the child must show that the parents sought the doctor's professional advice and that they relied on the negligent information provided to them by the doctor. But even that is not enough for a cause of action in tort. The child must further show that the doctor's negligence actually resulted in the injury. What injury? Birth as a defective human. It is the birth and not the defect that must be causally linked to the doctor's negligent actions. In other words, all of these requirements of tort may be satisfied and the determination of damages remain utterly problematic.

Tort theory traditionally maintains that the monetary amount awarded to the plaintiff must be sufficient to return the victim to the position he or she would have occupied had the injury not been suffered. There's the rub. Since the child would not have existed but for the doctor's negligence, how much money will it take to return the child to the position of nonexistence? Obviously no monetary figure can accomplish that. The cost of hiring an assassin does not establish the baseline! Consequently a number of courts have denied actions in wrongful life.

Those courts are captives of a nasty little legal myth: the idea that unless a tort victim is restored to the preinjury state by a financial award, no damages should be assessed. When the monetary measure of damages is inadequate, the tortfeasor escapes responsibility. The issue of damages can be approached in a constructive way, however, if the restoration myth is cast aside for the unjustified fiction it is. There are definite and obvious costs involved in the defective children cases. Medical and education bills can be astronomical. Of course those are not costs of returning the child to the preinjury state—that's impossible. The child never had a preinjury state. The cost of maintaining the child's life, however, is a determinable sum of money. Why not treat that sum as the amount of damages the child has a right to recover from the negligent health-care provider? This would be consistent with basic tort law principles. It was, in fact, the decision of the California court in *Curlender*. The problem of measuring the value of nonexistence is effectively skirted.

Does anything control the extent of recoverable damages? The answer provided by the court in *Curlender* was that recovery ought to be limited to the pain, suffering, and care costs the child would endure and incur only during the lifespan limited by the child's disease.[12] The child should not be allowed to measure its loss against the life expectancy of a normal child. Further, in accordance with tort principles the child should be able to seek punitive damages if he or she can prove fraud or malice on the part of the doctor. Suppose the doctor withheld the pertinent information from the parents because of his or her antiabortion views.

There is one social policy reason for adopting this limited-actual-damages approach. There can be little question that a society's general utility is lowered by the birth and maintenance of a severely defective child. Social costs also may include medical and educational bills. It is both efficient and fair for society to place the burden of such costs on those whose negligence is causally responsible for the problem. That does not, of course, speak to pain and suffering and other general damages.

The *Turpin* court addressed those issues. It awarded Joy Turpin only extraordinary medical expenses and denied her claim for pain and suffering. In doing so it relied on another legal myth: the benefit doctrine, which provides that damages should be reduced to the extent the plaintiff has received a benefit as a result of the injury. There is a great deal of common sense in that notion. If you got more good than harm from an injury, you should not be able to recover—you are already ahead of the game. But what benefit is conferred on severely defective children by the negligent health-care providers responsible for their being born? The *Turpin* court had an answer: the benefit received is "existence with the capacity both to receive and give love and pleasure as well as to experience pain and suffering."[13] When they applied that formula, they determined that the pain and suffering of the defective child did not outweigh the benefit of existence. Thus the child was not entitled to general damages. This notion may be a remnant of the wrongful birth *Shaheen* case (Pennsylvania, 1957)[14] in which the court judged it a matter of law that the countervailing joys of parenthood outweigh the sorrows of giving birth to a defective child. But how are we to determine the extent to which a Tay-Sachs or a spina bifida or a Down's syndrome child gives and receives love and pleasure? Many of them do, of course, but to what degree? Have we not, if we adopt the benefit doctrine, presupposed in favor of exactly what the tort throws in doubt: the value of life over nonexistence? In other types of tort cases, pain and suffering are recoverable without driving the court to the edge of a metaphysical abyss. Why must the matter be so difficult in wrongful life? The answer is obvious. Wrongful life perches on a very unstable rock wavering on the edge of that chasm. The matter of the value of life as opposed to nonexistence cannot be avoided.

Perhaps the most repeated attack on the wrongful life tort is that it violates American public policy. The sanctity of life, we believe, defeats any judgment that an individual's life is so wretched that he or she would have been better off not existing. If the tort of wrongful life compensates the child for existing, it is an affront to some of our most dearly held moral and metaphysical principles.

One way of approaching the question is to calculate the expenditures in money, suffering, pain, and so on required to maintain one's life against the benefits received from living. There has been considerable movement of late in our society, with judicial support in some instances, towards acknowledging that people may reach a point in life of diminishing returns, where death is a justifiable option. There is, however, a notable difference between suicide and euthanasia decisions, on the one hand, and preventing existence on the other. It is much easier to grasp what people mean when they say that they have reached the point in life where they can expect no more valuable experiences than to understand what a person might mean by "I would be better off had I never been born." Who among us has never been born?

That's the catch, yet that is what the plaintiff in a wrongful life suit seems to be claiming. The child cannot claim that it would have been better off had it been born nondefective, for that is not a possibility. Either the child is conceived and born with the defect or it is never conceived or it is aborted. The world in which the child is not defective *cannot* exist.

Although the *Berman* court was reluctant to admit that a life can become so impaired as to be of negative social worth, the court in the famous case of Karen Ann Quinlan expressed quite a different view.[15] The *Quinlan* court sanctioned the cessation of life-prolonging treatments and allowed nature to take its course, ending Karen's life. The *Turpin* court cited *Quinlan* in support of the view that, as a matter of public policy, life in any state is not always preferable to nonlife. That is a major shift in thinking. Despite the fact that *Quinlan* is cited in wrongful life suits, its issues are not relevant, in my opinion, to the crucial matters involved in wrongful life. *Quinlan* is a right-to-die case. Cases like *Quinlan* are concerned with a privacy right: to determine one's own medical treatment. In *Quinlan* that right was held by the court to be constitutional. But at the other end of life there is no parallel right. How can one determine not to exist before one does exist? Hence, even though *Quinlan* establishes that some lives can be of negative social and personal worth, it does not ground the notion that there is a right of never existing that can be invoked by those who, when they come into existence, lead lives of negative personal and social worth and so may claim the *Quinlan* right to die.

Quinlan has lent support to the notion that rough standards can be developed for determining which lives are worth living. But how? And how could what would probably be a scale of meaningfulness in lives be incorporated into law? Surely using any statutory criteria for a meaningful life could have frightening consequences. They might open the door for a political discussion about whether all impaired life should be extinguished at birth, and that is a slippery slope down which humans already slid earlier in this century, a slope down which we ought not again start to slide. At its bottom one finds the quicksand that devours all life that does not conform to standards of quality set by those in political power.

Courts have shied away from standard setting because, as in *Turpin*, they are reluctant to say what constitutes a perfect human being and "what condition less than perfect will be recognized as a cognizable injury or defect? . . . All human beings have some imperfections. Would partial deafness in one ear or poor vision qualify? Will a large, uncorrectable, disfiguring, discolored, facial birthmark or a cleft palate be so recognized? What about an albino?"[16]

Distinctions, important and fine ones, can be and have been drawn and utilized in law. In fact, we can distill crucial distinctions from the legal literature on wrongful life. First, the defect must be one that could have been discovered before birth by use of the existing technology. Second, it must be neither amelioratable nor curable. Partial deafness, poor vision, and the like can be remedied. Tay-Sachs disease and Down's Syndrome cannot, yet both can be detected prior to or during pregnancy and the birth prevented. And what of fetuses infected with AIDS?

Perhaps the first problem for the health-care provider is that allowing this tort will drive up already high insurance costs. Perhaps many obstetricians will elect not to practice. These are definite negatives, but there are also pluses. The liability that this tort would create for the doctor should encourage greater care at the prenatal and pregnancy stages. Physicians would be virtually legally responsible for performing amniocentesis, regardless of whether or not they personally object to abortion. They would certainly have a duty to advise those in high risk groups to have amniocentesis and other relevant tests. Recognition of the tort should deter negligence in genetic counseling and prenatal care, and that is a big social benefit, even though it will be achieved at the price of turning one element of a doctor's practice into "defensive medicine." That itself may be a concern, for obstetricians are likely to urge abortion in even slightly risky cases to protect themselves against suits that would leave them responsible for the expenses of the defective child's care.

Social benefits and costs with respect to the tort seem to be about equal, but a potentially serious problem arises from the technical side. Amniocentesis sometimes identifies healthy fetuses as defective, and there is a risk that amniocentesis can induce premature stillborn delivery. The benefits of reducing the number of severely impaired children burdening society could be offset by the social costs of aborting perfectly healthy fetuses. There is a relevant difference between these and run-of-the-mill abortions: the child would have been carried to term but for the fact that amniocentesis revealed an impairment when the fetus was healthy.

Another concern arises because the counsel of the doctor is the sole determining factor in the decision to abort. Some have argued that if wrongful life is allowed, there will be enormous pressure on doctors to euthanize defective infants right after birth in order to protect themselves from the fiery breath of the dragon that is this tort.

What then ought to be done with the tort of wrongful life? I believe the determining factor should be whether or not wrongful life lies outside the traditional boundaries of tort law. Tort honors the principle of the sanctity of human life by embodying the general doctrine that people should be able to seek remedies for the wrongs that they are caused by the intentional and the negligent acts of others. That is one of the major practices that grounds our concept of responsibility as discussed in chapter two. All human beings, no matter how deformed and impaired, should have the opportunity to recover for the harms inflicted on them. Courts and legislatures should not permit wrongs that result in major financial injuries to go uncompensated and unredressed. That would promote irresponsibility generally, and in the case of wrongful life, irresponsibility in a profession that is crucial to social welfare.

Cases in wrongful life are somewhat embarrassing to philosophers, because they tend to reveal that abstract metaphysical arguments about the value of existence over nonexistence have pathetically little practical value. A starting point, however, might be to examine what would occur if certain rights are granted to children at birth, rights that give them an interest in their existence and physical form.

Courts all over the country have agreed that a child cannot claim a cause of action based on its status at birth, but the matter of whether children should have rights to their existence and form is much in dispute in the legal literature. The following four rights are candidates:

1. a right to develop prenatally;
2. a right to injury-free formation;
3. a right to be born free from defects that with reasonable care could have been detected and treated before conception or birth; and
4. the right to be born a whole functioning human being.

I do not claim these are natural rights. They are useful legal tools to improve the responsibility situation illuminated by the tort of wrongful life. Each of the four rights would be vested at birth in the child. All are subject to other rights already established in the courts. The right to prenatal development is currently limited by *Roe v. Wade* and other rulings extending the mother's right to abort.

But this right is important if the child is to be allowed to state a cause of action claiming that its impairment occurred because the wrongful actions of a health-care provider altered the natural course of its prenatal development. The second right buttresses the first, again focusing on alterations in development induced by poor care.

The third right is teased out of what are now called wrongful birth suits brought by parents. It would vest in the child at birth the right not to be mal-formed because of preconception or prenatal negligent care. Granting this right is saying that children have legal control of the quality of their physical being. Again, other rights recognized by the Supreme Court will take precedence over this one. For example, if the parents were properly counseled and chose not to have appropriate tests or treatments, then parental immunity will defeat any claim on behalf of the child that this right was violated. It is important to note that damages with respect to a violation of this third right are not measured against nonexistence, but are found by calculating the difference between the cost of caring for the defective child and caring for the same child had it not suffered the defect. No metaphysics, just basic accounting.

The fourth right is the one most likely to bother the courts. If we vest in the child at birth the right to be born a whole, functioning human being, are we not thrown back into the existence versus nonexistence quagmire? We don't need to be. The notion of a whole, functioning human being provides nothing more than a solid legal ground for allowing damages for actual care costs.

Seeing the problem in this way makes it obvious that wrongful life is a misno-mer; we really have two different classes of responsibility failures causing injuries for which redress should probably be sought under a single tort. One injury is suffered by the parents, who were deprived of exercising their right to decide to abort the impaired fetus by the negligent treatment they received. *Roe v. Wade* insures that a woman may not be denied an opportunity to make an abortion decision. The other injury is to the child, who was born severely impaired be-cause the parents were deprived of their right. The rights of the parents and the child coincide on the matter of damages that are both reasonable and measur-able.

The interests of all parties would probably be best served by a new cause of action for wrongful impairment—a consolidating action, an action that captures preconception, prenatal, and in-uterine treatment negligence responsibility for the birth of defective children, an action that joins the parents and the child as plaintiffs.

The typical charges against the wrongful life tort can be addressed in terms of the proposed wrongful impairment cause of action. It is said that wrongful life extends the doctor's responsibility to care to persons not yet conceived. That is already true of wrongful impairment, and there is a good public policy reason to apply this doctrine to wrongful life as well: the promotion of better medical care in the society. Wrongful life seems to fly in the face of the sanctity of life doctrine; certainly many courts have viewed it that way, and antiabortion groups have been livid over it. The creation of a new cause of action for wrongful impairment, though probably not acceptable to the antiabortion lobby, takes a giant step away from existence/nonexistence evaluations.

Damages in wrongful life, it is said, are virtually impossible to ascertain. Perhaps this is true if the comparison is made to never being born, but it is not true for wrongful impairment. Furthermore, a cause of action in tort for wrongful impairment, responding to advances in technology, would be a reasonable extension of medical malpractice principles honored for nearly a century in American law. If such a cause of action were created, the legitimate responsibility aims of wrongful life would be accomplished with a minimum of metaphysical baggage.

15 · Faustian Bargains

The famous physician of eighteenth-century London, Samuel Garth, was also a drunkard who could regularly be seen slumped over drunk in a chair in his club. A member once roused him and said, "Come on Garth old boy, you ought to be off seeing your patients." Garth grunted, "It doesn't matter whether I see them today or not. Nine of them have such bad constitutions that all the physicians in the world couldn't save them; and the other six are hearty enough that all the physicians in the world couldn't kill them."

I suppose all of us would like to think that Garth was wrong and that he was behaving in an irresponsible manner, but many of us probably suspect that he is right. The history of medicine is anything but a confidence builder. Recent studies purport to show that the professional practice of medicine, though it is popularly credited with extending life expectancy in the last two centuries, has really only a meager claim to that accomplishment. If anything has improved the population's chances of living longer, it has been the measures taken by governments in the fields of public health and pollution control. The routine practice of medicine by professional physicians has probably made only a nick in the problem of disease control.

But what should we expect? The vast majority of doctors are as insulated from the major social health problems as government officials, college professors, scientists, or lawyers. Rank and file physicians are hired professionals. Traditionally they are hired by individuals who have complaints they want relieved. This doctor/patient relationship is so central to our grasp of the practice of medicine that it controls the focus of our ethical concerns about the field. It tends to drive our ethical outlooks on the profession in two ways: one is crucial to the understanding of the moral responsibility of most doctors, and the other creates a smokescreen that obscures that understanding.

158

I will discuss the smokescreen first. The regular practice of medicine involves choices by physicians that amount to nothing more than routine diagnoses: for example, the prescription of treatment, tests, and drugs for many complaints. The patient has certain symptoms and the doctor responds in the standard manner—"Take two pills every four hours with plenty of liquids." There seem, on the surface, to be no substantive ethical or responsibility assessments in the process. Moral ambiguities are at a minimum. Hence, this sort of practice is often called technical-medical decision making.

Technical-medical practice is typically contrasted with those high-profile situations in which the doctor's office is invaded by moral ambiguity. Occasionally physicians must make choices which appear to go well beyond simply doling out the approved drugs for the common maladies. They decide how and even whether to treat the terminally ill or those born severely handicapped. They have input into the determination of the proper distribution of scarce resources. They decide whether to perform an abortion. They determine whether or not to consent to a patient's desire to have life support systems discontinued. These sorts of choices are contrasted with the standard ones and are called medical-ethical issues. In these cases, doctors do not focus on types of treatment, but ask, "Given the nature of the illness, the treatment, and the patient's values and preferences, is the normally prescribed treatment morally defensible?"

Most doctors will readily agree that technical-medical decisions are the body and soul of their practices, and many will insist that the medical-ethical issues are wholly external to medicine. They are seen as outside responsibility matters that have been smuggled in via the backdoor by philosophers in search of work. It is disturbing for doctors, then, that as new technologies are introduced, these medical-ethical issues attract more and more public interest. In fact, many doctors have become antagonistic to the introduction of ethical questions in medicine. They are persuaded, to the point of fanaticism, that there is a dichotomy between technical-medical and medical-ethical issues. Generally they display their creed by proclaiming that medicine, as they practice it, is a science and hence primarily a value-free, objective analysis and treatment of biological disorders. If there are medical ethics problems to be confronted, they are in the domain of research scientists who probably will discover the knowledge needed to solve them. In other words, in the minds of a number of doctors, medical ethics problems are problems of ignorance. The new technology may create new tangles, but it will also untie them. That is the profession of blind faith.

The main difficulty with such a view, as a little reflection reveals, is that it is not possible to reduce a patient's own values to factors that can be scientifically weighed. For example, there is no technical answer (it is hard to imagine there ever will be) to the problem of deciding whether one should administer a painful regimen of chemotherapy to a terminally ill cancer patient when there is no guarantee it will work. Even in daily practice, the technical options are exhausted at some point, and the physician must make medical-ethical choices. The most general of those choices involves the question, Will the contemplated treatment really benefit the patient? Any answer to that question involves consideration of the patient's overall well-being and the quality of life the patient is living and will live during and after the treatment.

Medicine is, in the end, and despite what the technologists and accountants want us to believe, patient centered. Its goal is, and has always been, the total well-being of the patient—every doctor worth his or her stethoscope will attest to that. But to reach that goal with any degree of success, doctors must take quality of life issues seriously in routine, everyday practice. As David Schultz writes, "All decisions in medicine (whether you like it or not) implicitly appeal to normative quality-of-life questions."[1] There simply are no technical/scientific answers to those questions. They are moral in nature, and so medical practice in all of its aspects is intricately interwoven with ethics and questions of responsibility. There is no escaping ethical entanglement in the practice medicine.

Even those prepared to admit that ethics and medicine are natural bedfellows are still likely to focus attention on such high-profile issues as abortion, euthanasia, and AIDS policy, thereby judiciously avoiding discussion of the moral problem most closely associated with routine medical treatment today. Perhaps the most important moral issue in medicine currently is cost containment and related practices that are injected between doctor and patient.

Cost containment is a euphemism for the constraints under which doctors allow themselves to be placed by striking Faustian bargains with third parties. These bargains look terrific going in, but they turn out to cost the doctor his or her ethical soul by perverting the ethical structure of medical practice. The Mephistophelian tempters are well known: HMOs, PPOs, hospitals, insurance companies, and the like. In all of these deals the doctor trades away his or her control of the primary treatment of the patient. Preapproval for medical services required by insurance companies, for example, means that someone with often no more than a nurse's training is placed in authority to second-guess the doctor's judgment regarding the best interests of the patient. (Usually the decision maker has never interviewed the patient.) Nothing cuts closer to the heart of the responsibility relationship between doctor and patient.

The doctor lured into an open-panel HMO accepts a set of conditions that restricts his or her ability to treat the patient and leaves the patient totally in the dark with regard to the doctor's judgment. Doctors are being turned into dependents of third parties who call the tune; patients are seldom apprised of the limitations on the doctor's care that may threaten their well-being.

What is the moral effect of this new way of doing medical business? The relationship between doctor and patient, which I described earlier in terms of moral responsibility, also takes a legal description: it is a fiduciary relationship. In the state of Texas, for example, giving something of value to a doctor to influence his or her treatment of a patient constitutes a kind of racketeering. A comparable fiduciary relationship exists between a bank trust officer and the principal of the trust he or she administers. If the trust officer is paid by a real estate agent to invest the funds in a development handled by that agent's firm, the trust officer violates the law, even if the trust is benefited by the investment. What many doctors in America are doing by signing up with one or another of the Faustian tempters would, in comparable terms, land a bank trust officer in jail. Disregard for the principles of fiduciary responsibility plagues the practice of medicine.

It is important to understand that there is no distinction in law, nor should there be one in morality, between good and bad bribes. Hence, even if the insurance companies and the HMOs and the hospitals bribe the doctor to do good (or what the doctor would do anyway) with respect to the treatment of patients, the doctor breaches the fiduciary relationship with the patient by participating in those Faustian bargains. Quite simply, if the doctor is getting certain hospital privileges and perks to treat patients in specific ways, he or she has breached the responsibility relationship and is acting unethically (if not also illegally). Considerations other than those regarding patient welfare are propelling his or her practice.

A doctor's motives are morally suspect when the doctor-patient responsibility relationship is controlled by third parties. Legally, the fact that the patient may still receive adequate or even excellent care is irrelevant to the doctor's breach of duty. Morally, however, the matter may not be so cut-and-dried. From a consequentialist's perspective, the fact that the patient's treatment is not compromised could be a prevailing reason to overlook any damage done to the fiduciary relationship. The consquentialist narrows the scope of responsibility to that for which the patient primarily seeks the services of the doctor and determines whether or not that end was accomplished. As the primary reason is usually the restoration or maintenance of health, if that is achieved, the doctor's responsibility will have been met.

Evidence that these Faustian bargains do not affect patient care is inconclusive, and a growing volume of anecdotal material suggests the contrary. Nonconsequentialistic ethicists, however, do not worry about whether the patient's well-being is appropriately protected. Their major interest is in the purity of motives.

Little needs to be said about the way such ethicists perceive the insurance, HMO, and hospital controls on the doctor/patient relationship. It is difficult for a doctor to sound convincing when he or she claims that a certain type of surgery or treatment is being done solely because it is in the best interests of the patient, if he or she is receiving all manner of gifts, from secured parking places to disguised kickbacks.

Purity of motives in routine practice is a complex matter in the current business climate. Perhaps we should give up the idea of evaluating the ethical character of a doctor's actions on the basis of motives and focus totally on outcomes. If we were to do that, however, the patient/doctor responsibility relationship would have to be radically redefined. Perhaps that is happening de facto. Are we not reracking the categories of medical practice by representing the doctor as a technician and laying the responsibility for patient care and treatment on the well-padded shoulders of the corporate provider? I cannot think of any persuasive moral blockades that should be thrown up against such a new understanding of medical practice, but doctors may no longer be able to claim the prestigious role they have enjoyed in our society for over a century. They may have to settle for the status currently held by plumbers.

The law should come to grips with the realities of the business of medicine and redefine the patient/doctor relationship in a way that is consistent with the doctor's new business role, the later twentieth century station of the physician in our society. In other words, the law ought to treat the doctor as a service provider and not as a trust depository. By revising our view of the role of physicians in that direction, we could actually relieve doctors of the kinds of conflict of interest and racketeering burdens that now weigh on the profession. The mythology of the American Doctor, however, is not likely to be altered so easily in the American mind. A new image of free enterprise medicine would be a very large pill to swallow, but it would be closer to the facts.

At the recent convention in San Antonio of the American Society for Hospital Marketing and Public Relations, sessions were entitled: "Maximizing Results from Unpaid Advertising," "Making Marketing Everybody's Business," "Physician Marketing: Techniques That Work," and "Developing a Physician's Sales Program: How to Sell without Guilt." At the meetings of the Texas Medical Association a two-and-one-half hour workshop on "Marketing Tips for a Successful Practice" was featured. Hospitals are definitely becoming less secretive about the business aspects of medicine. Tom Sunde of the Santa Rosa Hospital System unabashedly told me, "Our job is to show the doctors what we . . . can do for them. . . . The hospital's mission is to get physicians predisposed to sending their patients to that hospital."

And doctors are falling right in line by accepting all manner of gifts and perks and inducements. Is this where doctors' responsibility problems in patient guidance lie? Should a doctor tell a patient what the hospital gives the doctor in return for performing the surgical procedure the doctor prescribes?

I think a radical proposal is in order. Recent talk about patient advocacy and worry about the moral dilemmas in guiding a patient's choices is a product of a misdescribed situation—maybe even a delusion—that has been nurtured by the medical profession. Let us take the matter of patient advocacy out of the doctor's hands. Why do doctors think it should be there anyway? It could be fruitful to ask how the problem of guiding the patient through medical decisions differs from guiding any consumer through a purchase in any other part of the marketplace? Of course the physician has much more knowledge than the patient. But more of what kind of knowledge? Certainly not more knowledge of the patient's values and conception of a worthwhile life than any other sensitive and concerned person.

The knowledge doctors have is technical medical knowledge, and that is what they are selling. Few doctors spent as much time in the humanities as they did in the laboratory. Medical training gives them license to medical expertise, no more than that. If they find themselves in muddles about what to tell patients, it may be because, as Bradley would insist,[2] they are overstepping their stations. Adopting a spatial ethical position could significantly help us reconceive the responsibilities of the members of the medical profession.

If we relieve doctors of the burden of patient guidance, there are two places where such a responsibility might fall. One is on the patient; the other is on the government. If it falls to the government, it could take a variety of different forms or schemes. Most of those, I suspect, would not be welcomed by the medical profession, though they are not forms of socialized medicine. An agency of government might serve as a kind of watchdog or ombudsman for patients, offering them information about the hospital, HMO, or other entanglements of the doctor and perhaps providing them with the latest information on the type of care being prescribed, the success rate of the doctor in the performance of certain procedures, and so on. That agency would not regulate the medical industry, but it would offer advice to its consumers, at least in a general way. (The Consumer Protection Agency could also play a role.) In any event, the market would remain about as free as any other market in America, and patients/consumers would be at liberty to purchase whatever services they want or can be convinced to buy. The fiduciary cord, then, would be cut. Caveat emptor would govern. The doctor's position would be comparable to that of an automobile mechanic. He or she would still try to convince consumers of the need for a regular checkup or surgical procedures, but the boundaries of a doctor's moral responsibilities would shrink. They would no longer encompass providing guidance as to what choice of service the consumer should make.

Unless I miss my guess, America's doctors will not rejoice in such a redescription of their roles in the medical industry. That is a real puzzler, for the old adage "actions speak louder than words" has always seemed a reliable guide to beliefs. In short, if doctors really want to be held responsible for providing fiduciary-based guidance to their patients, then volunteering full disclosure of the business bargains into which they have entered would be one step in the right direction.

If, however, financial/business considerations are to rule the practice of medicine, then as a society we should insure, by whatever intervention is required, that the level of health care responds directly to the human needs of the patients, regardless of their remunerative capacities.

"Patient advocacy" is a fashionable slogan. High cost is a serious matter, but the current breakdown in the doctor/patient responsibility relationship threatens the fiduciary understanding that has ethically grounded the practice of medicine in the United States.

For decades doctors have enjoyed very high regard in the American mind. The image of the country or family doctor—trusted friend, attendant to all of the ills of his or her patients—made its mark. However, it will not take much to put the medical profession on the same plane in the public's view as the legal profession. Nothing could tip over the pedestal faster than the proliferation of Faustian bargains that work to the general detriment of the doctor-patient responsibility relationship, especially if they are rightly perceived as made in the interests of profitability.

16 · Enforced Corporate Responsive Adjustment

The weekly *Corporate Crime Reporter* in a typical issue ran stories on:

1. A felony involuntary manslaughter charge filed in Los Angeles against a construction company,
2. Environmental Protection Agency knowing endangerment convictions returned on fifteen charges against a Denver concrete additive manufacturer,
3. A national bank in Massachusetts indicted on currency-reporting violations,
4. New York commodities salesmen convicted of conspiracy and mail fraud,
5. An eighteen-count federal grand jury indictment for racketeering and other violations brought against four associates of the Wedtech Corporation, and
6. Ivan F. Boesky sentenced to three years imprisonment for Securities and Exchange Commission violations.[1]

It was an ordinary week in the annals of corporate crime.

The impression conveyed by the *Reporter* is that the number of corporate crimes is escalating, and most sociological indicators suggest that corporate and white-collar crime has increased since Sutherland's studies in the 1940s (1949). Even if a significant portion of that rise is attributable to better reporting and more concise definitions, we cannot deny that corporate crime is a fact of American life. How can we control it?

Before we can take a stab at the problem of social control of corporate criminality, we must distinguish between corporate and white-collar crime. By "corporate crime" I mean crime attributable to a corporate entity or any responsible person acting on its behalf. "White-collar crime," in the strict sense I prefer, refers to offenses committed by persons from within their professional or corporate stations, generally for personal reasons, and including actions taken against the corporations that employ them.[2] To commit a white-collar crime one must occupy a certain kind of position in the professional/business world (including, of course, government service). An executive's taking a bribe from a supplier as an inducement to place an order is a white collar crime; dumping the waste of the company's factory into a river is a corporate crime. I will leave discussion of the white-collar criminal for another occasion. (However, strategies for dealing with the white-collar criminal can, I believe, be based on the same moral foundation I will construct for the handling of corporate criminality.)

Brent Fisse and I, both jointly and separately,[3] have challenged the orthodox view that corporate responsibility for crime depends on proof of corporate intentionality for the causally relevant acts at or before the time of the untoward event. We have argued that corporate responsibility may best be assessed on the basis of the corporate defendant's response to the harm it has caused. Fisse has called this the concept of reactive fault, and I have developed the corresponding Principle of Responsive Adjustment (PRA), as discussed in chapter one.

Reactive corporate fault, according to Fisse, is an unreasonable corporate failure to undertake appropriate preventative and/or corrective measures in response to the corporate commission of the *actus reus* of an offense.[4] The idea of reactive corporate fault reflects, as Fisse notes, two practical realities worthy of our attention:

1. Communal attitudes of resentment toward corporations that fail to react diligently when they have caused harm; and
2. The common managerial practice, in accordance with the principle of management by exception, of treating compliance as a routine matter to be delegated to inferiors unless major problems, generally involving the reputation or image of the corporation, occur.[5]

PRA requires that the corporate intention that motivates a lack of responsive corrective action (or the continuing of the offending behavior) look back to retrieve the actions that caused the offense, regardless of the fact that they were not intended by the corporatation at the time of the offense. Intentionality has a significant role to play in PRA. However, the time-frame focus on corporate policy (needed to generate the relevant corporate *mens rea*) must be extended to block nonattribution of responsibility to the corporate offender when its only relevant policy at the time of the *actus reus* was ordinary, boilerplate compliance. (A version of the old *ultra vires* problem.) If the time frame is expanded to encompass what the corporate offender has done in response to its commission of the *actus reus* of the offense, then the compliance policy that appears in its annual report will be irrelevant. What will count is what the corporate offender has done or proposes to do by way of implementing internal reform to prevent repetitions.

Since I first offered it, a number of criticisms of PRA have been made, though most seem to be based on a persistent misreading: the claim that PRA rewrites history. Time's arrow continues to fly its inevitable course from past to future, but the shotgun of moral evaluation scatters its pellets in many directions. There is a major difference between thinking that the past can be changed by actions in the present (backward causation) and thinking that we can, and ought to, change our moral evaluations of those who were the cause of harmful things happening. And most importantly, it is in the present and into the future that PRA licenses holding someone responsible for a past deed where a *mens rea* cannot be ascribed in isolation from subsequent behavior. PRA does not say that if we had access at the crucial time, we would have discovered a *mens rea*. It says that now we have the intentional reactive fault that includes the past action within its scope.

It would misrepresent PRA to suggest that we can learn of the intentionality of the original act from the subsequent one. However, in forming the intention that motivates the subsequent act, the actor cannot (except in very special circumstances) ignore the original act. (This may capture the point of Bradley's observation that "in morality the past is real because it is present in the will.") The intention that motivates the subsequent relevant act retrieves the past act and then either endorses or rejects it. It is not the case that we can, or need to, deduce anything about the intentionality of the original act from the subsequent act. That it was or was not intentional no longer matters. That the event occurred does matter. We may never be able to pinpoint the relevant intention. Hamlet might himself be unclear as to what, if any, specific intentions motivated him to kill Polonius. Perhaps the act was impulsive. His killing Polonius may not have been intentional (I do not say it was unintentional), though done quite deliberately and even on purpose. (Recall Austin's accounts of those distinctions in "Three Ways of Spilling Ink."[6])

One modification of PRA is required. It was pointed out by economist Kenneth Koford. PRA, especially when used in corporate cases, is not meant to supplant proactive Bayesian judgments of the probability of events and the taking of morally appropriate avoidance measures. If a fair Bayesian judgment is that a harmful result will likely occur, the benefits of avoiding it are greater than the costs, and if most people would agree that one should not do it, then moral responsibility for doing it can be assigned without reference to subsequent actions. This, of course, covers only those cases in which the risks of causing harm should be obvious to ordinary people. These are the "How could anybody do that?" cases. They are rare, but unfortunately they do happen. Koford's example was leaving a loaded shotgun with a group of seven-year-old children. In such cases PRA would offend our intuitions, because it suspends judgment unreasonably; thus it should not come into play in such cases. The more numerous and interesting cases, however, are those in which there is little or no agreement as to the likelihood of bad results. In those cases we cannot say what the ordinary reasonable person is likely to believe with respect to the probability of untoward outcomes. Once the harm has been caused, the moral demands change and PRA provides the structure for the evaluation of moral responsibility.

PRA offers a promising way of avoiding contentious attribution of criminal intentionality to a corporation. It is rare that a company displays any criminal intention at or before the time of commission of the *actus reus* of an offense. The typical legal solution at present is either to impose strict liability or to impose liability vicariously on the basis of the intent of a representative. The former approach avoids the issue by making intention irrelevant at the level of attribution of liability, though intentionality may be relevant in relation to sentence. The latter approach, which is essentially a form of strict liability, is based on a representationalism that utterly ignores the fundamental criminal element of *mens rea*. To generate the relevant corporate intentionality that will displace strict or vicarious liability, focus must be on a corporate defendant's policy. That focus is achieved in a relevant way by a PRA-sanctioned extension of the time frame of judicial inquiry to encompass what a defendant has done *in response to* the commission of the *actus reus* of an offense. What matters, then, is not a corporation's general policies of compliance, but its implementation of a program of internal discipline, structural reform, and compensatory or restitutionary relief. This temporal reorientation flushes out blameworthy corporate intentionality more easily than is possible when the inquiry is confined to corporate policy at or before the time of the *actus reus*. Remember the Firestone 500 tire affair in which defective ties were responsible for many deaths? It is impossible to show any palpable flaw in Firestone's general compliance policies. It is easy, however, to expose Firestone's intentional adoption of a reactive policy that did not include prompt implementation of a recall program in response to the overwhelming evidence that the tire was defective.

The expansion of corporate criminal liability into a responsive time frame invites innovative ways to tackle stubborn problems of corporate criminal liability. I want to focus on three: the role of interventionism, the due diligence plea, and the design of penal sanctions.

Philosophers and legal theorists have joined a slew of social commentators in developing proposals for controlling corporate behavior through government intervention in the internal decision structures of corporate offenders. Christopher Stone's *Where the Law Ends: The Social Control of Corporate Behavior* led the parade. Stone championed[7] such court-ordered intrusions into a convicted corporation's decision making as mandating new boxes in the flow chart occupied by watchdog directors. Stone was reluctant to recommend application of interventionism across the board. He limited its use to recidivism cases and to hazardous industries. Stone expressed the belief that in what must be the vast majority of cases, the interventionist strategy is too drastic. But what is to be done in such cases?

The American Bar Association proposed a continuing judicial oversight sanction in 1980. But the ABA recommends that such a sentence only be imposed when the criminal behavior is serious, repetitive, and the result of inadequate internal accounting or monitoring procedures, or when a danger to public safety exists. The ABA proposal takes no account of the corporate offender's responsive compliance activities unless the case is extremely severe. In cases that are not serious or repetitive, the only sanction recommended is a fine. We may suppose that misleading advertising cases fall in that category, yet such cases may be paradigmatic of defective standard operating procedure cases and so prone to repetition. Fines, even hefty ones, do not have a record of producing the significant changes in corporate decision structures and standard operating procedures that would be desirable if the corporations are to be brought into compliance. The Hopkins Report[8] supports the common intuition that effective changes in defective or deficient corporate operating procedures cannot be expected as a result of fines, though more data is needed where fines are truly stiff. Hence, the courts must wait for repetitions before more effective sanctions are utilized according to the ABA proposal.

If interventionism is too limited and injects the government too much and too deeply into corporate life (as does the ABA continuing oversight sanction) and fines are often ineffective, is there a better way to guarantee an appropriate corporate response to its harm-causing behavior? I think there is. The common assumption in the Stone and ABA approaches is that the courts can examine corporate responses to the commission of criminal offenses only by inserting themselves in the corporate decision process. That assumption, however, ignores the alternative of requiring convicted corporations to file compliance reports that detail their own internal responses to the offense. Judicial intervention could, and should, be held in abeyance, to be used only if the corporation's own reaction is judged unsatisfactory. I call this approach Enforced Corporate Responsive Adjustment (ECRA).

ECRA brings PRA to bear on the judicial handling of corporate offenses. It demands an adjustment in the legal framework for dealing with the majority of such offenses. A two-stage judicial hearing procedure is required. In the initial stage the issue before the court will be whether the *actus reus* of an offense was committed on behalf of (or by) the corporate defendant. Once that is established to the satisfaction of the court, the defendant corporation will be required to prepare a compliance report that spells out what steps it has taken or will take by way of internal discipline, modification of existing compliance procedures, and, as appropriate, compensation to victims. The second stage of the judicial procedure will determine whether the corporate offender has satisfactorily responded to its harm causing or risk imposing (as established at the first trial stage). If adequate measures have been taken to adjust, the corporation will be acquitted. If not, the corporation will be convicted on the basis of PRA and be liable to a variety of further penal sanctions that could include extreme forms of interventionism and judicial supervision. What is important is that use of such drastic violations of the integrity of the corporate internal decision structure will be contingent on the corporate defendant's own failure, intentional and/or deliberate, to make a responsive adjustment to insure that there are no repetitions of its harm-causing behavior.

In short, ECRA preserves managerial freedom, as long as the court is satisfied that effective responsive adjustment has been undertaken. In notable ways ECRA is a cousin of John Braithwaite's model of Enforced Self-Regulation,[9] in which corporations are required to formulate their own regulatory standards and intervention is restricted to the development and enforcement of overarching principles and social goals. ECRA is not so sweeping. It requires corporate offenders to formulate their own reactive programs in response to specific violations. ECRA has the virtue of minimizing state intervention while not, as in the case of fines, excluding it altogether. It has the virtue of placing the onus of managerial alterations on shoulders both best trained and most likely to be effective in bearing it: the managers of the firm. This then responds to the fact, also noted by Braithwaite and Fisse, that though there probably are some fundamental, minimal requirements for effective corporate compliance systems, the variables differ greatly from corporation to corporation without necessarily affecting the compliant outcome. Furthermore ECRA will not be restricted to only the more serious and/or repeated offenses. The lesser offenses will be more effectively dealt with by ECRA than by purely monetary sanctions.

The application of ECRA will undoubtedly produce a hue and cry because it does acquit an offending corporation that "cleans up its act" in response to its harm causing. But it would be a greater shortcoming, I think, if we were to adopt a theory of sanctions that undermines our "commitment to the moral force of the criminal law"[10] by breaking all links to intentionality. ECRA preserves that link and thereby blocks the move to stricter and stricter liability offenses. The downside is that corporate offenders may be perceived as getting a free "first bite of the apple." It might be thought that a significant amount of harm will escape punishment. In the criminal sense that is strictly true, but ECRA is not recommended as a principle in tort law. Hence, existing grounds for suit in tort, including punitive damages, are available to victims. It is imaginable that ECRA could be put to excellent use as the limiter/regulator of punitive damages in tort. It would then effect some desirable tort reform. Certainly it will be the case that the so-called first bite is not taken without producing a desired effect: a change in procedures and/or policies within a corporation that has committed a criminal offense.

The adoption of the responsive adjustment time-frame approach corrects some nasty problems with the due diligence defense. Recall the first case cited from the *Corporate Crime Reporter*: a Los Angeles construction company was indicted for felony manslaughter. A worker died in a cave-in at the construction site. He was cleaning dirt out of trenches when an embankment collapsed, burying him. The indictment charged that the soils engineer's report was grossly inadequate because he did not recommend shoring for a vertical cut. It also charged that the excavation contractor had informed the general contractor about safety concerns, but no shoring was installed. This is not a strict liability offense, and so it might admit a defense of due diligence. The offense revolves around not taking due care to prevent the harm. What standard of due diligence or care would have been relevant in a proactive time frame? Would it really have been adequate to the situation?

Due diligence purports to impart an objective standard of care which takes the practices prevailing in the industry as a benchmark. That objective standard may be adjusted to meet the needs of particular circumstances, but there are clear limits on the amount of alteration allowable, as the standard must still be applicable across the industry. Another problem is that in many industries no generally accepted standard for a compliance system exists. Still, if a customary compliance system does exist in the industry and the corporate defendant has adopted it, should that exculpate the corporation?

Suppose, from a proactive point of view, that the Los Angeles construction firm had met all of the safety standards normally upheld by construction firms in that area. It exercised due diligence and, according to the traditional theory, should be acquitted of the manslaughter charges. If it did nothing to change its excavation methods after the first death and industry standards have not appreciably changed, and another death occurs in similar circumstances, it could again plead due diligence and should again look forward to acquittal. But something surely is wrong. Due diligence, proactively understood, flies in the face of basic intuitions about justice. If the industry standard does not set the benchmark on which the plea rests, then a corporate offender is not provided with clear prior notice of conduct subject to criminal liability. Furthermore, if a court should determine that the industry standard was set too low, then good faith compliance with the standard may not shield a corporation from criminal liability. What then happens to fundamental fairness? It is surely unjust to disallow a due diligence plea on the grounds that the corporation should have anticipated a failure in its procedures that only came to light in the industry after the injury occurred. Also, the advance specification of acceptable standards only invites the search for loopholes.[11]

The proactive due diligence defense cannot help but pull the standard down to a common denominator level that would put the force of the law behind older, traditional compliance technology. No legal incentives would be provided for corporations to find innovative solutions or to apply state-of-the-art techniques to prevent harm. Law tied to a proactive time frame for offenses is stuck in a dangerous rut that deprives potential victims of adequate protection. It can extricate itself only by imposing higher standards that the defendant can rightly claim "descend from the blue." Legal/moral deficiencies with due diligence also arise because existing industry standards lack particularity, thus inviting myriad interpretations by company lawyers.

In measuring the significance of these problems, account should be taken of various ways in which they are now minimized. First, standards tailored to individual corporations have been imposed under an injunction or consent order. This is not uncommon in the enforcement of antitrust laws, securities regulations, and corruption offenses.[12] Second, broad standards of due care for an industry have been made more precise by using injunctions to crystallize their meaning and application to particular situations.[13] Third, some dynamic thrust has been shown to be possible through the imaginative use of negotiation and bargaining in enforcement,[14] prospective standard setting in judicial decisions,[15] and administrative techniques for inducing technological change (like forced technology through offsets against penalties[16]). These methods are valuable, but they do not provide rules of criminal liability that are particularistic rather than universalistic, focused rather than rife with loopholes, and dynamic rather than static or, at best, tortuously incremental.

However, standard setting (in conjunction with ECRA) that is dominated by a reactive time frame overcomes the problems. Using the ECRA model, a corpo-

rate offender would be required to produce a compliance report in which it spec-
ifies the standards it will attempt to meet in response to its harm causing. Standard setting is then neither a cataloging of routine prevention nor an excursion
into possible world scenarios. The standards are tailored both to the particular
corporation and its activities, but also to the particular case that exposed its de-
cision-structure weaknesses. The old due diligence defense would not succeed,
even if the company could not have foreseen the harm produced by following
the existing standards of the industry. In fact, due diligence and due care would
have a small or no role to play.

ECRA provides fair notice of criminal prohibitions while eliminating loop-
hole-prone rules. The focus is shifted from industry-wide standards which may, in
fact, be too low (the harmful result is evidence that they may indeed be too low)
to the adequacy or inadequacy of the corporate offender's response to the need to
develop a higher standard of care. Proactive due diligence, as noted above, im-
poses static and often undemanding requirements of care. ECRA, unconfined to
ex ante due diligence, extends to the care that *should be* taken regardless of the
existing industry standard, and so it is more dynamic and demanding, often perhaps requiring state-of-the-art technology to satisfy its demands. ECRA then
works to reduce the tension between stability-inducing rules of law and the rapidly changing corporate, technological, and social world to which they are to be
applied.

In addition to the advantages of the ECRA approach that I have cited, there
is also a moral/social payoff. ECRA should bring exemplary corporate responsive
adjustments to the attention of the general public and instill models of good
corporate citizenship across an industry.

Because the emphasis in ECRA is on the way the offending corporation's
actions will be seen subsequent to its harm causing, ECRA responds well to
the shame-based morality characteristic of the contemporary corporate scene.
Shame is a visual concept that relates to the way actions look to others, but its
effectiveness depends on a certain degree of self-respect. To be shameable one
must want to maintain a certain level of social acceptability or reputation: an
essential element of most business. This leads to the third way to look innova-
tively at problems with corporate criminal liability: penal sanctions.

The proactive time-frame commitment that has governed most thinking
about corporate criminality produces a bias toward the adoption of the notion of
vicarious liability, which locks the judicial system, by and large, into a very restricted number of applicable sanctions, dominated by fines. Fines have been
used because, viewed from the proactive perspective, it is seldom possible to
prove that a corporation committed the *actus reus* of an offense with the appro-

priate corporate *mens rea*. Boilerplate compliance policies, as noted earlier, are intended to display the absence of the corporate *mens rea*. For example, they typically tell us that the corporation only engages in legal activities. With access to the corporate *mens rea* effectively blocked, many U.S. jurisdictions have adopted the vicarious liability approach for corporate cases. All that is required is demonstrable fault on the part of an employee acting on behalf of the corporation. The *mens rea* of a manager or employee is typically easier to expose, of course, than corporate intentionality, and no published policy of compliance will serve as a shield.

Vicarious liability, as Fisse has argued, "projects a noninterventionist attitude toward corporate decision making."[17] No wonder it is championed by the staunchest defenders of free enterprise. The emphasis in vicarious liability is almost solely on the state of mind of a single representative, rather than on the corporate internal decision structure. Avoidance of interventionism, conjoined with the historical relationship between vicarious liability and vicarious tortious liability, generates the bias in favor of momentary remedies of damages and the offending corporation's identification of fines with enterprise costs.

Fines, however, have serious limitations and can be passed on to blameless populations in the form of higher prices, layoffs, and so forth. Although the 1973 report of the Task Force on Corrections of the National Advisory Commission on Criminal Justice Standards and Goals found the fine "far less costly to the public, and perhaps more effective than imprisonment or community service,"[18] fines against most corporations have proven to have little deterrent capacity. The problem of easy affordability is exacerbated by the fact that many corporations can recoup fines by raising prices or reducing production costs. Both Oliver Wendell Holmes, Jr.,[19] and H. L. A. Hart[20] noted that though there is a difference, or should be, between a fine and a tax, in many cases the line between the two becomes so blurred it disappears. In most corporate criminal cases drawing the line may be extremely difficult in practice. Taxes are often imposed to discourage activities that have not been made criminal. "Conversely, fines payable for some criminal offenses . . . become so small [in relation to the offender's income] that they are cheerfully paid and offenses are frequent. They are then felt to be mere taxes because the sense is lost that the rule is meant to be taken seriously as a standard of behavior."[21]

Interventionist sanctions, such as punitive injunctions, are not so easily assimilated. But some noninterventionist sanctions should prove almost equally successful in producing the desired alteration in corporate procedures and policies. Furthermore, at least one of those can be derived directly from the previously mentioned shame base in morality with which ECRA is compatible: court ordered and directed adverse publicity, or what I have elsewhere called, the Hester Prynne Sanction after the central character of Hawthorne's *Scarlet Letter*.[22]

If the proactive time-frame approach is in force and we are blocked from adequate information about the "corporateness" of the *actus reus* of the offense, the implementation of an adverse publicity sanction may appear to be too severe and thereby unwarranted. Fines seem the only justifiable option. However, by shifting to the ECRA approach, corporate policies and procedures are no longer shielded, and so willful, deliberate noncompliance by the corporate offender may be exposed and the offending corporation appropriately targeted for Hester Prynne or other innovative sanctions.

I agree with some of my most fervent critics, particularly John Ladd,[23] who see Hester Prynne as a drastic punishment, an ideal of ignominy and disgrace, and an assault on image and even identity. That is exactly why it is so devastating and hence effective in the corporate world. It attacks the heart of business: reputation. But that is also why it should only be used when there is no doubt as to the corporate offender's criminality. ECRA insures that condition is met.

I do not champion Hester Prynne over other types of sanctions in corporate criminal cases. I only argue that the innovative noninterventionist sanctions that a number of legal theorists have proposed as alternatives to fines, because they promise to be more effective in producing compliance, will be supported by far more reliable sentencing data if ECRA replaces the proactive perspective in our corporate criminality theory.

Monetary sanctions are, at best, only oblique ways of changing defective corporate practices, though with some corporations and some crimes a monetary penalty may be sufficient to produce the desired change. There is, however, no need to settle on only one type of sanction. An incremental escalation strategy or a mix of sanctions should prove both efficient and effective. Stone's interventionism is among the more severe options, just short of revocation of business permits and corporate charters. Insofar as protection of the integrity of the corporate enterprise is and ought to be a major commitment of our society, intervention should only be used in extremely serious cases—where the sentencing data unequivocally demonstrates violation of PRA. Still, even in such cases, Fisse seems to favor punitive injunctions requiring recalcitrant corporate offenders to install state-of-the-art technology at accelerated speed, instead of interventions of the *Where the Law Ends* variety. Stone has moved further away from his early position to what he now calls a volunteerist approach intended to foster "a measure of mutual trust and respect" in corporate/social relations.[24]

Another advantage of the ECRA approach to corporate criminal liability is that it generates the desirable reliable sentencing facts. The focus of the crucial second phase of the ECRA trial is not on the *actus reus*, but on whether the company had failed to respond appropriately. That issue will be the subject of detailed evidence.

Furthermore, PRA helps to expose the need for sanctions capable of effecting a smooth transition between less and more drastic means of regulation. Suppose that a corporate offender has been subjected to a civil injunctive order stipulating that effective pollution control devices are to be installed in its plant. Efforts at compliance were made but then abandoned as a result of competing cost pressures. The company is held liable on the basis of PRA. Something needs to be done to ensure compliance, but imposing a fine is only an oblique method of making the company comply. Given the defendant's recalcitrance, issuing a further civil injunction would fail to capture the gravity of the reactive noncompliance. Fisse argues that the ideal sanction for both of these concerns is a punitive injunction requiring not only that the defendant corporation install the necessary device, but also that it do so in some punitively demanding and constructive way (at accelerated speed, for example, or by going beyond state-of-the-art technology).[25]

Two major objections to ECRA should be raised: that it is prone to be too lenient and that it will be inefficient. The first objection is that "first free bite of the apple" mentioned earlier. As Clinard and Yeager[26] have demonstrated, negotiated settlement is the most commonly used method of applying sanctions in cases of corporate criminality today. Big chunks of the apple are regularly devoured and no fines assessed. However, it would be a complete misunderstanding were one to think that ECRA allows a free first bite. For any corporate offense ECRA requires a responsive adjustment from the corporation that may be very costly. In the absence of a satisfactory response, it would also require injunctions, adverse publicity orders, and other recommended measures. The pressure and costs brought to bear on the convicted corporate offender could well exceed any simple monetary penalty.

The second objection is a bit more challenging. It would argue that ECRA is inefficient because it will impose significant burdens of investigation, supervision, and management on the justice system. Admittedly, these kinds of cost factors will increase under ECRA, and surely they will be more costly than the application of totally noninterventionist monetary sanctions. How can they be justified as alternatives to fines?

The simple answer is that

> the level of fines required to satisfy the economic calculus for the deterrence of serious corporate offenses is so high as to be beyond the resources of

most corporate offenders, and hence we need to resort to alternative means of social control that, although regrettably more costly in terms of enforcement resources, is more likely to achieve effective prevention of unwanted harms.[27]

A more complex answer challenges the very basic assumptions of the Posner-led economic analysis of law. In effect, it challenges the application of the economic calculus to the problem in the first place. Applying the calculus requires one to make probability predictions with respect to the occurrence of harm, the extent and gravity of that harm, and the chances of detection and conviction. John Byrne and Steven Hoffman have persuasively argued that such calculations at the level of exactitude required are impossible in corporate cases.[28] Furthermore, the calculus method assumes "a unified managerial rationality" that is a figment of the economist's imagination. Skepticism about the results of these economic analyses would seem to be in order. Even if we admit the probabilistic calculation method as our guide to the development of an efficient general criminal liability system, two rules of thumb emerge when it is impossible, as in the corporate cases, to adequately assess the required probabilities. Fisse and I have framed those two rules[29] in the following way: (1) develop proscriptions based on considered assessments of the nature of unwanted harms in society; and (2) use fault concepts and sanctions geared to provoke responsive corporate reactions to violations of those proscriptions.

I leave it to other moral and social philosophers to tell us what should fall under the first rule. Doing so is to tell us what the social world ought to look like and how it ought to function. With respect to corporate offenders, ECRA meets the demands of the first part of the second rule, while an innovative mix of sanctions (including Hester Prynne and punitive injunctions) should respond to its second part.

17 · The Responsibilities of Military Law, or How to Make Military Justice Just

In Title 1 of Book II of the *Theodosian Code* the issue of jurisdiction is tackled. The second edict under that title, attributed to Emperor Constantius Augustus on July 25, 355, contains the following: "In criminal cases, if any person in the imperial service should prosecute an accused person, the governor of the province shall try the case. If it should be affirmed that any military man has committed *any crime* (italics mine), it shall be tried by the person to whom the direction of military affairs has been entrusted."[1]

The accompanying interpretation of Constantius Augustus's edict, supplied by the Theodosian scholars, made crystal clear the intent and force of the edict. It was that civil cases and military cases were to be treated as falling under separate jurisdictions. If a private citizen brought criminal charges against a military person, the case was heard before military superiors. Only if the military person initiated an action against a private citizen was the case removed to the civilian courts. Furthermore, the only two kinds of cases in which the military person was assured of the same outcome as the civilian were established in the next entry in the *Code*: "forceful violation of the chastity of anyone" and robbery. All other cases were apparently left to the wisdom of the courts-martial.

It is not difficult to imagine why the Romans and most of the societies that succeeded them have maintained a distinction between civilian and military justice. Discipline, which usually translates to "obedience to superiors," surely is essential to successful military operations. It is commonly believed that direct access to nonmilitary courts and civilian rights protections could lead to difficult command situations. The military has been traditionally viewed as a body of persons apart from the ordinary members of society. Since the earliest times, the maintenance of a self-contained judicial control has been seen by the military hierarchy as crucial, if not essential, to good order, high morale, and the self-

178

discipline of the service person. In other words, it is believed (and stated in the Naval Institute's comprehensive work on *Military Law*[2]) that military justice is intended to promote a certain state of mind in the individual serviceperson, "so that he (or she) will instantly obey a lawful order, no matter how unpleasant or dangerous the task may be. . . . In this way, law supports the military mission, which it must do if the nation's freedom is to be protected and preserved."[3]

Congressional enactments are almost the exclusive source of American military law. Congressional responsibility and authority are derived from section 8, Article I of the Constitution, in which Congress is empowered to raise, support, and maintain army and naval forces and to govern those employed in military service by making all laws "necessary and proper."

From 1789 to 1862 Congress enacted several pieces of legislation in the area of naval law. The common characteristic of these statutes was that each aimed at decreasing naval law's dependence on British maritime customs and the common law. In 1862 Congress passed the "Articles for the Government of the Navy" ("Rocks and Shoals"). These were superseded in 1951 by the Uniform Code of Military Justice (hereafter UCMJ).

The history of American army law is comparable, if more active, than its naval counterpart. The British Articles of War (1765), which contained a section on military justice, were the model for the first American military code, adopted by the Continental Congress in 1775. That code was revised in 1776 into the American Articles of War, which remained in force until 1806, when a new code was adopted. That code was superseded by the Articles of War of 1874. They were in turn replaced by new articles in 1917, then again in 1921 and 1948. The Uniform Code superseded the 1948 articles and was made applicable to all branches of the armed services. In 1962 the Uniform Code was amended, and in 1968 it was significantly altered by the Military Justice Act. In 1969 the executive branch, in the name of the president, drafted the *Manual for Courts-Martial*, directives that implement the UCMJ.

The Constitution is the authoritative source of American military law, just as it is the source of the authority of the president, Congress, and the Supreme Court. It is of interest that in the UCMJ Congress delegates its constitutional authority in substantial areas of military justice to the president. Article 36 is of particular import. It reads:

Pretrial, trial, and post-trial procedures, including modes of proof for cases arising under this chapter triable in courts-martial, military commissions, and other military tribunals and procedures for courts of inquiry, may be prescribed by the President by regulations which shall, so far as he considers practicable, apply the principles of law and the rules of evidence generally recognized in the trial of criminal cases in the United States district courts, but which may not be contrary to or inconsistent with this chapter.

Article 36 of the UCMJ thereby empowers the president to create the *Manual*. Article 56 further delegates to the president the authority to set the maximum punishments for violations of the Code. It has been argued, though without vigor, that Congress cannot constitutionally transfer its powers in this area to the executive branch, so both the UCMJ and the *Manual for Courts-Martial* should be declared unconstitutional. There is little reason, however, to pursue this argument, for it is most unlikely that the titanic military justice system will founder on such an ice cube. Our focus from the point of view of responsibility should be on the difficulties that have been associated with the attempt to reconcile military justice with the provisions of the Constitution.

Two problems for the constitutionalist confronting military law seem prominent, even dominant. One is jurisdictional, and the other concerns the extent to which constitutional rights and protections can and ought to be available to those accused under the UCMJ and standing trial in the military justice system. Many if not most of those rights are not encoded in military law. The jurisdictional and rights issues are entangled in a number of landmark military law cases of both the Supreme Court and the Court of Military Appeals (CoMA). I will tell a story that interrelates a few of those cases and highlights the constitutional development. But first it is important to remember that in the struggle to "constitutionalize" military law there are (and have been) two main combatants. I refrain from identifying them with political positions, because matters of constitutionality where the military is concerned are political footballs. Conservatives might be expected to champion only that level of constitutional protection that is consistent with full-fledged support of the defense establishment. On the other hand, support of personal constitutional rights has frequently been a conservative rallying cry. In any event, I am uncomfortable with trying to pin political labels on the polar positions. Suffice it to say that on the one side a military law in which constitutional protections are not provided is defended (perhaps on utilitarian grounds) as essential to the constitutional purpose of the military. This argument typically contains the claim that armed service personnel must forego the constitutional protections of civilians in order that those protections can be preserved for civilians. The constitutionalist's position, on the other hand, argues that military law not only ought to incorporate the rights and protections of the Constitution, except perhaps in time of war, but that military law must be absorbed into the federal court system where constitutional remedies will be available to military personnel as part of our fundamental law. Francis X. Gindhart, clerk of the Court of Military Appeals (CoMA) writes, "How ironic it is that the dedicated and valiant members of the armed forces, on whom we all ultimately depend to preserve and defend our constitutional government and way of life, must spend their own personal and professional lives in constitutional alienage."[4] The constitutionalist argues that entering military service ought not entail renouncing one's rights as an American.

As in most debates of this type, the middle ground, though severely trampled and shell-shocked, is regarded as uninhabitable without much investigation by the polar combatants. I think a story can be told in terms of CoMA cases that shows that our military justice system actually has been consistently moving to occupy the middle ground and, with one major adjustment, that ground should be viewed as the appropriate location with respect to responsibility, justice, equity, and fairness.

Because CoMA is a product of the UCMJ, it exists solely at the will of the Congress. (It is an Article I court.) The UCMJ states that CoMA decisions are final, and the Supreme Court has made only a few attempts since the early 1950s to intercede or supervise CoMA's administration of justice. Jurisdictional issues, however, have prompted the most significant constitutional attention. It is on such cases that I shall focus.

The 1955 case of *Toth v. Quarles*[5] is the earliest major decision after the UCMJ was enacted in which the Supreme Court intervened in a CoMA case. The confrontation was over Article 3(a) of the UCMJ. While serving as security guards on a post in Korea, Robert Toth and a fellow airman murdered a Korean. By the time the crime was discovered, Toth had been honorably discharged and returned to civilian life in Pittsburgh. Article 3(a) states that a person charged with an offense against the code while in military service can be tried by court-martial even though that person has left the service. The air police were sent to apprehend Toth and bring him back to Korea to stand trial. Toth's sister filed for a writ of habeas corpus in federal district court in Washington, D.C., claiming that Article 3(a) is unconstitutional.

The district court issued the writ on the grounds that the arresting officers had not followed the Federal Rules for Criminal Procedure since Toth had not been brought before a federal commissioner. The air force appealed. The court of appeals reversed the lower court decision and remanded Toth to air force custody. The appeals court's primary reason was that customarily an accused is subject to stand trial in the jurisdiction in which the offense was committed. (That, by the way, is a principle also spelled out in the *Codex Theodosianus*.[6]) Toth's sister was undeterred. She appealed to the Supreme Court, which ruled Article 3(a) unconstitutional.

The Supreme Court applied a jurisdictional test in *Toth*, but not the Theodosian test of location of the crime. Instead of the facts of the offense being the determining factor, the status of the accused was made the central test for jurisdiction. The Supreme Court (by a 6-3 margin) found that Toth lacked the requisite status because he had been honorably discharged, so he "could not constitutionally be subjected to trial by court- martial." He was set free.

Associate Justice Hugo Black's opinion for the majority contained a number of relevant points. He maintained that the assertion of military authority over civilians cannot rest on the president's powers nor on any theory of martial law. The Fifth Amendment, he argued, does not grant to Congress court-martial power with respect to the due process clause. Furthermore, Black stated that considerations of military discipline cannot warrant the expansion of military legal jurisdiction at the expense of the constitutionally preferable system of trial by jury. All civilians, including ex-service personnel, must have all benefits afforded by the constitutional (Article III) courts.[7]

In effect, Black was voicing for the majority of the Court the view that military law was not good enough for civilians, even if it suffices, given the need to maintain discipline, for those in the armed services. Associate Justices Reed and Minton wrote dissenting views. Reed's opinion ostensibly focused on the heinous character of the crime and on the fact that it would now go unpunished, but beneath the surface was the jurisdictional issue. "If Congress enacts the substitute law as the Court suggests [i.e., trial by federal district court] . . . the accused must face a jury far removed from the scene of the alleged crime and before jurors without the understanding of the quality and character of a military crime. . . . Or perhaps those accused will be extradited and tried by foreign law."[8]

The elements that fueled Reed's opinion are obvious. He defined jurisdiction not primarily in terms of status, but traditionally, in terms of the location of the crime. Secondly, he opted for a United States military court rather than trial under a foreign legal code. We may assume that Reed believed that military law is more likely to protect a U.S. citizen's rights than is any foreign legal system. He was probably right, at least with respect to many countries in which the U.S. military has a presence. Although there are, as mentioned above, no constitutional protections in military justice, many of the rights associated with the Constitution are available to armed service personnel, and some of the provisions for the accused in the civilian courts, such as representation by counsel, are arguably better supplied in the military courts.

Toth was used by the attorney for Dorothy Krueger Smith to gain a Supreme Court reversal of a court-martial sentence against her. Dorothy Smith, a civilian, murdered her husband, a colonel, while they were stationed in Japan. She was tried by court-martial under Article 2(11) of the UCMJ and convicted. Her attorney filed for a writ of habeas corpus. The Supreme Court consolidated the case with a similar one from Europe (*Reid v. Covert*) and on June 11, 1956, decided (5-4) not to intervene. Justice Clark, writing for the majority, maintained that Americans accompanying our troops overseas "would enjoy greater protections under the UCMJ than in foreign courts."[9]

Mrs. Smith's attorney petitioned for a rehearing, which was granted. After the new hearing on June 10, 1957, the Court reversed its earlier decision. Justice Black wrote the principal opinion, arguing that the Constitution only permits Congress to regulate land and naval forces, not those who might have some relationship with them. No statute, Black maintained, can be framed to force a civilian to submit to court-martial. He noted the constitutional inadequacies of military law: no trial by jury, no indictment by grand jury, no Bill of Rights protections.

There can be little doubt that in 1957 the Supreme Court had good reason to denigrate military justice. But military law did not remain intransigent in the face of constitutional criticism. The CoMA case of *Jacoby* in 1960 marks a significant move towards the Constitution.

Loretta Jacoby was an airman third class. She was convicted by a court-martial (a special, not a general, court-martial[10]) on charges of violating Article 134 of the UCMJ by bouncing checks. She received a bad-conduct discharge, forfeiture of $70 per month for four months, confinement at hard labor for four months, and reduction to the grade of basic airman. The issue on which the CoMA decision on her appeal turned was whether "it was proper to receive in evidence certain dispositions taken upon written interrogatories over the accused's objection that she was thereby denied her constitutional right to be confronted by the witnesses against her."[11]

Over the objections of Jacoby's attorney, three bank officials testified against Jacoby by written deposition. The trial counsel cited two CoMA decisions [*Sutton* (1953) and *Parrish* (1956)] as stare decisis for permitting the admission of written depositions even though the accused and her counsel were not present at the time the depositions were taken. CoMA Judge Ferguson noted that Jacoby's position had merit and that "in the light of the Constitution" he was convinced that CoMA had "erred in so giving effect to the doctrine of *stare decisis*"[12] (with respect to *Sutton* and *Parrish*). He went on to argue that though stare decisis generally ought to apply, it should not "perpetrate a mistaken view" in military law, especially when it stands in direct opposition to both the letter and the spirit of the Constitution. In *Jacoby* (as well as *Sutton* and *Parrish*) the Sixth Amendment right that guarantees the accused a chance to confront the witnesses was clearly abridged.

Ferguson writes, quoting from the Supreme Court decision in the *Mattox* case (1895):

> The substance of [the Sixth Amendment's] . . . protection is preserved to the prisoner in the advantage he had once had of seeing the witness face to face, and of subjecting him to the ordeal of cross-examination. This, the law says, he shall under no circumstances be deprived of, and many of the very cases which hold testimony such as this to be admissible also hold that not the substance of his testimony only, but the very words of the witness, shall be proven.[13]

The majority in *Jacoby* ruled that with respect to Article 49, the UCMJ conflicted with the Sixth Amendment. They reversed the finding of the review board on Jacoby's court-martial and ordered that the case be returned to the judge advocate general of the air force to determine whether a new court-martial proceeding against the accused would be initiated.

CoMA did a number of significant things with *Jacoby*, but perhaps the most important was to identify the Constitution, with respect to rights, as overriding expediency and the UCMJ. In effect, it ruled that the UCMJ has to pass constitutional muster and, as in the case of Article 49, it frequently cannot do so.

The *Jacoby* decision was not, however, a unanimous one. Judge Latimer wrote the dissenting opinion. He strongly objected to what he called the "civilianizing" of the interpretation of military justice—to warping "the Code to make military law on all fours with civilian law."[14] The military, Latimer argued, cannot be removed from military law; hence there must be a "fundamental distinction between the two." The Constitution, he maintained, "entrusted to Congress the task of striking a precise balance between the rights of men in service and the overriding demands of discipline and duty."[15] It is of some note that though Latimer expressed such a sweeping defense of the separation of the courts doctrine, he actually justified his dissent in *Jacoby* on the narrow point that the evidence gathered in the interrogatories was redundant because the accused had herself testified to its truth during the trial. Nonetheless, Latimer endorsed the traditionalist's view that Article 49 properly relieves the military of the onerous burden of transporting the accused under guard in the company of attorneys to take depositions at locations remote from the base at which the court-martial is

to occur. (The traditionalist's view is that given the frequency of military personnel relocations, the costs of prosecuting run-of-the-mill offenses could become
excessive; hence, many crimes might go unpunished and the disciplinary structure of the military could be severely weakened as a result.) Even Latimer allowed that if the accused could demonstrate before the convening authority that
"the taking of depositions might make it impossible for him to defend [himself]
properly,"[16] relief from Article 49 could be granted. That had not been the case in
Jacoby; hence, Latimer argued, the lower court decision should have been affirmed.

The major effect of *Jacoby* was the further extension of the Constitution over
the UCMJ. Nufer writes, "The Opinion of the Court declared that Article 49 of
the UCMJ *infringed* on a servicemember's *inherent* rights under the Sixth Amendment: that anyone, whether civilian or military, should be able to 'confront witnesses against him.' "[17] Simply, *Jacoby* establishes that constitutional relief is always available to the accused serviceperson who feels his or her basic liberties
and rights have been unduly restricted or abridged by military law. It is especially
noteworthy that it was the highest military court, not a civilian court, that put
forth this doctrine. The military courts were shoving military law into the middle
ground.

The story continues into the mid-seventies with the watershed case of *McCarthy* (1976), in which CoMA had to determine the extent to which military justice extends into the civilian community when the accused is a soldier and the
offense occurs off post. Again, the issue was jurisdictional.

McCarthy was convicted in a general court-martial at Fort Campbell, Ken-
tucky, of selling marijuana to a fellow soldier outside the gate of the fort. McCarthy contended that the offense was not service connected and so not properly
heard in a military court. He cited the Supreme Court's 5-3 decision in *O'Callahan v. Parker*[18] in which the court held that a service member is entitled to a
civilian court for crimes that are not service-connected. In the civilian system,
the Supreme Court stressed that the service member's constitutional rights to a
grand jury indictment and trial by jury are protected. The court maintained, "the
expansion of military discipline beyond its proper domain is a threat to liberty"[19]
and "courts-martial are singularly inept in dealing with the nice subtleties of constitutional law."[20] The *O'Callahan* decision produced a series of criteria for determining whether or not an offense was service connected: the service member
must have been properly absent from the base when the crime was committed;
the crime must have been committed in the United States during peacetime, and
off base in an area not under military control; there must be no connection between the accused's military duties and the crime; there must be an available

civilian court in which the case can be prosecuted; and the alleged crime must not involve a threat to the military post or military property.

CoMA had to admit that the fact that McCarthy was a soldier was not sufficient to establish the service connection, but it added a new factor to the *O'Callahan* criteria: "whether the military interest in deterring the offense is distinct from and greater than that of civilian society and whether the military interest can be vindicated adequately in civilian courts."[21] This turned out to be a reformulation of the old argument against assuring that constitutional protections are provided to the military personnel because of the potential disruption of authority and discipline.

CoMA ruled that despite the fact that McCarthy apparently passed the *O'Callahan* tests, he was properly tried in a court- martial. It set forth two sets of reasons (actually two different opinions, one by Chief Judge Fletcher and one from Judge Cook) in support of the same result. Fletcher accepted the Supreme Court's *O'Callahan* criteria as governing jurisdiction but went on to argue that *McCarthy* did not meet the criteria in crucial ways. According to Fletcher the formation of the criminal intent must have occurred on the base, and there was a distinct threat to the military personnel by the introduction of marijuana to the base.

Judge Cook first attacked the earlier Supreme Court's denigration of the military courts. He argued that courts-martial members are "the functional equivalents of the jurors in a civilian criminal trial."[22] Hence, trial by jury was provided in the military courts. Judge Fletcher himself had decried such a preposterous claim, but Cook was undeterred. He sallied forth with the contention that the civilian courts are too lenient with respect to punishing marijuana trafficking, as is evident at rock concerts, so to let such courts prosecute military personnel would "foster disregard of and even contempt for the military prohibitions."[23] In other words, retreat to the necessity of maintaining discipline. Surely this argument demonstrates that the military interest in the case was distinct from the civilian.

Cook's opinion aside, the important step taken in *McCarthy* was that the highest military court acknowledged the superseding authority of the Supreme Court in jurisdictional matters—the relevance of the *O'Callahan* criteria. In so doing, it again limited the exercise of its own authority over those in uniform, edging further into the middle ground.

These cases cannot adequately represent almost four decades of military law decisions, but they do tell a coherent story of progress down a certain track undeterred by other decisions of either CoMA or the Supreme Court. The story is one of the "civilianization" (using Latimer's term) of military justice, or rather, it is the story of the rapid movement since the advent of the UCMJ toward constitutional protection during military prosecution. It is of note that these decisions do not call for recasting of the military law to include a military version of constitutional rights. Instead, they attest to the authority of the Constitution over the military justice system. In simple terms, they reject the notion that military law must be distinct from civilian law, regardless of what the old soldiers claim about discipline, responsibility, and morale.

But elements of these cases, and especially the *O'Callahan* criteria, suggest that there should be significant differences between military law and constitutional law. The military discipline argument has never been totally discredited, and it is not likely to be. Who can doubt that the military must have more control over the prerogatives of soldiers, sailors, and aviators than a wide-open extension of constitutional rights would permit? Few would disagree that in wartime fine points of constitutionalism cannot be allowed to deter or interfere with military action.

There is a major difficulty, however, with the wartime-necessity defense of the suspension of constitutional rights in military law. When is the military in a state of war? As is well known, the power to declare a state of war constitutionally resides with the Congress. Since World War II, however, there have been few periods when the American military was not in combat or stationed under arms in volatile regions where hostilities could erupt at any moment. One could argue that if there is no official state of war, then there is not sufficient legal reason to enforce substitution of military regulations for constitutional protections. The war-peace distinction crucial to such an argument is, for all practical purposes, a distinction without a difference. The age of executive-ordered engagements, missions, and alerts has been upon us for nearly five decades. Hence, if the military law defender (hereafter "militarist") is right that wartime conditions require strict adherence to the code, there is no room left for the constitutionalist. Still, we must not forget that the conditions of undeclared warfare that prompt support for the militarist's views are created by actions of the executive that are themselves of dubious constitutional status. One of the effects of the militarist's position, then, might be the destruction of the authority of the fundamental law of the land—the very law the military is maintained to protect.

I am afraid we owe this problem to the shortsightedness of the framers of the Constitution, for they seem not to have imagined that the country would have a large standing armed force in a time when no war has been declared. This could also explain why the framers say so little about military law and justice. The world they knew was one in which the military was only active in declared wars. Offenses committed within the ranks of the military were handled expeditiously, with little concern for the niceties of judicial review. Standing armed forces and a world spasmodically erupting in the kind of hostilities to which executive order is the only effective response may be so alien to the underlying conceptions of the Constitution that hope of salvaging constitutionality in military law becomes a pipe dream.

Since 1951 the military justice system has shown remarkable flexibility and little resistance to being molded by Supreme Court interventions on behalf of personal rights. But how far has military law really come? The case of Lieutenant William Calley [USCMA 534, 48 CMR (1973)] provided an excellent test. In 1971 Calley was found guilty in a general court-martial held at Fort Benning, Georgia, of the murder of 22 Vietnamese civilians in the village of My Lai. Calley's attorney went collateral by seeking a writ of habeas corpus from the U.S. District Court at Columbus, Georgia. The writ was obtained, and a federal judge ordered Calley released. The army refused to honor the order and appealed to the circuit court of appeals in New Orleans, which sustained the court-martial verdict. The army's primary reason for appealing the district court order was to derail a precedent that would have occurred: that a civilian court other than the Supreme Court could overrule a military court's decision. The Supreme Court refused to review the Calley conviction, thereby sustaining the verdict of the circuit court and the general court-martial.

The Calley case is important not only because the high court sustained the court-martial verdict, but also because collateral interference in the case by the civilian inferior court was disallowed. Of particular note is that *Calley* was one of the first cases to come to trial after the enactment of the Military Justice Act of 1968, which provided for independent single-officer courts and trained counsel for defendants. Calley's defense rested on the claim that he was following superiors' orders and that the massacre at My Lai was nothing more than an instance of ordinary army operations in Vietnam. It is unlikely that a defense of this type would have been used in a court-martial before 1968. The reason, as noted by Generous, is that until that time the law officer in a court-marital was appointed from the local staff judge advocate's office. "He was normally subject to the convening authority, [and] would risk his career if he permitted a defense such as the one Calley used."[24] Because the Military Justice Act made the military judge independent of command pressure, the door was opened for most any defense, even one intended to draw the military itself into the dock with the accused. This freedom granted to the military judge responded to Supreme Court complaints in *O'Callahan* about tribunals appointed by the very commander who had preferred the charges. Independent judges are not exactly jury trials, but they are laudable improvements on past procedures.

Much more important to the reform of military law than the independence of the judges would be placing all offenses in the armed services within the jurisdiction of the reformed UCMJ. Even critics agree that "once a GI's case reaches a point where the Uniform Code takes over, he will be treated about as fairly as he might be on any other jurisdiction."[25] Requiring that all cases, whether they involve senior officers or buck privates, be brought before a court-martial would create a much fairer system. As it stands, senior officers can often avoid court-martial for offenses for which lower ranking service members stand trial.

Suggestions like the change of jurisdiction, though practical, do not go to the heart of the issue. They do a little interior decorating within the military justice system, but they do not confront the major constitutional inadequacies cited by the Supreme Court. Intuitively, it seems irresponsible and unfair to subject those in the armed service of their country to a legal code that is basically alien to all of their previous legal experiences. A simple distinction is sometimes drawn to defeat this objection. The armed forces are usually composed of two different types of servicepersons: those who entered the military by free enlistment and those who are conscripted. Although the draft now is inactive, registration is still required, and the draft may be revived if conditions warrant it. Therefore the distinction does not seem to be an artificial one. Those who volunteered for military service of their own free will, it can be argued, expressly agreed to abide by the rules and regulations of the armed forces, including the UCMJ. That commitment should stand, this argument continues, despite the fact that it means losing some or even all of the constitutional protections of ordinary citizens. Enlistees should be viewed as responsible adults contracting, in part, to be bound to the decisions of an alternative way of resolving disputes, the UCMJ. The model here might be a private arbitration court to which parties to a conflict submit their cases and agree to be bound by the arbitrator's judgment without recourse to the federal system and its rights. The idea is that of justice between consenting adults based on contract. The only segment of the military for whom the constitutional inadequacies of the UCMJ might need to be remedied, then, are those who did not freely accept the authority of the code: those who were conscripted.

But this argument bounds too fast and too far. We may imagine two sorts of arguments put forth to buttress the significance of the enlistment/conscription distinction. The first was suggested above: that a contractual relationship exists for the enlistee that has the effect of superseding the constitutional protections. This argument looks specious. Admittedly there are superficial similarities between ordinary contractual relationships and enlistments. However, the conditions crucial to supporting the conclusion that the enlistee gets what he or she contracted for are missing. For example, it is a cornerstone of the theory of contract that contracts without consideration are legally unenforceable. Consideration in contract is typically seen as a benefit conferred by the promisee on the promisor or a detriment incurred by the promisee. In fact, as Holmes noted, "It is . . . thought that every consideration may be reduced to a case of the latter sort, using the word 'detriment' in a somewhat broad sense."[26] In enlistment, who is the promisor? Who the promisee? It seems reasonable to say that the enlistee promises to serve the military and abide by the UCMJ: that would make the enlistee the promisor conferring a benefit upon the military. After all, the enlistee usually initiates the relationship. The television recruitment spots would only constitute binding offers to the general public if they were clear, definite, and explicit and leave nothing open for negotiation and show that some performance was promised in positive terms in return for something requested. Could a navy enlistee sue for breach of contract if he joined because, after seeing the ad, he decided he wanted to see the world and yet he was never stationed outside of Norfolk, Virginia (which happens to be his hometown)? In enlistment, what is the detriment incurred by the military? This business begins to stretch the normal notions of contract well out of fit. Holmes rejected the account of consideration in terms of benefits and detriments. In its place he offered the "bargain theory," the view that "the root of the whole matter [of consideration] is the relation of reciprocal conventional inducement, each for the other, between consideration and promise."[27] Here again, however, the enlistment situation only satisfies the criteria if we perform semantic gymnastics. An enlistment may surely have elements of reciprocal inducement, especially in times of peace and an all volunteer force, but they are far from essential to the enlistment. A private citizen motivated by patriotism, or perhaps by poverty, wanders into a recruitment center and signs up for three years in the army. Maybe the army has induced this person by posters and slick advertisements, but how has he or she induced the army? By being able-bodied? The more one tries to fit the situation into the conventional contract scenario, the further from conventional it moves, and that is not to ignore the fact that the army provides food, shelter, training, and pay in return for service.

I do not argue that enlistment does not create a binding responsibility relationship. It surely does. But it seems to do so outside of contract law. When the army prosecutes an AWOL soldier, it does not plead breach of contract. That is one of the reasons military law was created.

It might be further argued (though I think the point of doing so is now lost) that even if enlistment creates a contract, that contract cannot place one of the parties (the enlistee) outside the realm of basic constitutional rights, even voluntarily. It cannot alienate the enlistee from the fundamental protections of the basic law of the society. Contract law neither is, nor should be, that powerful.

The second sort of argument that might be set forth to buttress the enlistment/conscription distinction under military law associates military service with ordinary employment. There seems to be a good deal of value in thinking in such terms about the military. The soldier does have something like an employment relationship to the army. But if we press this too far, we will be in danger of losing the distinction between mercenaries (for whom the contractual description is most clearly appropriate) and soldiers. Still, if we say that enlistees are, in important ways, seeking employment in the military, we might go so far as to invoke an assumption of risk doctrine to cover their dealings with the code.

Enlistees should know, it might be argued, that while in service they will be governed by the UCMJ. They assume the risk that is coincident with the loss of constitutional protections. Drafted soldiers do not assume such a risk, as they did not seek association with the military.

The old doctrine of assumption of risk was captured in *Farwell v. The Boston and Worcester Rail Road Corporation* (1842) by Chief Justice Shaw of the Supreme Judicial Court of Massachusetts. "The general rule, resulting from considerations as well of justice as of policy, is, that he who engages in the employment of another for the performance of specified duties and services . . . takes upon himself the natural and ordinary risks and perils incident to the performance of such services."[28] The test is whether the employment was voluntary and whether the perils were likely to be known to the employee. In *Pouliot v. Black* (1960), the Massachusetts court affirmed the doctrine: "As a matter of law, by his voluntary conduct in exposing himself to a known and appreciated risk, plaintiff assumed the risk."[29]

One might wonder if the risks the enlistee assumes when entering the military should include those of its judicial system. The enlistee, we may suppose, is well aware of the dangers of combat and accepts those, but should the doctrine be extended to the administration of the UCMJ's brand of justice?

If we were to apply the assumption of risk doctrine to the enlistee, consider what we would have to do with the conscripted soldier. The draftee certainly did not voluntarily assume any risks, yet in combat and during other military duties there is almost no way to distinguish the risk assumers from those who did not assume the risk. Should draftees have the right to remedies that enlistees do not when work conditions produce injuries?

The assumption of risk doctrine, however, has been significantly reformulated since *Siragusa* (1962). Workmen's compensation legislation, the doctrine that "an employer has a duty to his employees to exercise reasonable care to furnish them with a reasonably safe place to work,"[30] and contributory negligence have rendered assumption of risk a relic in the work place. Of course, one could claim that because such doctrines are hardly at home in the military, assumption of risk should still govern there. Retaining the doctrine simply to preserve an impractical distinction intended to overcome an unfairness has little to recommend it. We cannot escape the fact that both enlisted and conscripted service members stand in the same position vis-à-vis the lack of constitutional protections under military law. If it is unfair to impose such a legal system on a draftee, it is equally unfair to impose it on an enlistee.

It could be considered fair to deprive service members of constitutional rights, I suppose, for two reasons: One would be that the rights themselves were trivial, meaningless, vacuous, or inherently distributable only in such a way as to foster untoward or inequitable conditions between the members of the society. Surely our basic constitutional rights cannot be described in any such fashion. A second case would be that rights were substituted that were as good or better in promoting fairness, justice, and equity as those in the Constitution. That, as noted in a number of Supreme Court decisions, is not the case. Yet there remains the persuasive consequentialistic argument of the militarist: there are important and undeniable military reasons for military law. The continuing advance of military court decisions towards the standard of the federal courts seems destined to be repelled when it finally reaches the lines of military necessity. But a responsible compromise might still be reached. I shall try to sketch what it might look like.

Let us grant that the military legal system must be, to some extent, independent of the civilian courts for legitimate command and discipline reasons. To achieve that end, appeals of courts-martial decisions should run only through the superior military courts, and only CoMA decisions should be appealable into the federal system and then directly to the Supreme Court. This would disallow collateral attacks on military court decisions in the federal district courts. However, "going collateral" will not be a viable option if the offenses tried by courts-martial are restricted to genuine military crimes—crimes peculiar to military service. In that category there are two types of offenses: those that do and those that do not place the lives of other military personnel in jeopardy. Included in the latter group are failure to show appropriate respect for a superior officer; failure to obey certain kinds of orders in noncombat situations (not swabbing a deck when ordered, for example); wearing an improper uniform (such as wearing a yarmulke[31]); and the like. The former class will include such offenses as failure to obey a direct order in combat; willfully disobeying such an order; being AWOL, sleeping on watch in a war zone. Specifically in reference to the UCMJ, the first category of offenses would consist of crimes set forth in Articles 88 (contempt toward officers), 89 (disrespect toward superior commissioned officers), 90 (willfully disobeying a superior commissioned officer), 91 (insubordinate conduct toward a warrant officer, noncommissioned officer, or petty officer), 112 (drunk on duty) and 115 (malingering). The second group would contain UCMJ crimes set forth in Articles 85, 86, 87, 94, 99, 100, 101, 102, and 104 (desertion, absence without leave, missing movement, mutiny or sedition, misbehavior before the enemy, subordinate compelling surrender, improper use of a countersign, forcing a safeguard, and aiding the enemy).[32]

If military courts were to deal exclusively with military crimes, then all other criminal cases that involve military personnel could be tried in the federal district courts or other civilian courts, whether or not the crimes were committed on a military post. Found under the Punitive Articles of the UCMJ[33] are murder, manslaughter, rape, larceny, robbery, forgery, maiming, sodomy, arson, extortion, assault, burglary, housebreaking and the like. These should fall under the jurisdiction of civilian courts, removing in effect, the status of the accused test for jurisdiction and excluding military property as a relevant factor in the location test for jurisdiction. Service members would have full constitutional rights for all standard civilian crimes. Furthermore, because the usual penalties for the more heinous civilian crimes far exceed the normal time of enlistment and/or the length of conscripted service, military law would no longer be in the position of depriving a person of his or her liberty (in some cases for 25 years at hard labor) without constitutional protections or remedies.

Strict militarists will no doubt raise any number of objections to this attempt to carve out a middle position in the constitutional "crisis" of military law. They will worry that bringing civilian law onto the base will undercut command discipline and prerogatives. That worry may be justified, but the undercutting of such prerogatives also has been a product of the UCMJ and the Military Justice Act of 1968. We may well imagine that hard-line militarists would prefer the older approach of leaving all matters of prosecution in the hands of commanding officers. In wartime combat the old approach may be necessary for discipline, but the peacetime standing army creates a different world, one that the framers of the Constitution seemed to fear.

Although the Constitution does not expressly forbid a standing army, it tries to exert legislative control by requiring that military appropriations never be for a period in excess of two years. Presumably, the need to maintain a large standing force would be evaluated at the end of the two years. In *Federalist*, Number 8, Hamilton goes much further: "Standing armies, it is said, are not provided against in the new Constitution; and it is therefore inferred that they may exist under it. Their existence, however, from the very terms of the proposition, is, at most, problematical and uncertain."[34] He warns that standing armies necessarily strengthen the executive arm of government at the expense of the legislative, so the state will "acquire a progressive direction towards monarchy." Hamilton regards a standing army as the "engine of despotism." The framers did not want to create a bifurcated society under parallel legal codes. In wartime the civilian and military populations can be efficiently separated, but in peacetime the borderline between them blurs.

The civilian criminal codes are not now, and should not become, interested in the purely military crimes mentioned above. While it is the treatment of just those sorts of crime that provides the militarist with his strongest case, how they are handled is likely to affect the maintenance of discipline and morale. Hence military law ought to focus in that direction. Its administration of justice, however, should incorporate as much fundamental fairness and due process as circumstances will allow. Granted, enormous discretionary latitude must be extended to commanding officers in combat. However, for the sake of the constitutional aim of a unified society under law, the movement in military law to incorporate its own versions of the constitutional protections afforded the accused must be continually encouraged.

There is a striking similarity between the military-civilian legal bifurcation in our society and the dual and separate jurisdictional issue that confronted early Plantagenet Britain. As William of Newburgh notes, "criminous clerks" had committed hundreds of murders and were receiving nothing greater than prison sentences and reduced diets so Henry II decided to act.[35] But because those in religious orders who committed crimes were tried only in the ecclesiastical courts, so Henry "came face to face with the fact that a large and important part of the people were beyond the control of the state courts."[36] Henry's response to this situation was the monumental Constitutions of Clarendon (1164).

The first article of the constitutions established that the right of advowson[37] belonged not to the church, but to the landowner. Disputes over the right (even if both parties were members of the clergy) had to be heard in the king's court, not in the ecclesiastical courts. Article 3 became the most famous part of the constitutions. It required that when a cleric was suspected of a crime, he was accused in a lay court, where he entered his plea. If he pleaded innocence, he was taken to an ecclesiastical court for trial. If found guilty there, he was defrocked and then returned to the King's court, where either the results of the church court were accepted or a further trial was conducted. If the accused was found guilty, he would receive the same kind of sentence an ordinary layperson would receive for the crime.

Thomas Becket, the Archbishop of Canterbury, refused to assent to the constitutions, defending to the death the separation of the church courts from the king's court. The murder of Becket tempered the king's attempt to unify the jurisdiction of criminal law under his own court, for it gave birth to the infamous doctrine of "benefit of clergy," which allowed a cleric to be tried for any felony less than treason in the ecclesiastical courts. Treason and all misdemeanor charges against those in holy orders were heard in the lay courts. (It was not until the "benefit" was abolished by statute in 1826 that Henry's goal of joining two major segments of his society under a common legal system was finally accomplished.) The church courts were left to deal with purely ecclesiastical matters in whatever ways they felt to be consistent with their institutional purposes.

I propose that a version of the defrocking penalty for the guilty in the Constitutions of Clarendon be adopted by the military. If a service member is convicted in the civilian court of a crime that warrants long-term incarceration or supervised probation, then a discharge from the service should be forthcoming. (I agree with Generous that distinctions among types of discharges should be eliminated.[38]) The prosecution of minor offenses, such as disturbing the peace and public drunkenness, would occasion little interruption in service duties, though the conviction would be a matter of public record and may be noted with interest by the offender's superiors.

What Henry II saw as definite injustice—a virtual guarantee of unequal treatment in parallel courts for the same offense—we can explicate in more extensive legal terms. Not only are dual legal systems liable to deal differently with similar offenses, they are likely to have incompatible rules of evidence, different notions of due process, dissimilar senses of fairness and equity, different conceptions of fundamental rights and responsibilities, and so on. In a society that expects its law to deliver the basic principles of the Constitution to all of its citizens, such rifts between legal systems must be minimized. Although the military courts themselves have been steadily moving in that direction, they are confined to act within the UCMJ, which is distinctly socially disjunctive. The proposal I have outlined recognizes the fact that military law's only constitutional raison d'etre is to promote the efficient operation of the land and naval forces. It is analogous to what Henry viewed as the ecclesiastical law's legitimate purpose: regulating the religious lives of those in holy orders. But my proposal also affords military personnel all of the rights guaranteed by the Constitution that are consistent with their service duties. To do less is to relegate those in the armed forces to second-class citizenship, and that is definitely unconstitutional.

Another issue must be confronted, an issue raised by Associate Justice Reed in the *Toth* case. My proposal focuses only on peacetime applications of military law within the territory of the United States. One of Reed's concerns with the majority opinion in *Toth* was that if the military were not granted jurisdiction over nonmilitary crimes committed by those in service while stationed in a foreign country, the accused's fate would rest with a foreign legal system in which our constitutional guarantees may be totally absent. Would it be fair to place an American serviceperson, even one accused of a heinous crime, under the jurisdiction of foreign law? Yes, I believe it would be fair. In this regard the American in the armed forces is no worse off than any private American citizen who, while living or traveling in a foreign country, violates its criminal code. The United States Constitution does not protect Americans everywhere on earth. Why should American military law do so? Military personnel should be subject to the criminal code of the jurisdiction in which they are based, whether at home or abroad. At home they should, in as full a measure as possible, enjoy the same rights, privileges, and protections as their fellow citizens.

18 · Dinner with Auden

W. H. Auden was invited to speak at my college when I was still an undergraduate. Although at the time I had not read much of his work, I was invited, for some long forgotten reason, to join him and two faculty members for dinner. Auden was a prodigious consumer of alcoholic beverages. The two faculty members who completed the party made it plain that for at least two reasons I was not to drink. First, as the college was picking up the tab and I was underage, they did not fancy a reprimand from the dean. Second, I was to be what today would be called the designated driver. It would be my responsibility to return Auden to the hotel after dinner.

The meal itself was rather dull, with Auden only pausing between drinks to utter a few pleasantries about the college and to fish for compliments on his speech. He had spoken on the concept of tragedy, contrasting Greek tragic heroes with those of Christian authors, such as Melville. (He had published an essay on the subject in the *New York Times Book Review*[1] some years before.) He had received an enthusiastic response. The consensus was that his lecture had been most helpful to the students studying literary foundations, a required course. He nodded and ordered another drink.

The two faculty members may have dedicated themselves to the task of matching Auden's intake of booze, or they may simply have been intimidated. In any event, they were not in his league as far as drinking was concerned. On reflection, I think he was well aware of what he was doing to them, and that he rather enjoyed watching them slip further and further "under the table" until they virtually dropped out of the conversation. Auden, on the other hand, appeared not only fresh, but positively chipper, as though he had gotten his intellectual second wind. After the dessert tray was offered and politely refused, the two faculty members made what even at the time I thought were lame excuses and staggered out, leaving me in the restaurant with Auden. He made some unkind remarks about their inability to hold their liquor, then ordered a bottle of brandy.

"So then," he asked, "you learned a lot from my lecture, did you? I'm sorry, what is your name?"

My name cast him into deep thought. He muttered "French" over and over, fell silent for a moment or two, then asked me if I was a fan of Freeman Willis Crofts.

I admitted to never having heard of Crofts, who, as Auden informed me, was the author of detective fiction and who had created a detective Auden especially admired. The detective's name was Inspector French. Auden went on at length to explain why Inspector French should be held in high regard and, more importantly, why detective novels like those by Crofts ought to be studied by those claiming an interest in moral and social philosophy. Much of what he said about detective fiction he had published in a famous essay called "The Guilty Vicarage."[2]

Auden insisted that a genre distinction be drawn between detective stories and crime fiction. Milieu, he maintained, is the basic differentiating element from which the other major differences flow. Detective stories must be set in what Auden called the "Great Good Place." Crime stories occur in the "Great Wrong Place." Think of the basic differences in settings between the novels of Agatha Christie and Dorothy Sayers on the one hand, and Raymond Chandler and Dashiell Hammett on the other. Chandler's and Hammett's stories take place in ugly, corrupt, depressing places. Their characters are, by and large, unsavory mobsters and professional killers. Even the good guy is tainted and only a short step from criminality. No one in the stories is really concerned about defending society or the interests of the community. Auden writes, "In a society of professional criminals, the only possible motives for identifying the murderer are blackmail and revenge, which both apply to individuals, not to the group as a whole, and can equally well inspire murder."[3]

The detective story, on the other end of the spectrum, occurs in an apparently innocent society existing in a state of grace. The murder, specifically the corpse, is a shock to the social system because it is out-of-place there. It is unexpected and disruptive. Corpses litter *The Godfather* film epic and clutter Mickey Spillane's novels; there they seem perfectly appropriate and expected. The settings require dead bodies, ripped to shreds with machine gun bullets. The Great Wrong Place is saturated with wanton, gratuitous killing. The score is kept in corpses. In *The Godfather* even the representatives of society—the police, the clergy, and elected officials—are complicitious in all manner of criminality. There is no stable sense of good or right. What counts as good is but a modicum of peace arrived at in compromise agreements among criminals, a tenuous balance of terror usually on the verge of being tipped even as the agreement is ostensibly being struck. There is never a return to grace, just a continual downward spin into wider and wider circles of wickedness and corruption. Society at large is the victim in *The Godfather*, yet it is conspicuously absent from the film. We seldom see the people on whom the families prey, the faceless victims of their illegitimate enterprises. No one speaks for those victims or attempts to make restitution, in the name of and for the sake of the community, for the wrongs done to them. The implication is that there is nothing much to save and that the only interesting story is that of the cycles of vengeance among the unredeemable. The contrast between the baptism of a baby of corruption and the murders of criminal rivals that marks the climax of the first film in the series is stark and revealing. This is the Great Wrong Place through and through.

Saint Mary Mead and Cabot Cove, however, are places where people seem to live in harmony, peace, and even joy. They are Great Good Places through which snakes occasionally crawl. The primary task for the detective is to apprehend the murderer so the community can punish or exterminate him or her, and the place can be restored to its former tranquility—at least until the next novel in the series. The community must not only take an interest, but the apprehension and punishment of the murderer must be done in its name. Vengeance is not an acceptable motive; truth, compensation, and communal retribution are. The disruption of the tranquility of the Great Good Place is not a private matter. It is a very public concern. The detective's job is completed when the murderer has been identified and caught. There is an obvious plot-line similarity between the detective story and the magical barrenness themes of Celtic literature discussed in chapters eight and nine. Like those themes, the fantasy of the detective story is the fantasy of restoration.

The concept of the Great Good Place that gives structure and motivation to the detective story plays a comparable role in moral and social justification. It provides what might be called the deep structural motivation for responsibility and justice theories. By that I mean that it functions in justification at the level Wittgenstein called "bedrock." The concept of the Great Good Place serves to ground, in the sense of "end," moral justifications for social practices while also motivating social reforms. No one, from the moral point of view, can question why anyone would want to realize the Great Good Place or bring about a society like it. We can dispute the description of that place, but we cannot argue about it as a proper moral goal.

It will no doubt be suggested that there is a problem with the view that the Great Good Place provides a primary support for our common conceptions of morality and justice, because the term "good" that appears to describe the place would seem in need of a moral definition that is independent of the conception of that place. After all, how can one know this or that place is the Great *Good* Place unless one's notion of good is well worked out? It is not necessary, in my opinion, to be able to specify which thing is "good" of its kind prior to settling on an exemplar that gives meaning to "good" with reference to the kind. I have in mind something that can happen in pretheoretic aesthetic evaluation. A person with no prior conception of what would make paintings good ones might see a work that so attracts him or her that it becomes his or her model for "good" in painting. From it the elements of an idiosyncratic definition of "good" in painting (or paintings of that sort) may be derived. For a painting to be good in the eyes of that person, it must resemble the examplar in some respect. To question him or her about whether that exemplar painting is really a good one would be profoundly out of order, because the esteem in which it is held is not justified by appeal to rules and principles of aesthetics. In fact, it may open up new approaches, break the old rules, found a new style, and serve as a landmark for others. It is the justification of whatever, if any, rules and principles of aesthetics that person may consequently formulate with respect to paintings. It carries them along with it, so that it may be misleading to say that its status as "good" can be justified at all. It takes on a mythic character; it is the standard against which paintings (or paintings of a certain type, style, medium, etc.) are evaluated. It becomes an aspirational ideal. I suppose that in some cases it could reach such an elevated position in the person's mind (or in a culture, for that matter) that it transcends itself. It functions then as the exemplar of mythic proportion against which it may even fall short itself as time, lighting, and grime alter its appearance in the gallery. At that point it exists no longer on the canvas, but only in the conceptual scheme. The Great Good Place has taken on such a role in moral and social theory.

The more mundane attempts to found morality in rationality do not satisfy our sense of the deeper purposes of moral principles, rules, and constraints. The restoration or creation of the Great Good Place, the fantasy of moral responsibility, resists rational justification. If our culture were to forsake the Great Good Place as a meaningful symbol, however, it would do so at the cost of relinquishing many of the convincing justifications for its morality and its theories of justice—even the meaning of basic concepts.

David Gauthier has written, "Morality faces a foundational crisis."[4] He quotes MacIntyre, Williams, Mackie, and Harman as suggesting that "moral language fits a world view that we have abandoned."[5] But what world view? Gauthier thinks it is the idea that the world is purposively ordered. He maintains that unless we locate an acceptable alternative, we will no longer be able to understand the moral claims we make on each other and ourselves. For Gauthier, moral constraints on behavior can only be justified on deliberative rationality grounds. Simply, rationality requires that people keep their rational agreements, and so it requires that people "comply with the constraints of a contractarian morality."[6]

Though I have supported the argument that rational self-interest recommends the rule of retaliation (RR) that is at the core of morality and the stable community (as discussed in chapter two), Gauthier, I think, has misidentified the world view on which moral responsibility practices are founded. He seems to have done so because his commitment to the precepts of liberal atomistic individualism has him focusing on individual reasons to be moral rather than on the practices of morality, in particular those of responsibility. When questions about the reasons for, or grounds of, moral practices are raised, the answers do not always come back in terms amenable to individual rational choice theory. Sometimes they are framed in terms of communal or cultural aspirations, traditions, and myths so deeply embedded in the cultural identity of a society that they have long since become invulnerable to the challenge of individual rationality. They lie beyond justification, because with respect to the practices they give justification its sense. They are, in Wittgenstein's terms, "something animal."[7] He writes, "What people accept as a justification-is shewn by how they think and live."[8] The Great Good Place seems to be one of those embedded conceptions.

Gauthier, along with a number of other rational choice theorists, gives short shrift to the possibility that when members of a community share a sociopolitical vision, they are sufficiently motivated over the short and long haul to constrain their actions despite the counsel of rationality. H. L. A. Hart's account of the internal aspect of rules sheds some light on what is involved.

> Chess players do not merely have similar habits of moving the Queen in the same way. . . . In addition, they have a reflective critical attitude to this pattern of behavior: they regard it as a standard for all who play the game. Each not only moves the Queen in a certain way himself but "has views" about the propriety of all moving the Queen in that way. These views are manifested in the criticism of others and the demands for conformity made upon others when deviation is actual or threatened.[9]

For Hart, the necessary element in the internal aspect of rules in a community is that there should exist a critical reflective attitude with respect to certain ways of acting, and that such an attitude is manifested in demands for conformity and criticism of deviation. In certain circumstances, doing something that does not accord with the adopted (or traditional) rules may be rational for an individual, but it will not be condoned by the community. An appeal to principles of rationality will not be an acceptable defense. You will be punished for doing it, even if the community at large were to garner some net gain from your doing it. It is just not done. Mythic concepts like the Great Good Place are often found at the bottom of such critical reflective attitudes, grinning residually up at us like the frog at the bottom of Austin's beer mug.[10]

The vision of the Great Good Place can motivate justice theorists who, even though they reject the possibility of its realization, defend principles, rules, and laws intended to support the existence of the next best thing. Not even Hobbes tried to reform the Great Wrong Place. Locke, Kant, Bentham, Mill, Rawls, and Walzer all aim for the Second Best Place, the corrupted Great Good Place, the society for which Plato's Athenian Stranger proposed the *Laws*.

Many of the claims moral responsibility makes on us are founded in the shared vision or myth of the perfect human society. It is intriguing, however, that in the Great Good Place morality does not function as it does in our conceptual world. There morality is not a matter of constraint. It passes from the normative to the descriptive.

Auden begins his attempt to identify the conceptual content of the Great Good Place by noting that, "Every adult knows that he lives in a world where, though some are more fortunate than others, no one can escape physical and mental suffering."[11] Many people, perhaps most, wish that the world were radically different than it is. Many dream, at least occasionally, about better worlds where serious conflicts between personal taste and moral responsibility never occur, where pain and suffering are avoided, where duty and desire are not opponents, where individual aesthetics and social ethics are one, where people invariably do the right thing. Morality begins in dreams.

In the Great Good Place there are no normative moral laws, no rules. The residents are by nature happy and moral. (Wouldn't Kant, but not Hume, be surprised?) They act on inclinations that always produce the morally appropriate behavior. In the Great Good Place, as Auden described it, universal moral imperatives are unknown because they are unnecessary.[12] Like unrestrained, happy children, inhabitants do whatever they choose, but what they choose to do is always morally right. They do not act on moral principles; sentiment motivates behavior that accords with moral principles. Moral laws, if there were any, would be predictive, like laws of nature. They would tell *how* the people there behave, not how they *ought* to behave. Aesthetics (or matters of individual taste) and ethics (matters of universal law) are never in conflict. I do not mean that they are indistinguishable. Ordinary aesthetic issues, such as interior decorating, are not, or usually are not, matters of morality. Still, in the Great Good Place no one displays bad aesthetic taste in anything. Choices of decor, like choices of action, are always appropriate to the time and place.

In all things the residents of the Great Good Place act on preferences, without regard to the rationality of their choices. Yet, their choices are unswervingly correct, both morally and aesthetically. That does not mean that the Great Good Place must be boring and devoid of all argument. Andrew Hacker writes, "The kinds of disputes we have nowadays will be obsolete. . . . Politics and economics, armies and navies, diplomacy and wars—all these as we know them will be quite passé. But there may well be raging controversies on, say, the merits of sea-shell vs. butterfly collecting, surfboarding vs. mountain-climbing, or Bach vs. Britten."[13]

Whatever the inhabitants of the Great Good Place do is for them a form of play. Nothing there is done for reasons beyond itself or the pleasure it gives. Sexual or erotic behavior occurs, but, as Auden notes,[14] it is confined to only two sorts: the merely potential sexual relationships of perpetually courting couples (think of the novels of Jane Austen or the movies of Doris Day) or the "polymorphous promiscuity" of children or child-like adults.

Allowing for certain differences in particulars, the vision of the Great Good Place has motivated (should I say provoked?) two radically different world historical perspectives (megamyths) that have contested for dominance in Western thought from the earliest of times to the present.

Those megamyths are Eden or The Garden of Innocence or Arcadia *and* Heaven or Utopia or The New Jerusalem. Temporal geography constitutes the major conceptual difference between them, but that produces the "characterological gulf"[15] between them that explains something of their different social motivational capacities. Eden is long past, the golden age in which the evils and contradictions of contemporary life [understood as any epoch subsequent to Eden] have not yet occurred. Utopia is future, but maybe not distant future—only a little ways down the yellow brick road (but also across the intoxicating field of poppies). In Utopia all social problems are justly, fairly, equitably resolved. Troubles will be over and all needs satisfied on, as they sang in *Finian's Rainbow*, "That Great Come and Get It Day."

The Edenite scenario is given in Genesis, of course, though the concept of a Great Good Place that once existed is found in most Indo-European cultures. Comparisons between different versions of the Eden myth (Eden, the Greek Golden Age, Shangri La, Brigadoon, and so forth) would prove edifying, no doubt, but the central elements that mark a mythical place as Edenistic are more to the point of the present concern. It seems important that outsiders do not, or should not, enter Eden (entry of outsiders is viewed as a severe threat and typically marks its decline).

Detective story writers must adopt an Edenistic perspective on the Great Good Place, because the idyllic nature of the locale must be established to motivate restoration. Detectives are not social reformers; they merely attempt to return things to their proper places. Perhaps that is why so many of them are described by their authors as fastidious (think of Hercule Poirot, Sherlock Holmes, Miss Marple, Lord Peter Wimsey, Inspector Morse, Inspector French). Repair and revival is their business, not reformation and revolution. Detective stories occur in closed social units. The murderer is never an outsider, so he or she is generally an amateur (Professor Moriarty, a more or less permanent snake in the garden, is the major exception). In real life, people are murdered on the streets of their neighborhoods by career criminals who have no "legitimate business" being there, and who steal off into the shadows never to be detected and punished.

The crucial fact of human (mythic) history for those with an Edenite perspective is the Fall, the loss of paradise. Disharmony disrupts the garden. A corpse is found in the library of a prominent citizen, a dead body lies in the vicarage, and so on.

Eden is a myth of loss. Recovery is not an essential element of the perspective, and in some versions it is not possible. Incorporated in the myth is the notion that humans have not only the capacity, but also the inclination to destroy the good they create or into which they have been created. Edenites see the Great Good Place as a momentary, very temporary society of the past, doomed by a flaw in at least some of its members. Locke writes:

> The Golden Age (before vain Ambition, and *amor sceleratus habendi*, evil Concupescience had corrupted Mens minds into a Mistake of true Power and Honour) had more Virtue, and consequently better Governours, as well as less vicious Subjects.[16]

Understanding how that idyllic state (arguably not Locke's state of nature but a perfect civil system) comes to be corrupted requires, Locke tells us, the careful examination of the "Rights of Government"

> to find out ways to restrain the Exorbitances and prevent the Abuses of that Power which they having entrusted in another's hands only for their own good, they found was made use of to hurt them.[17]

Hence, the theory of justice emerges as a corrective either to restore the Golden Age or more likely, to maintain a second-best civil system, one that acknowledges the reality of the Fall, the corruption inherent when taste and duty diverge.

The Edenite conception of the Great Good Place invites entropic pessimism with respect to the prospects for the human race. The detective story avoids this by invoking the restoration fantasy. Its antientropic message rubs off the otherwise gloomy stain on human potential embedded in the Eden scenario. Detective stories are, despite the murders, homilies of hope.

Most Edenite political theories, however, are truer to the myth of loss. Thus they focus only on what may be possible in the corrupt world where inhabitants are presumed to be persuadable by appeals to long-term rational self-interest, despite their whims and destructive urges.

Outside of detective fiction, memorable Edenite characters living in the corrupted post-Expulsion world have been created by novelists, playwrights, and screenwriters. Comedy is often teased from the circumstances of the inexplicably innocent adult trying to cope with the corruption of everyday life. Auden's favorite example was Dickens's Mr. Pickwick. (Mine is Steve Martin's *The Jerk*. Tom Jones is arguably a candidate.) The same scenario can be viewed from the tragic side, as it is in Melville's *Billy Budd*. The protagonist, whether in comedy or tragedy, begins his or her adventures believing the world to be populated by well-meaning, honest, fun-loving, entertaining people. Then he or she discovers a fair share of dishonest, wicked, malevolent, and cruel people. East of Eden is a far cry from paradise.

The Fall as crucial to the explanation of human history and human nature was classically championed by St. Augustine.

> God . . . created man good; but man, corrupt by choice and condemned by justice, has produced a progeny that is both corrupt and condemned. . . . Thus, from a bad use of free choice, a sequence of misfortunes conducts the whole human race . . . from the original canker in its root to the devastation of a second and endless death.[18]

For Augustine, human history is the story of a continual degeneration from that happy, but lost, place of Eden.

> The race of mortal men has been a race condemned. Think first of that dreadful abyss of ignorance from which all error flows and so engulfs the

sons of Adam in a darksome pool that no one can escape without the toll of toils and tears and fears.[19]

Augustine's world was the Great Wrong Place of crime fiction. (It is difficult to imagine the Bishop of Hippo writing detective stories! His times and world are so out of joint, that they cannot be put right by the actions of mere mortals.) But the Augustinian world, though depressing, is remediable. The grace of God alone, Augustine believed, can save the human race. Human actions are otherwise impotent to reverse the degeneration of human life, because the human predicament is human nature itself.

Americans seem to believe, according to surveys taken on such matters, that despite technological advances and the staggering growth of scientific knowledge, the human race cannot save itself and will fall prey to its own devices. That is a favorite theme of fundamentalist Christianity which shows itself in the expressed pessimism among the contemporary collegiate generation. According to recent polls, college students believe that, despite the political changes in Europe and the supposed dawning of the "New World Order," their lives will end in a nuclear holocaust. Maybe such expectations can be ascribed to a twisted sort of romanticism or Edenite degeneration seen through the romantic eyes of youth, rather than a careful assessment of the political climate. Why don't college students believe their lives will end in an uncontrollable epidemic of AIDS—that the world will end not with a bang but a whimper?

The degeneration conception of human history that is generally correlated with the Edenite perspective on the Great Good Place is characteristically politically conservative. It is also a mainstay of the message of televangelism. Television preachers proclaim that if there is again to be a Great Good Place for the human race (or for some special class of humans—the blessed), it will be created by forces outside us, and we will become its residents only through the intervention of a supernatural power. Perverse as it may sound, some electronic ministers encourage provoking nuclear war in order to hasten an act of God that will "rapture" the blessed to Heaven and destroy the rest of the corrupt human race.

Women have been co-opted into various types of political Edenisms, convinced, no doubt, that they are revolting against traditional feminine role models. But, as John Passmore argues, "it is Eve, not Adam, who must vanish if the 'original state' of perfect humanity is to be regained."[20] Eden is the male myth version of the Great Good Place. Why then should women want to participate in any social movement whose victims they must become if it is to succeed? Except for the detective story version (interestingly dominated by women authors such as Christie, Sayers, and James, not to slight Doyle and Crofts), the logic of

Eden is that "you can't go home again." The chances of success are less than minimal. The best you can do is cope with the steady degeneration of human life through Hesiod's metallic ages, from the Golden Age of pure play to that of Iron and now, maybe, Rust.

Utopia, the other megamythic vision of the Great Good Place is also rooted in biblical literature. It emerges in the idea of deliverance from suffering and oppression. It typically involves the notion of liberation in this world and even revolution. Its dominant image is the escape from bondage. It is Exodus.

Exodus is a linear tale, a quest, whose end, the promised land, is laid out in the beginning as a realizable hope. It is important to remember, as Michael Walzer argues,[21] that the social end state of the story is radically different from the starting state. "Exodus is a journey forward—not only in time and space. It is a march to a goal."[22] It is a progress. It is progressive.

It is no wonder, Walzer notes, that Exodus has been a symbol to generations of radicals who reconstruct it as movement from a corrupt political system to a better one. It has come to represent the idea of the social perfectibility of humanity by its own actions. That, of course, is not the received interpretation of the biblical text; God is the force behind the punishment of Pharaoh and the destruction of the Egyptian army. Still, the ideas of political independence; of advancing to a more perfect state of civil justice and human freedom; of positive forward social movement and the transformation, both literal and figurative, of the people in the process: all these key elements of the Exodus story have figured prominently in the works of social and political writers for centuries. Writers from widely diverse political positions have written about these subjects, writers ranging from Benjamin Franklin to the early Boer nationalists, from Adolph Hitler to the leaders of the American civil rights movement. Regardless of the role assigned to God, the Utopia myth offers a linear conception of human history moving onward and upward to sociopolitical perfection.

Just as the degenerative theorists have champions in the history of Christian theology, so too does the perfectibility hypothesis. Two are particularly prominent. The first is St. Irenaeus, who wrote during the second century. Irenaeus was concerned with the significance of the expulsion from Paradise in light of the teachings of Christ. Irenaeus argued that the sin of Adam and Eve could not have been the oft-described fall from grace, the loss of perfection without any hope of restoration by human actions. Instead, he maintained, human beings must have been created in an imperfect state. The original sin was simply an act of immaturity. And because human beings were created with freedom of will, they are capable of self-improvement, of shaping themselves into more mature, God-like creatures, or what Irenaeus called "children of God."

God made man lord of the earth . . . but he was small, being but a child. He had to grow and reach full maturity . . . man was a child; and his mind was not yet fully mature; and thus he was easily led astray. . . . How could he be trained in the good, without the knowledge of its contrary? . . . The mind learns by realizing of what sort of thing is contrary to goodness. . . . How then will any man be a God, if he has not first been made a man? How can any be perfect when he has only lately been made a man? . . . Our duty is first to observe the discipline of man and therefore to share in the glory of God.[23]

By the fifth century the possibility of human perfection found an even stauncher defender in Pelagius, a British monk. Pelagius's favorite biblical text was not from Exodus; it was Matthew 5:48, from The Sermon on the Mount. "Be ye therefore perfect, even as your father which is in Heaven is perfect." In that passage Jesus seems to be commanding human beings to perfect themselves. How, Pelagius wondered, can humans obey that holy command if perfection is not within their power? He argued, if God through Christ commanded it, it must be possible for the human race to perfect itself, to progress through better and better states, until Utopia, or heaven on earth, is achieved. If perfection is not possible because of something in our very natures, it would be cruel for God, an all-powerful being, to order his underlings to do something they can only fail to do. Therefore, we must be capable, Pelagius believed, of producing the Great Good Place on earth.

The adverse effects of utopian thinking are all too obvious in human history. Achievement of the perfect social system can be, and has been, used to justify all manner of violence. Moses, it should not be forgotten, commanded the Levites to "go in and out from gate to gate throughout the camp and slay every man his brother, and every man his companion, and every man his neighbor"[24] as a cleansing of the tribes of those who worshipped the golden calf and longed to return to the fleshpots of Egypt. Progress to advertised promised lands is characteristically recorded in blood. Utopian versions of the Great Good Place, it is painfully evident, permit indulgence in aggressive and violent fantasies that make little sense to Edenites.

Social utopian visions have come in many different and incommensurable guises. Each licenses and demands positive action to create it, regardless of the cost in human life. IRA terrorists have a conception of the perfect future state. Achieving it, they might argue, requires assassination and indiscriminate bombings. Zionists, though they have a different vision of the Great Good Place, share the same violent tactics. The same may be said of Palestinian terrorist groups and many others.

Hitler was a utopian. His vision of the Great Good Place, as Auden noted, was a world in which, among other things, "there are no Jews, not a world where they are being gassed by the million day after day in ovens."[25] But the ovens played a major role in Hitler's attempt to move European civilization (indeed, the world) from the imperfect to the perfect, as he imagined it. Once Utopia is achieved, it is like Eden; there is no aggression, unhappiness, or evil. To reach that state, however, utopians must exclude the unredeemable, even if doing so is a gruesome business.

The checkered history of utopian thinking is intimately linked to racism. By the middle of the last century, the ideas of progress and race were so interlocked that many utopian thinkers believed there had to be a racial basis beneath perfectibility. Only one race could hope to achieve civilized greatness. This perverse notion has ironic origins in the Enlightenment. One of the two impelling forces that forged the racist-utopian weld was a form of Golden Age regression—in this case to Greek and Roman culture. During the Enlightenment, for example, Greek and Roman statues were widely regarded as models of perfected humanity. The second factor in the equation was the Enlightenment faith that science could reduce all things, no matter how complex, to principles and measurements. The historical union of these two ideas gave birth to the notion that one could determine, through scientific testing and measurement, which peoples and cultures of any period were closest to the Greek and Roman ideals and which were farthest away—the inferior stock. The quasi-scientific popular literature of the nineteenth century was filled with talk of discrete races and "triumphs of civilization" attributed to that insidious conception: the Aryan race and culture. Perverse logic of this sort becomes especially clear when one realizes that the Arcadian ideal, by its very nature, resides in a degenerative conception of human history, even though it was touted as the model of utopian achievement in a purportedly progressivist ideology.

The linkage of racism with perfectibility dominated utopian thought for nearly two centuries on both sides of the Atlantic. The catalog of its monuments of shame is very thick. It includes Dachau and Auschwitz, but also Sand Creek, Wounded Knee, and the Trail of Tears.

Should it be of concern that there are many, perhaps too many, versions of Utopia competing for attention? Yes, to the extent that some versions of Utopia fall far short of the basic requirements of the Great Good Place. Usually their primary failing is that they refuse access to potential inhabitants on the basis of morally insignificant factors, such as race, religion, ethnic origin, sexual orientation, and so forth. These factors are real concerns when utopian dreams are translated into political and social actions, because utopian activists tend to start their constructivist campaigns by eliminating or destroying those they regard as unredeemable. Walzer notes that the purging of the people is one of the first crucial steps in political reform.[26] This feature of utopian thought, though important practically, is not central to my interests. The legion of instances of violence in the name of the Promised Land does, however, speak to a major difference between Edenistic and utopian visions of the Great Good Place. Utopians have a motivational capacity that is drained from Edens. For utopians, the fantasy of restoration is readily recognized as nonrealizable and the myth of social engineering is not exposed as mythic so easily.

Lewis Mumford talks of two types of Utopias.[27] I want to make use of his insight, but not his terminology. Edenistic and utopian conceptions of the Great Good Place can be distinguished in that the Edenistic conception is escapist, the utopian is constructionist. Edenistic escapist conceptions are merely imaginative substitutes for the world in which we find ourselves. They are intellectual and emotional refuges, dreamy and enchanted places whose realization, even on mild reflection, is not taken seriously anymore. Perhaps that is why detective stories are often, and rightly, catalogued as escapist literature, in the same category as pulsating romantic fiction. Though we appreciate the serenity and beauty of the settings in detective fiction, we are not tempted to use them as models for altering the existing social world. Perhaps we see them as places that might have been, or as places that once were, but not really as places that can be or can be again.

The constructionist visions of the Great Good Place are quite a different matter. They are always utopian. They purport to engineer real social systems that will approach, if not actualize, the Great Good Place. And, though not actually produced, many have at least made a significant impact on the way less grandiose endeavors in law and morality have taken shape in our culture. Mumford writes:

The Icarians who lived only in the mind of Etienne Cabet, or the Freelanders who dwelt within the imagination of a dry little Austrian economist, have had more influence upon the lives of our contemporaries than the Etruscan people who once dwelt in Italy, although the Etruscans belong to what we call the real world, the Freelanders and Icarians inhabited-Nowhere. Nowhere may be an imaginary country, but News from Nowhere is real news.[28]

In the same category with the Etruscans are to be found most of the so-called indigenous tribes. Study of their cultures may have a broadening effect on education, but their impact on our lives has surely been minimal, and their cultural and social schemes, if they are put forward in a favorable light, can only be seen as Edenistic, not utopian. *Dances with Wolves*, for example, is escapist, not constructionist.

The Great Good Place is a mythic ideal that operates in our moral, social, and legal thinking as role or station exemplars function at the microcosmic level. It is the unachievable *telos* against which the success or failure of our institutions is measured. Its place and function in morality reveal the basic scaler character of our conceptions of justice, fairness, good, and the other moral notions used to evaluate social practices.

I safely returned Auden to his hotel. The next day he conducted a class on Kafka that he began with the quotation, "Perhaps there is only one cardinal sin: impatience. Because of impatience we were driven out of Paradise, because of impatience we cannot return."[29]

Notes

Chapter 1. Principles of Responsibility Ascription and the Responsibility Barter Game

1. J. L. Austin, *Philosophical Papers* (Oxford, 1961), p. 273.
2. Aristotle, *Nicomachean Ethics*, trans. M. Ostwald (Indianapolis, 1962), Book III.
3. Austin, *Philosophical Papers*, p. 273.
4. J. L. Mackie, *Ethics, Inventing Right and Wrong* (Harmondsworth, 1977), p. 208.
5. Daniel Dennett, "Conditions of Personhood," in *Identities of Persons*, ed. Amelie Rorty (Berkeley, 1976), p. 179.
6. Ibid.
7. See Donald Davidson, "Agency," in *Essays on Actions and Events* (Oxford, 1980), pp. 43–61.
8. Peter A. French, "The Corporation as a Moral Person," *American Philosophical Quarterly* 16 (1979): 207–217.
9. What I have called the Corporate Internal Decision (CID) structure is really just a redescription license of the required sort. A CID Structure has two elements of crucial interest: (1) an organizational system that delineates stations and levels of decision making and (2) a set of decision/action recognition rules of two types, procedural and policy. These recognition rules provide the tests that a decision or an action was made for corporate reasons within the corporate decision structure. The policy recognitors are particularly relevant to the attribution of corporate intentionality. Borrowing the distinction from Wittgenstein (Ludwig Wittgenstein, *Philosophical Remarks* [Oxford, 1975], no. 39), the organizational structure of a corporation gives the grammar of its decision making, and the recognition rules provide its logic. The CID structure accomplishes a subordination and synthesis of the decisions and acts of various human beings and other intentional systems into a corporate action, an event that under one of its aspects may be truthfully described as having been done for corporate reasons or to bring about corporate ends, expectations, purposes, and so on.
10. Davidson, "Agency," p. 47.
11. Ibid., pp. 52–60.
12. Ibid., p. 59.
13. Dennett, "Conditions of Personhood," p. 180.
14. Thomas Donaldson, *Corporations and Morality* (Englewood Cliffs, N.J., 1982), p. 22.
15. Austin, "Three Ways of Spilling Ink," in *Philosophical Papers*, pp. 272–87.

16. Peter A. French, *Collective and Corporate Responsibility* (New York, 1984), chapter 10.

17. Ibid., chapter 11.

18. F. H. Bradley, *Ethical Studies* (London, 1876), p. 46.

19. Aristotle, *Nicomachean Ethics*, p. 51.

20. Joel Feinberg, *Doing and Deserving* (Princeton, N.J., 1970), p. 134.

21. Bradley, *Ethical Studies*, p. 31.

22. Aristotle, *Nicomachean Ethics*, p. 57.

23. Dennett, *Conditions of Personhood*, p. 181.

24. Kurt Baier suggested this aspect of responsibility to me in a discussion of corporate responsibility, as did Herbert Fingarette in another context.

Chapter 2. Responsibility, Retaliation, and TIT FOR TAT

1. Edmund L. Pincoffs, "The Practices of Responsibility Ascription," *Proceedings and Addresses of the American Philosophical Association* 61, 5 (June 1988): 825–839.

2. F. H. Bradley, "The Vulgar Notion of Responsibility in Connexion with Theories of Free Will and Necessity," in *Ethical Studies* (Oxford, 1876).

3. Aristotle, *Nicomachean Ethics*, trans. M. Ostwald (Indianapolis, 1962).

4. The difference between the first two purposes is reflected in the distinction between punitive and compensatory damages in tort law, or perhaps more obviously, that between criminal liability and tort. In *Prosser and Keeton on the Law of Torts* (W. Page Keeton, gen. ed., St. Paul, Minn. 1984) the distinction between tort and criminal liability is explained in terms of the interests affected and the remedies provided. Punishment in criminal law is designed to protect the interests of the public. That protection may be achieved either by eliminating the offender from society (permanently or for a limited period of time) or by reforming the offender or by deterring others from committing similar crimes. In tort law, on the other hand, the action is brought by the injured party for the purpose of gaining compensation for the damage suffered. The law in tort cases serves to enforce the judgment won by the injured party against the harm causer. Society at large has only a kind of "rooting-interest" in the proceedings. The dominant notions are restitution and compensation.

There has developed a secondary level of damages in tort that is not directly related to compensation: punitive damages. Such awards are intended to punish or discourage the commission of acts comparable to the injurious one for which the suit was brought, and so constitute an invasion of criminal law into the field of compensation. The award of punitive damages is generally dependent, however, on the injured party's proving that more than the commission of the tort was involved in the injury. "There must be circumstances of aggravation or outrage, such as spite or 'malice', or a fraudulent or evil motive...or such a conscious and deliberate disregard of the interests of others that the conduct may be called willful or wanton. (Ibid., pp. 9–10.) For that to have occurred, the border between individual and social interests must surely have been crossed. In any event, the distinction between compensatory and punitive purposes for making responsibility ascriptions should be clear.

5. Plato, *The Laws*, Book IX, 860 d–e.

6. Ibid., 860 a–b.

7. Ibid., 862 b–c.

8. J. L. Mackie, *Persons and Values* (Oxford, 1985), 2:214.

9. Ibid., 2:215.

10. *The Code of Hammurabi*, section 229.

11. Exodus 22:22–25.

12. Hans Jochen Boecker, *Law and the Administration of Justice in the Old Testament and Ancient East* (Minneapolis, 1980), p. 174.

13. V. Wagner, "Rechtssatze in gebundener Sprache und Rechtssatzreihen in israelitischen Recht," in *Beihefte zur Zeitschrift fur die altestamentliche Wissenschaft* (1972), p. 14 (trans. Jeremy Mosier).

14. Boecker, *Law and Administration of Justice*, p. 175.

15. Robert Axelrod, *The Evolution of Cooperation* (New York, 1984), chapter 2.

16. Hobbes, *Leviathan* (1651), chapter 14.

17. William Shakespeare, *Henry V*, Act III, Scene I.

18. Axelrod, *The Evolution of Cooperation*, chapters 2 and 3. See also Robert Axelrod, "The Emergence of Cooperation among Egoists," *American Political Science Review* 75, 2 (1981): 306–318.

19. Ibid., p. 48.

20. Peter Danielson, "The Moral and Ethical Significance of TIT FOR TAT," *Dialogue* 25 (1986): 449–70.

21. Ibid., p. 453.

22. Ibid., p. 454.

23. Axelrod, *The Evolution of Cooperation*, p. 212.

24. Ibid., pp. 213–214.

25. Ibid., p. 136.

26. Ibid., p. 137.

27. Ibid., p. 44.

28. Danielson, "Moral Significance of TIT FOR TAT," p. 462.

29. Mackie, *Ethics, Inventing Right and Wrong*, p. 216.

30. Ibid., p. 207.

Chapter 3. Losing Innocence for the Sake of Responsibility

1. Herbert Morris, "Loss of Innocence," in *On Guilt and Innocence* (Berkeley, 1976), pp. 139–161.

2. Genesis 3:7.

3. Morris, "Loss of Innocence," p. 140.

4. J. L. Austin, *Philosophical Papers* (Oxford, 1961), p. 190.

5. John Searle, *Speech Acts* (Cambridge, 1969), pp. 141–146.

6. Ibid., p. 144.

7. N. R. Hanson, *Patterns of Discovery* (Cambridge, 1965), p. 22.

8. See Soren Kierkegaard, *The Concept of Dread*, trans. Walter Lowrie (Princeton, N.J., 1946), chapter 1, section 6, chapter 2, and chapter 3.

9. Donald Palmer, *Looking At Philosophy* (Mountain View, 1988), p. 362–363 (Try as I have, I cannot find the specific point in Sartre's works where this example is given. I will trust Palmer's sources.)

10. Genesis 3:22.

11. Thomas Hobbes, *Leviathan* (1651), part 1, chapter 13.

12. Sean O'Faolain, "The Man Who Invented Sin" in *The Finest Stories* (Boston, 1957), pp. 176–177.

13. Ibid., p. 181.

14. See Morris, "Loss of Innocence," p. 142.

15. Ibid., p. 143.

16. Seneca, *Letters of a Stoic* (Baltimore, 1969), Letter XC, pp. 176–177.

17. Morris, "Loss of Innocence," p. 146.

18. Steven Cohan, *Violation and Repair in the English Novel* (Detroit, 1986), p. 20.

19. Ibid., p. 29.

20. Emily Bronte, *Wuthering Heights* (1847), pp. 72, 74.

21. Ibid., chapter 12, p. 107.

22. Aristotle, *Nicomachean Ethics*, trans. D. Ross (Oxford, 1925), Book 3, p. 51.

23. Gunter Grass, *The Tin Drum* (New York, 1961), p. 53.

24. Bertrand Russell, *Problems of Philosophy* (Oxford, 1912), chapter 5.

25. Ibid., p. 46.

26. Ibid., p. 47.

27. Ibid., p. 58.

28. See Morris, "Loss of Innocence," p. 156–157.

29. William Golding, *The Lord of the Flies* (New York, 1954), p. 156–157.

Chapter 4. Fate and Responsibility

1. G. W. Hegel, *The Philosophy of History*, trans. J. Sibree (New York, 1956), p. 8.

2. Aeschylus, *Prometheus Bound*, trans. G. Murray (New York, 1950), p. 44.

3. Steven M. Cahn, *Fate, Logic, and Time* (Atascadero, 1967), p. 8.

4. Ibid., p. 9.

5. Ibid., p. 10.

6. Richard Taylor, "Fate," in *Reflective Wisdom*, ed. J. Donnelly (Buffalo, 1989), p. 339–340.

7. A. J. Ayer, "Fatalism," in *The Concept of a Person and Other Essays* (New York, 1963).

8. Adolf Grunbaum, "Causality and the Science of Human Behavior," in *Readings in the Philosophy of Science*, ed. Feigl and Brodbeck (New York, 1953).

9. Cicero, *De Fato*, trans. H. Rackham (Cambridge, 1960), p. 225.

10. Ibid., p. 225–227. Steven Cahn cites these two ancient arguments on p. 22.

11. Cahn, *Fate, Logic, and Time*, p. 21.

12. Aristotle, *De Interpretatione*, trans. E. M. Edghill, in *The Basic Works of Aristotle*, ed. R. McKeon (New York, 1941).

13. Ibid., 19a, 9–20.

14. For a discussion of this argument see Cahn, *Fate, Logic, and Time*, chapter 3.

15. W. V. O. Quine, *Word and Object* (Cambridge, 1960), and *Elementary Logic* (New York, 1965), p. 6.

16. Jan Lukasiewicz, "On Determinism," in *Polish Logic, 1920–1939*, ed. S. McCall (Oxford, 1967), p. 36–37.

17. Cahn, *Fate, Logic, and Time*, chapters 7 and 8.

18. Ibid., p. 113.

19. Ibid.

20. Harry Frankfurt, "Alternate Possibilities and Moral Responsibility," *Journal of Philosophy* 66, 23 (December 4, 1969): 828–839.

21. Noted by Cahn, *Fate, Logic, and Time*, p. 135.

22. Immanuel Kant, *Critique of Pure Reason*, trans. J. M. D. Meiklejohn (New York, 1901), p. 73.

23. F. H. Bradley, *Appearance and Reality* (Oxford, 1959).

24. Cahn, *Fate, Logic, and Time*, especially chapter 8.

25. Ibid., p. 136.

26. Frankfurt, "Alternate Possibilities," p. 829.

27. Ibid., p. 834.

28. Ibid., p. 836.

29. Peter Van Inwagen, "Ability and Responsibility," *Philosophical Review* 87 (April 1978): p. 201–224.

30. John Martin Fischer, *Moral Responsibility* (Ithaca, N.Y., 1986), p. 55.

Chapter 5. Time, Space, and Shame

1. Charles Dickens, *Bleak House* (1853), chapters 1 and 2.

2. Ibid., chapter 3.

3. For an excellent example see Geoffrey Thurley, *The Dickens Myth* (London, 1976).

4. Dickens, *Bleak House*, chapter 15.

5. F. H. Bradley, *Ethical Studies* (Oxford, 1876).

6. Charles Dickens, *A Tale of Two Cities* (1859), chapter 3.

7. Barry Cunliffe, "The Tribal Islands," in *The Ages of Britain* (New York, 1983), p. 19.

8. "The Wanderer," trans. G. K. Anderson, in *The Literature of England*, ed. Woods, Watt, Anderson, and Holzknecht (Chicago, 1958), p. 517.

9. "The Seafarer," trans. G. K. Anderson, in *The Literature of. England*, p. 59.

10. Jeremy Bentham, *An Introduction to the Principles of Morals and Legislation* (1789), chapter 1.

11. Bradley, *Ethical Studies*, pp. 174, 187.

12. Ibid., p. 187.

13. Ibid., p. 173.

14. Ibid., 173.

15. Peter A. French, *Collective and Corporate Responsibility* (New York, 1984).

16. Bradley, *Ethical Studies*, p. 166.

17. See, for example, D. L. Hall and R. T. Ames, *Thinking through Confucius* (Albany, 1987).

18. See Cicero, *On Duties* (Cambridge, 1991), and Seneca, *Letters from a Stoic* (Baltimore, 1969).

19. Bradley, *Ethical Studies*, p. 194.

20. Hilary Putnam, *Meaning and the Moral Sciences* (London, 1978), pp. 90–91.

21. Bradley, *Ethical Studies*, p. 179.

22. Ibid., p. 197.

23. See Robert Nozick, *Philosophical Explanations* (Cambridge, Mass., 1981), pp. 29–71.

24. Friedrich Nietzsche, *On the Genealogy of Morals*, trans. Kaufmann and Hollingdale (New York, 1967).

25. Ibid., p. 70.

26. For a brief but insightful discussion of the features of both guilt and shame see Herbert Morris, *On Guilt and Innocence* (Berkeley, 1976), pp. 59–63. He makes this point on p. 61.

27. J. O. Urmson, "Saints and Heroes," in *Essays in Moral Philosophy*, ed. A. Melden (Seattle, 1958). See chapter 12 for a discussion of the aspirational level of morality.

28. Erik Erikson, *Childhood and Society* (New York, 1950).

29. Morris, *On Guilt and Innocence*, p. 62.

30. Mark Twain, *Puddenhead Wilson's New Calender* (1894), chapter 27. (This business about blushing was a major topic of science in the nineteenth century. Darwin's remarks are found in *The Expression of the Emotions in Man and Animals*. In 1839 Thomas Burgess published *The Physiology of the Mechanism of Blushing* in which he argued that blushing is

evidence of the spirituality of humans. Havelock Ellis produced an essay on blushing. The point of this flurry of interest was to locate a mark of humanity, and, sadly, that was thought to be an important matter with regard to justifying the treatment of nonwhites in the colonial empires of the European nations).

31. Stanley Cavell, *Must We Mean What We Say?* (Cambridge, Mass., 1969), chapter 10. See also Gabriele Taylor, *Pride, Shame, and Guilt* (Oxford, 1985), pp. 82–84.

32. Taylor, *Pride, Shame, and Guilt*, p. 83.

33. Jane Austen, *Pride and Prejudice* (1813), chapter 18.

34. For a more detailed account of the various problems with shame therapy and other aspects of shame, see Helen Merrell Lynd, *On Shame and the Search for Identity* (New York, 1967), and Gerhart Piers and Milton Singer, *Shame and Guilt* (New York, 1971).

35. A point owed to Herbert Morris.

36. Taylor, *Pride, Shame, and Guilt*, p. 60.

37. W. Somerset Maugham, *Of Human Bondage* (New York, 1915), p. 60.

38. Helen Lynd, *On Shame*, pp. 58–59.

39. For a discussion of its use in criminal punishment see Peter A. French, *Collective and Corporate Responsibility* (New York, 1984), chapter 14, and Brent Fisse and Peter A. French, *Corrigible Corporations and Unruly Laws* (San Antonio, 1985), chapter 8.

40. Plato, *The Laws*, trans. Thomas Prangle (New York, 1980).

41. Ibid., p. 27.

42. Aristotle, *Nicomachean Ethics*, 1128b 10–35.

Chapter 6. Power, Control, and Group Situations

1. See Peter Morriss, *Power* (New York, 1987), especially chapter 4.

2. For a detailed version see Peter A. French, *Collective and Corporate Responsibility* (New York, 1984), chapter 5.

3. This analysis is based on Alvin Goldman's "Toward a Theory of Social Power," *Philosophical Studies* (1972) 23: 221–268.

4. John Martin Fischer, "Responsibility and Failure," *Proceedings of the Aristotelian Society*, (1985/86): 251–270.

5. Ibid., p.262.

6. Ibid., p. 266.

7. Ibid., pp. 267–268.

8. A most wonderful movie provides a wealth of examples as to how these matters may be settled, if they can be settled at all. It is *The Flight of the Phoenix*.

9. This formulation is derived from Goldman's analysis. See footnote 2.

10. French, *Collective and Corporate Responsibility*, chapter 5.

11. Morriss, *Power*, p. 39.

Chapter 7. The Responsibility of Inactive Fictive Groups for Great Social Problems

1. Norman Care, *Sharing Fate* (Philadelphia, 1987).

2. Larry May, "The Responsibilities of Inactive Groups," *Nous* 24 (1990): 269–278.

3. May's term.

4. John Martin Fischer, "Responsibility and Failure," *Proceedings of the Aristotelian Society* (1985/86): 251–270.

5. Virginia Held, "Can a Random Collection Be Morally Responsible?" *Journal of Philosophy* 67 (July 23, 1970): 471–481.

6. May, *Responsibilities of Inactive Groups*.
7. Ibid.
8. Ibid.

Chapter 8. Hobbes and the Hobbits

1. See, for example, Peter Vallentyne, *Contractarianism and Rational Choice, Essays on David Gauthier's Morals by Agreement* (Cambridge, 1991).
2. St. Augustine, *City of God* (New York, 1950), chapter 22.
3. Thomas Hobbes, *Leviathan* (1651), part 1, chapter 13.
4. Ibid.
5. Ibid., part 2, chapter 17.
6. Ibid., chapter 18.
7. J. G. Frazer, *The Golden Bough* (London, 1949), p. 2.
8. For a detailed account of this see John Darrah, *The Real Camelot* (London, 1981).
9. See S. Evans, *The High History of the Holy Grail* (London, 1898).
10. Darrah, *Real Camelot*, p. 54.
11. Polydore Vergil, *Anglica Historia* (Basel, 1534).
12. Thomas More, *History of King Richard III* (London, 1557).
13. For a more detailed account of this aspect of the play, see George Lyman Kittredge's introduction to William Shakespeare, *The Tragedy of King Richard the Third* (New York, 1968).
14. More, *Richard III*.
15. See the Kittredge introduction noted in 13 above.
16. *The Letters of J. R. R. Tolkien*, selected and edited by Humphrey Carpenter (Boston, 1981), p. 404.
17. Ibid., p. 406.
18. Ibid., p. 121.
19. Ibid., pp. 178, 120, 200.
20. J. R. R. Tolkien, *The Fellowship of the Ring* (Boston, 1965), Prologue.
21. Robert Graves, *I, Claudius* (London, 1934), and *Claudius the God* (London, 1934).
22. *The Letters of J. R. R. Tolkien*, p. 215.

Chapter 9. The Wasteland

1. J. B. Frazer, *The Golden Bough* (London, 1949), p. 2.
2. See John Darrah, *The Real Camelot* (London, 1981), especially part 1.
3. Peter A. French, "Responsibility and the Moral Role of Corporate Entities," in *Business and the Humanities*, ed. T. Donaldson (Oxford, forthcoming).
4. Brian Barry, "Justice Between Generations," in *Law, Morality, and Society* (Oxford, 1977), p. 270.
5. Ibid., pp. 272–273.
6. Michael Walzer, *Obligations* (Cambridge, 1970), Chapter 1.
7. I use the terms "corporation" and "corporation-like entities" to refer to any organizations that function through corporate decision structures. Hence, organizations like the various church, governmental, and so-called nonprofit organizations would qualify.
8. Peter A. French, *Collective and Corporate Responsibility* (New York, 1984), Chapters 3, 4, 12.
9. Roger Scruton, "Corporate Persons," *Proceedings of the Aristotelian Society* (forthcoming).

10. Robert Solomon, "Business and the Humanities: An Aristotelian Approach to Business Ethics," in *Business and the Humanities*, ed. T. Donaldson (Oxford, forthcoming).

11. Ibid.

12. Scruton, "Corporate Persons."

Chapter 10. Exorcising the Demon of Cultural Relativism

1. Norman Bowie, "The Moral Obligations of Multinational Corporations," in *Problems of International Justice*, ed. S. Luper-Foy (Boulder, Colo., 1988), p. 100.

2. Ibid., pp. 97–113.

3. See Richard Rorty, "Solidarity and Objectivity," in *Post-Analytic Philosophy*, ed. J. Rajchman and C. West (New York, 1985).

4. Donald Davidson, "Thought and Talk," in *Mind and Language* (Oxford, 1975), pp. 20–21.

5. Ibid.

6. David E. Cooper, "Moral Relativism," *Midwest Studies in Philosophy* 3 (1978): 101.

7. Philippa Foot, *Vices and Virtues* (Oxford, 1978), especially chapters 7–9 and 11.

8. Cooper, "Moral Relativism," p. 104.

9. Peter A. French, *The Scope of Morality* (Minneapolis, 1979), chapter 2.

10. John Searle, "Deriving Ought from Is," in *Speech Acts* (Cambridge, 1969).

11. Cooper, "Moral Relativism," p. 103.

12. Bowie, "Moral Obligations of Corporations," p. 110.

13. Ibid.

14. Ibid., pp. 110–111.

15. Colin Turnbull, *The Mountain People* (New York, 1972).

Chapter 11. Moral Responsibility and Heroism

1. Sarah Russell Hankins, "Archetypal Alloy," in *The Hero in Transition*, ed. R. B. Browne and M. Fishwick (Bowling Green, Ohio, 1983), p. 273.

2. Ibid.

3. Roger Rollin, "The Lone Ranger and Lenny Skutnik," in *The Hero in Transition*, p. 27.

4. John Rawls, *A Theory of Justice* (Cambridge, 1971), p. 117.

5. Aristotle, *Nicomachean Ethics*, trans. D. Ross (Oxford, 1925), Book 2.

6. J. O. Urmson, "Saints and Heroes," in *Essays in Moral Philosophy* ed. A. I. Melden (Seattle, 1958), pp. 198–216.

7. Immanuel Kant, *The Doctrine of Virtue*, trans. M. J. Gregor (Philadelphia, 1964), pp. 21–22.

8. Ibid., p. 120.

9. Ibid., p. 84.

10. Ibid., p. 86.

11. Ibid., p. 23.

12. Jeremy Bentham, *The Principles of Morals and Legislation* (1789), chapter 1, section 10.

13. Fyodor Dostoevsky, *The Brothers Karamazov*, trans. C. Garrett (New York, 1950) vol. II, book 5, chapter 4, p. 291.

14. Christopher New, "Saints, Heroes, and Utilitarians," *Philosophy* (April 1974): 184.

15. Sidney Hook, *The Hero in History* (Boston, 1943), p. 229.

16. Ibid., p. 235.

17. Daniel Boorstin, *The Image* (New York, 1962), p. 57.

18. Urmson, "Saints and Heroes," pp. 213–215.

19. Aristotle, *Nichomachean Ethics*, Book 3.

Chapter 12. The Burke of a Mill

1. John Locke, "Second Treatise," in *Two Treatises of Government* (1690), chapter 13, section 149.

2. Ibid.

3. Ibid.

4. James Mill, *An Essay on Government* (1820).

5. Ibid., section 7.

6. Ibid.

7. Ibid., section 8.

8. Robert Paul Wolff, *In Defense of Anarchism* (New York, 1970). See also Wolff's "On Violence," *Journal of Philosophy* 56, 19 (October 2, 1969): 601–616.

9. Immanuel Kant, *Foundations of the Metaphysics of Morals*, trans. Lewis W. Beck (Indianapolis, 1969), section 2.

10. Wolff, *In Defense of Anarchism*, p. 22.

11. Edmund Burke, *Collected Works*, Vol. 2 (Boston, 1865), p. 95.

12. Ibid., pp. 95–96.

13. See Hilary Putnam, *Meaning and the Moral Sciences* (London, 1978), especially lectures 5, 6, and part 2.

14. Peter A. French, *Ethics in Government* (Englewood Cliffs, N.J., 1983). See also Peter A. French, *The Scope of Morality* (Minneapolis, 1979).

15. Burke, *Collected Works*, vol. 7, pp. 71–87.

16. See French, *The Scope of Morality*, chapter 1, and J. L. Mackie, *Ethics: Inventing Right and Wrong* (Harmondsworth, 1977), p. 208.

17. William Wollaston, *The Religion of Nature Delineated* (1724), section 1.

18. Ibid., Section 1.

19. Mackie, *Ethics*, pp. 208–215. He is not, however, interested in the representation question.

20. Ibid., pp. 211–212.

21. Ibid., p. 164.

22. Burke, *Collected Works*, vol. 11, p. 96.

23. See Hanna Pitkin, *The Concept of Representation* (Berkeley, Calif., 1967).

24. Ibid., pp. 175–176.

25. Ibid., chapter 8.

26. Ohio Legislative Service Commission, *A Guidebook for Ohio Legislators* (Columbus, 1970), p. 72.

27. Edmund Burke, *An Appeal from the New to the Old Whigs* (1791).

28. John Rawls, *A Theory of Justice* (Cambridge, 1971), pp. 300–301.

29. An appeal of this sort was made by Edmund Beard in "Conflict of Interest and Public Service," *Ethics, Free Enterprise, and Public Policy*, ed. De George and Pichler (Oxford, 1978), pp. 232–247.

30. Rawls, *Theory of Justice*, pp. 300–301.

Chapter 13. Law's Concept of Personhood

1. For a deeper discussion of roman law on personhood see P. W. Duff, *Personality in Roman Private Law* (Cambridge, 1938).
2. R. H. Graveson, *Status in the Common Law* (London, 1953), p. 119.
3. Ibid., p. 121.
4. John Austin, *Lectures on Jurisprudence* (1885), lecture 42.
5. L. D. Solomon, D. E. Schwartz, and J. D. Bauman, *Corporations, Law and Policy* (St. Paul, Minn., 1988), p. 10.
6. *Trustees of Dartmouth College v. Woodward*, 17 U.S. (4 Wheat.) 518 (1819).
7. See Duff, *Personality in Roman Law*.
8. See Charles P. Sherman, *Roman Law* (Boston, 1917), vol. 2.
9. George Ellard, "Constitutional Rights of the Corporate   Person," *Yale Law Journal* 91, 8 (July 1982): 1646.
10. John Holdsworth, *A History of English Law* (London, 1942), vol. 3, pp. 409ff.
11. Ibid., vol. 9, p. 46.
12. H. H. Liebhofsky, *American Government and Business* (New York, 1971), p. 158.
13. Ellard, "Constitutional Rights," p. 1647.
14. Otto Gierke, *Das deutsche Genossenschaftrecht* (1887).
15. J. N. Figgis, *Churches in the Modern State* (London, 1914).
16. F. W. Maitland, *Collected Papers* (Cambridge, 1911), vol. 3.
17. Ernst Freund, *The Legal Nature of Corporations* (1897).
18. Ellard, "Constitutional Rights," p. 1649.
19. Peter A. French, *Collective and Corporate Responsibility* (New York, 1984).
20. Ibid., chapter 2.
21. Roger Scruton, "Corporate Persons," *Proceedings of the Aristotelian Society* (forthcoming).
22. Ibid.
23. Ibid.
24. F. H. Bradley, *Ethical Studies* (Oxford, 1876), p. 162.
25. See Maurice Hauriou, *Precis de droit Administratif* (Paris, 1892).
26. Scruton, "Corporate Persons."
27. French, *Collective and Corporate Responsibility*, chapter 3.
28. David Hume, *A Treatise of Human Nature* (1740) (Oxford, 1978   edition), p. 257.
29. Meir Dan-Cohen, *Rights, Persons, and Organizations* (Berkeley, Calif., 1986), pp. 46–49.
30. *Santa Clara v. Southern Pacific R.R.*, 118 U.S. 394 (1886).
31. Morton Horwitz, "*Santa Clara* Revisited: The Development of Corporate Theory," in *Corporations and Society*, ed. Samuels and Miller (New York, 1987), p. 14.
32. Ibid., p. 17.
33. *Hale v. Henkel*, 201 U.S. 43 (1905).
34. *First National Bank of Boston v. Bellotti*, 435 U.S. 765 (1978).
35. John Flynn, "The Jurisprudence of Corporate Personhood," in Samuels and Miller, *Corporations and Society*, p. 147.
36. James Coleman, *The Asymmetric Society* (Syracuse, N.Y., 1982).
37. Ibid., p. 13.
38. Ibid., p. 26.
39. Jean-Jacques Rousseau, *The Social Contract*, trans. Maurice Cranston (Baltimore, 1968), p. 65.
40. Bradley, *Ethical Studies*, p. 166.

41. Ibid., p. 171.
42. G. W. F. Hegel, *Philosophy of Right*, trans. T. M. Knox (Oxford, 1952), p. 154.
43. Ibid.
44. Ibid., p. 153.
45. Ibid., p. 154.
46. Scruton, "Corporate Persons."
47. Ibid.
48. Ibid.

Chapter 14. Better Off Unborn?

1. *Roe v. Wade*, 410 US 113 (1973).
2. *Zepeda v. Zepeda*, 41 Illinois App. 2d. 240, 190 N.E. 2d. 849 (1963) cert. denied, 379 US 945 (1964).
3. Amniocentesis is used between the fourteenth and the sixteenth weeks of gestation. A needle is inserted through the abdomen into the uterine cavity and amniotic fluid is withdrawn. That fluid is tested for enzyme deficiencies and is used to diagnose chromosomal abnormalities, X-linked recessive disorders, metabolic disorders, and malfunctions of the central nervous system. Amniocentesis is highly recommended for pregnant women over thirty-five and where there is a history of Down's Syndrome, spina bifida, hemophilia, muscular dystrophy, or mental retardation. It is also recommended when a parent is a positive carrier of the sickle-cell trait or when the parents have Eastern European Jewish ancestry.
4. *Gleitman v. Cosgrove*, 49 NJ 22, 227, A.2d 689 (1967).
5. *Berman v. Allen*, 80 NJ 421, 431–432, 404, A2d. 8, 14 (1979).
6. *Park v. Chessin*, 60 A.D. 2d 80, 400 NYS 2d 110 (1977).
7. *Curlender v. Bio-Science Laboratories*, 106 Cal. App. 3d. 811, 829, 165 Cal Rptr. 477, 488 (1980).
8. Ibid.
9. *Turpin v. Sortini*, 31 Cal. 3d 220, 643 P. 2d. 9954, 182 Cal Rptr. 337 (1982).
10. *Harbeson v. Parke-Davis, Inc.*, 98 Wash. 2d. 460, 656. P 2d. 483 (1983).
11. *Curlender v. Bio-Science Laboratories*.
12. Ibid.
13. *Turpin v. Sortini*.
14. *Shaheen v. Knight*, 11 Pa. D. & C. 2d 41, 45–46 (1957).
15. *In re Quinlan*, 70 NJ 10, 355 A 2d 647 (1976).
16. *Turpin v. Sortini*.

Chapter 15. Faustian Bargains

1. David Schultz, "Some Thoughts on the Relationship of Medicine to Ethics," *Newsletter on Philosophy and Medicine*, Fall 1987, p. 1.
2. See chapter 5.

Chapter 16. Enforced Corporate Responsive Adjustment

1. *Corporate Crime Reporter* (January 11, 1988), p. 1.
2. I developed this definition and defended it in Brent Fisse and Peter A. French, *Corrigible Corporations and Unruly Laws* (San Antonio, 1985), chapter 1.

3. See Fisse and French, *Corrigible Corporations*, especially chapter 10; Brent Fisse, "Reconstructing Corporate Criminal Law: Deterrence, Retribution, Fault, and Sanctions," *Southern California Law Review* 56: 1183–1213; and Peter A. French, *Collective and Corporate Responsibility* (New York, 1984), chapter 11.

4. Ibid., p. 187.

5. Ibid.

6. J. L. Austin, *Philosophical Papers* (Oxford, 1961).

7. Stone's book was published in 1975 and his views have changed significantly in recent years. See Christopher Stone, "Corporate Regulation: The Place of Social Responsibility," in Fisse and French, *Corrigible Corporations*, chapter 2.

8. Andrew Hopkins, *The Impact of Prosecutions under the Trade Practices Act* (Canberra, 1978).

9. John Braithwaite, "Enforced Self-Regulation: A New Strategy for Corporate Crime Control," *Michigan Law Review* 1982: 1466–1507.

10. John Braithwaite, "Taking Responsibility Seriously," in Fisse and French, *Corrigible Corporations*, chapter 3, p. 57.

11. Identification of these later difficulties with due diligence is owed to a discussion with Brent Fisse.

12. William Donovan and Breck McAlister, "Consent Decrees in the Enforcement of Federal Anti-Trust Law," *Harvard Law Review* 46 (1933): 885–932.

13. See note, "Declaratory Relief in the Criminal Law," *Harvard Law Review* 80 (1967): 1490–1513, and note, "The Statutory Injunction as an Enforcement Weapon of Federal Agencies," *Yale Law Journal* 57 (1948): 1023–1052.

14. See Keith Hawkins, *Environment and Enforcement* (Oxford, 1984).

15. See M. L. Friedland, "Prospective and Retrospective Judicial Lawmaking," *University of Toronto Law Journal* 24 (1974): 170–190.

16. See Richard Stewart, "Regulation, Innovation, and Administrative Law," *Yale Law Journal* 88 (1979): 1713–1734.

17. Fisse and French, *Corrigible Corporations*, p. 204.

18. Sally Hillsman, Barry Mahoney, George Cole, and Bernard Auchter, "Fines as Criminal Sanctions," *National Institute of Justice Research in Brief*, September 1, 1987.

19. See Oliver Wendell Holmes, Jr., *The Common Law* (Boston, 1949), p. 300.

20. H. L. A. Hart, *Punishment and Responsibility* (Oxford, 1968), pp. 6–7.

21. Ibid., p. 7, n.8.

22. Peter A. French, "The Hester Prynne Sanction," *Business and Professional Ethics Journal* 4, 2 (1985): 19–32.

23. John Ladd, "Persons and Responsibility: Ethical Concepts and Impertinent Analyses," in *Shame, Responsibility, and the Corporation*, ed. Hugh Curtler (New York, 1986), pp. 77–98.

24. Stone, "Corporate Regulation."

25. See Stewart, "Regulation, Innovation, and Administrative Law."

26. Clinard and Yeager, *Corporate Crime* (New York, 1980), p. 87.

27. Fisse and French, *Corrigible Corporations*, p. 209.

28. John Byrne and Steven Hoffman, "Efficient Corporate Harm," in Fisse and French, *Corrigible Corporations*, chapter 6.

29. Fisse and French, *Corrigible Corporations*, p. 210.

Chapter 17. The Responsibilities of Military Law

1. *The Theodosian Code*, trans. Clyde Pharr (New York, 1952), Book 2, Title 1.

2. Edward M. Byrne, *Military Law* (Annapolis, Md., 1981), chapter 1.

3. Ibid., p. 1.

4. Francis X. Gindhart, Foreword, in Harold F. Nufer, *American Servicemember's Supreme Court* (Washington, D.C., 1981), p. vii.

5. *Toth v. Quarles*, 350 U.S. 11 (1955).

6. *Theodosian Code*, Book 9, Title 1, Edict 10.

7. *Toth v. Quarles.*

8. Ibid., p. 24.

9. See William T. Generous, Jr., *Swords and Scales* (Port Washington, N.Y., 1973), p. 178.

10. There are three types of courts-martial: summary, special, and general. Officers are not subject to summary courts. Special courts-martial may award up to six month's confinement at hard labor, while the general courts-martial are the highest trial courts of the military system and they can award any sentence permitted in military law. Another difference is that the trial and defense counsel and the judge at a general court-martial are always certified military lawyers.

11. *United States v. Jacoby*, 11 U.S.C.M.A. 428, 29 C.M.R. 244 (1960), 429.

12. Ibid., 429–430.

13. *Mattox v. United States*, 156 U.S. 237, 15 S.Ct. 337, 39 L. ed. 409 (1895), 242–244.

14. *United States v. Jacoby*, 441.

15. Ibid.

16. Ibid., 442.

17. Nufer, *American Servicemember's Supreme Court*, pp. 87–88.

18. *O'Callahan v. Parker*, 395 U.S. 258 (1969).

19. See John T. Willis, "The United States Court of Military Appeals: 'Born Again,'" *Indiana Law Journal* 52, 1 (Fall 1976): 168.

20. Ibid.

21. *United States v. McCarthy*, 2 M.J. 26 (U.S.C.M.A. 1976) 28.

22. Ibid., 30.

23. Ibid., 31.

24. Generous, *Swords and Scales*, p. 199.

25. Ibid., p. 201.

26. Oliver Wendell Holmes, Jr.,"The Elements of Contract," *The Common Law* (1881), p. 227.

27. Ibid., p. 230.

28. *Farwell v. The Boston and Worcester Rail Road Corp.* (Supreme Judicial Court of Massachusetts, 1842), 45 Mass. 4(Metc.) 49.

29. *Pouliot v. Black*, 341 Mass. 531, 170 N.E. 2d 709 (1960).

30. *Siragusa v. Swedish Hospital* (Supreme Court of Washington, 1962), 60 Wash. 2d 310, 373 P. 2d 767.

31. Note S. *Simcha Goldman v. Caspar W. Weinberger, Secretary of Defense, et al.* (1986) in which the Supreme Court held that the First Amendment did not prohibit application of the air force regulation to prevent the wearing of a yarmulke by the plaintiff while on duty and in uniform.

32. I do not mean these to be exclusive lists, but they are representative.

33. *The Uniform Code of Military Justice* (1950), Subchapter 10, Articles 77–134.

34. Alexander Hamilton, *The Federalist*, Number 8 (New York, 1788).

35. George Burton Adams, *Constitutional History of England* (New York, 1921),p. 95.

36. William of Newburgh, *Historia rerum anglicarum* (1016–1198), in *Chronicles of the Reigns of Stephen, Henry II, and Richard I*, ed. Howlett (London, 1884–1885) vol. 1, p. 140.

37. The right to name the candidate for a vacancy in a parish church.

38. Generous, *Swords and Scales*, p. 206.

Chapter 18. Dinner with Auden

1. W. H. Auden, "The Christian Tragic Hero," *New York Times Book Review*, December 16, 1945.

2. W. H. Auden, "The Guilty Vicarage," in *The Dyer's Hand and Other Essays* (New York, 1948, 1962), pp. 146–158.

3. Ibid., p. 151.

4. David Gauthier, "Why Contractarianism?" in *Contractarianism and Rational Choice*, ed. Peter Vallentyne (Cambridge, 1991), p. 15.

5. Ibid., p. 16.

6. Ibid., p. 13.

7. Ludwig Wittgenstein, *On Certainty* (Oxford, 1969), no. 359.

8. Ludwig Wittgenstein, *Philosophical Investigations* (New York, 1953), no. 325.

9. H. L. A. Hart, *The Concept of Law* (Oxford, 1961), pp. 55–56.

10. J. L. Austin, "Ifs and Cans," *Philosophical Papers* (Oxford, 1961), p. 231.

11. W. H. Auden, "Dingley Dell and the Fleet," *The Dyer's Hand*, p. 409.

12. See Ibid., pp. 409–410.

13. Andrew Hacker, "In Defense of Utopia," *Ethics* 65 (January 1955): 137.

14. Auden, "Dingley Dell and the Fleet," p. 411.

15. The term is Auden's, see Ibid., p. 409.

16. John Locke, *Two Treatises of Government*.

17. Ibid.

18. St. Augustine, *The City of God*, trans. Gerald Walsh, Demetrius Zema (Garden City, N.Y., 1958), chapter 14, p. 278–279.

19. Ibid., chapter 22, p. 519.

20. John Passmore, *The Perfectibility of Man* (New York, 1970), p. 313.

21. Michael Walzer, *Exodus and Revolution* (New York, 1985).

22. Ibid., p. 12.

23. St. Iraneaus, *Adversus Haereses*, trans. W. W. Harvey (1857).

24. Exodus 32: 27.

25. Auden, "Dingley Dell and the Fleet," p. 410.

26. Walzer, *Exodus and Revolution*, chapter 2.

27. Lewis Mumford, *The Story of Utopias* (New York, 1962).

28. Ibid., p. 12.

29. Franz Kafka, *The Great Wall of China* (New York, 1936).

Index

Aeschylus, 45
Aristotle, 3, 38–39, 41, 49, 50, 70, 100, 116, 121
Assumption of risk doctrine, 191–192
Auden, W. H., x, 93, 197–198, 202, 203, 211
Augustine, Saint, 85, 205, 206
Austen, Jane, 37, 203
Austin, J. L., 3, 11, 31, 167, 202
Axelrod, Robert, 23, 25, 26
Ayer, A. J., 47

Barry, Brian, 99
Bentham, Jeremy, 118, 202
Berman v. Allen, 148
Boorstin, Daniel, 120
Bowie, Norman, x, 102, 103, 108
Bradley, F. H., 13, 16, 19, 51, 57, 60, 61–64, 70, 139, 143, 163, 167
Braithwaite, John, 170
Burke, Edmund, 122, 123, 124, 125, 126, 127, 131, 132, 133, 143
Byrne, John, 177

Cahn, Steven, 50–51
Calley, Lt. William, 188
Care, Norman, 79
Cavell, Stanley, 67
Celtic lore, 87–89
Children, rights of, 155–156
Chrysippus, 48
Cicero, 47
Coleman, James, 142
Control
  actual causal, 71–72
  regulative, 71–72, 81
  and responsibility, 72
Cooper, David, 104, 105, 106

Corporate Internal Decision Structures (CID Structures), 100, 139–141, 213(n.9)
Corporations and corporationlike entities, 100–101
  as moral persons, 6
  as legal persons, 135–137
Court of Military Appeals (COMA), 180, 181, 183, 184, 185, 186
Crime
  corporate, 165
  fictional, 198–199
  white-collar, 166
Curlender v. Bio-Science Laboratories, 148, 149, 150, 151

Dan-Cohen, Meir, 140
Danielson, Peter, 25, 26, 27
Davidson, Donald, x, 5, 6, 16
  on agency, 4, 5, 6, 12
  on agent causation, 9
  on principle of charity, 104, 107, 108
Deep play, 114–115
Dennett, Daniel, 4, 10, 16
Detective fiction, 198, 199, 204
Dickens, Charles, 56–58, 205
Due diligence, 171–173

Eden, 30–31, 203, 204, 205
Edenite perspective, 203–207
Enforced Corporate Responsive Adjustment (ECRA), 169–177
Extended Principle of Accountability (EPA), 12
Exxon Valdez incident, 96

Farwell v. The Boston and Worcester Rail Road Corporation, 191
Fatalism, 44–54

227